THE GOVERNANCE OF INNOVATION IN EUROPE

Science, Technology and the International Political Economy

Series Editor: John de la Mothe

The upheavals of the international political economy during recent decades have fundamentally altered the relationships between firms and states, citizenship and management, social institutions and economic growth. The changing pace of competition, firm performance and geo-economics is shifting the pressures on public policy and corporate strategy alike. As a result, our conceptual frameworks for analyzing key events, emerging trends and driving forces are being challenged. As unclear as the future is, what remains certain is that science, technology and innovation will occupy a central place. By looking at a wide array of issues – ranging from security and foreign affairs, the environment, international institutions, corporate strategy and regional development to research policy, innovation gaps, intellectual property, ethics and law – this series will critically examine how science and technology are shaping the emerging international political economy.

Published titles in the series:

Regional Innovation, Knowledge and Global Change, edited by Zoltan Acs

The Complexity Challenge, by Robert W. Rycroft and Don E. Kash

Evolutionary Economics and the New International Political Economy, edited by John de la Mothe and Gilles Paquet

Global Change and Intellectual Property Agencies, by G. Bruce Doern

Systems of Innovation, edited by Charles Edquist

Universities and the Global Knowledge Economy, edited by Henry Etzkowitz and Loet Leydesdorff

Forthcoming titles in the series:

Innovation and the Service-Based Economy, edited by Ian Miles and Mark Boden

Developing Innovation Systems, by Mario Cimoli

Science and Technology and Governance, edited by John de la Mothe

Proposals for books can be sent directly to the series editor:
  John de la Mothe
  Program of Research on International Management and Economy (PRIME)
  Faculty of Administration
  University of Ottawa
  275 Nicholas Street
  Ottawa, Canada KIN 6N5

The Governance of Innovation in Europe

Regional Perspectives on Global Competitiveness

Philip Cooke, Patries Boekholt and Franz Tödtling

PINTER

London and New York

Science, Technology and the International Political Economy Series
Series Editor: John de la Mothe

Pinter
A Cassell Imprint
Wellington House, 125 Strand, London WC2R 0BB, England
370 Lexington Avenue, New York, NY 10017–6550

First published in 2000
© Philip Cooke, Patries Boekholt and Franz Tödtling 2000

British Library Cataloguing-in-Publication Data
A catalogue record for this book is available from the British Library.
ISBN 1–85567–627–3 (hardback)
    1–85567–628–1 (paperback)

Library of Congress Cataloging-in-Publication Data
    The governance of innovation in Europe: regional perspectives on global competitiveness /
Philip Cooke, Patries Boekholt, and Franz Tödtling.
        p.   cm. – (Science, technology, and the international political economy series)
    Includes bibliographical references and index.
    ISBN 1–85567–627–3 (hardcover)–ISBN 1–85567–628–1 (pbk.)
    1. Research, Industrial–Government policy–Europe.   2. Technology and state–
Europe.   I. Boekholt, P.   II. Tödtling, Franz.   III. Title.   IV. Series.
T177.E8C67   1999
338.9407–dc21
                                                                                                99–17501
                                                                                                CIP

Typeset by York House Typographic Ltd, London
Printed and bound in Great Britain by The Bath Press, Bath

Contents

Figures

Tables

Preface

This book represents the findings of the European Union DG12-Targeted Socio-Economic Research Programme study entitled 'Regional Innovation Systems: Designing for the Future' (REGIS). The project brought together teams of researchers from eleven European regions, nine in the European Union and two from Central and Eastern Europe. The project was ably guided from DG12 by Mrs Virginia Vitorino to whom we express gratitude for her support and involvement in many of the team meetings. Gratitude is more generally expressed to Directorate G-RTD Actions: Human Capital and Mobility: TSER-Project Management, for providing the funding necessary for conducting the two-year research project. Finally, in bringing this book to fruition we thank Petra Recter and John de la Mothe, respectively Commissioning Editor and 'Science and Technology in the International Political Economy' series editor at Pinter for Cassell Academic.

The book synthesises research produced, discussed and written in report form for project meetings held in Cardiff, Tampere, Aveiro, Udine, Vienna, Budapest and Bilbao. All hosts are thanked for their efforts in arranging these meetings which were crucial elements in the successful evolution of the project. The overall project co-ordinator was Phil Cooke, assisted by Nicole Schall (Cardiff University), both also responsible for the Wales study. Partner teams were led and supported as follows: Baden-Württemberg – G. Bechtle, C. Kaufmann (University of Bamberg); Basque Country – G. Etxebarria, M. Gomez Uranga, G. Intxaurburu, L. Ozerin, B. Garcia (University of the Basque Country, Bilbao); Brabant – P. Boekholt (Technopolis, Amsterdam and Brighton); Centro – E. de Castro, C. Esteves, F. Nogueira (University of Aveiro); Féjer – C. Makó, T. Kuczi, A. Novoszath (Hungarian Academy of Sciences); Friuli – M. Schenkel, M. Grandinetti, S. Boffo, E. Pugliese (Universities of Udine and Napoli); Lower Silesia – A. Kuklinski, R. Galar (University of Warsaw); Styria – F. Tödtling, A. Kaufmann, S. Sedlacek (University of Economics, Vienna); Tampere – G. Schienstock, M. Kautonen (University of Tampere); Wallonia – M. Quevit, P. Van Doren, G. Faucheux.

Clearly, this was a complex and diverse project in which the key aim was to explore the viability of regions as an appropriate level at which a new kind of innovation-based enterprise support policy might be delivered. In developing the final synthesis report for the European Commission into this book, and to relate it to the Pinter series theme, we were invited to develop our ideas and findings in the context of changes in the international political economy. These are included in Chapters 1 and 8. Franz Tödtling wrote Chapters 3 and 4 while Patries Boekholt wrote Chapters 6 and 7, but we all commented on everything to make it a collective and interactive endeavour. We have tried to be as true as possible to the reports of our colleagues in all the regional economies investigated, so any errors of omission or commission are the responsibility of none but the authors.

Introduction: Systems of Innovation and Future Innovation Policy at the Regional Level

1. Introduction

Innovation is said to account for 80 per cent of productivity growth in advanced countries, and productivity growth accounts for some 80 per cent of Gross Domestic Product (GDP) growth overall (Freeman, 1994b). This places the importance of innovation in context. It is the key to improved competitiveness, growth and, in consequence, employment. What needs to be understood better in the European context is why, apparently, firms and policies to promote innovation seem to be less able to produce innovations, hence improved competitiveness, than their equivalents in the USA and Japan (CEC, 1996). This means, as a first step, deepening understanding of how innovation is conducted in the European Union, what problems arise which prevent innovative effort from being realized sufficiently to bear commercial returns, and what, in policy terms, can be done to improve the position.

Recently much attention has been devoted in the literature to demonstrating the interactive nature of innovation. Authors such as Freeman (1987), Rosenberg (1976) Lundvall (1992) and Nelson (1993) have presented convincing arguments that successful innovation is systemic. This means that, at its best, it involves users, intermediaries, and scientists in an iterative process of learning. Previously it was assumed that injections of capital in research eventually led through a linear process to commercial results in a technology-push mode of operation. But the work of Von Hippel (1988) and others showed that much of it was user-driven. The interactive practices of innovation are highly social, requiring high-quality communication skills, receptivity to cognitive dissonance, and a teamwork mentality. Regular opportunities for tacit-knowledge exchange are necessary and change may often, accordingly, be incremental not radical. These insights point to the probable importance of proximity in interactive innovation and may explain why innovation is frequently observed in specific geographical concentrations.

Whereas the research which drew attention to the systemic character of innovation concentrated its focus on the national level, the essentials of systemic interaction, tacit knowledge exchange, the building of 'untraded interdependencies' (Dosi, 1988), the forging of trustful relations and development of innovative networks are better understood at the subnational or regional level. In much the same way that innovation is now increasingly understood as systemically interactive (Edquist, 1997a) so, ever more, the essentials of competitive economic coordination on the ground are perceived as regional. Ever since Marshall (1919) it has been understood that an important aspect of economic growth and change derives from the external effects of agglomeration, inter-firm linkage, and the existence of skilled labour pools in specialized industrial locations. Although Porter (1990) explained competitive advantage in terms of national conditions, on closer inspection many of his examples of successful industrial 'clusters' were, in fact, regional. What is now termed 'new regional science' recognizes this and has demonstrated the growing salience of regional economies as key nodes in the increasingly globalized arena of production (Sabel, 1989, 1995; Cooke, 1992; 1998; Storper, 1995; Storper and Scott, 1995; Scott, 1996; Tödtling and Sedlacek, 1997; Boekholt and van der Weele, 1998).

What, until recently, had still to be done was to pose the question as to whether systemic innovation was capable of being understood in terms of regional innovation systems. The present report focuses precisely upon that question. Taking eleven European regions, nine in the EU and two in eastern Europe, the research explored both the nature and extent of regional innovation practices of firms and innovation support organizations, and examined ways in which, to the extent regional innovation systems could be identified, they could be improved. The results of these investigations, covering a variety of regional types, from apparently successful, competitive regions like Baden-Württemberg to reconversion regions like Styria and Wales, industrial districts regions like Friuli and transitional regions like Lower Silesia, have profound implications for policy to support innovation at EU, member-state and regional levels. Indeed, one of the pioneering aspects of the findings has been the teasing-out of the multi-level governance relations of innovation, and how these vary in certain regions with respect to higher levels in the overall governance system. In this introduction, outlines of the methodological approach, questions raised and important empirical findings are presented. These refer to regional firms, both large and small, regional institutions and organizations and policies pursued to support regional innovation. In our conclusions key findings will be drawn together and main policy recommendations highlighted to assist in the design of more accomplished regional innovation systems for the future.

2. The regional innovation system concept

The *regional innovation system* concept is new, recognizing a growing perception that the regional level of economic co-ordination has an important role to play as a functional correlate to the increasing power of globalization as a general economic force, especially with respect to innovation (see Lundvall and Borrás, 1997). Regions are to be understood as meso-level entities operating, in political and administrative terms, between local and national governments. Many, though not all, EU member-states have regional governments with varying degrees of influence over innovation policy (see, for example, Cooke *et al.*, 1997). Sometimes these are designated from above as an administrative reorganization by nation-states, as in France where they mainly handle budgetary functions decentralized from central government. On other occasions they have been created by pressure from below, as in the UK, where cultural heterogeneity has been expressed in demands for distinctive governance structures, e.g. Northern Ireland, Scotland and Wales. Yet other regions express a mixture of both, as in Italy which has special statute and ordinary statute regions, the former reflecting cultural distinctiveness as found in Friuli Venezia-Giulia, Sardinia and Sicily, or Spain where the Basque Country, Catalonia and Galicia have culturally-justified extra powers. There are also federal systems which result in equivalent powers amongst regions, more culturally originated in Belgium than, say, Austria or Germany. It is also noteworthy that a future EU accession country, Poland, has recently announced the designation of regions within its territory. One of these, Lower Silesia, is included in the research reported here. Another future EU member, Hungary, also represented in this study by the Féjer region, has not yet taken a regionalization route.

A large amount of EU policy, notably structural intervention and aspects of innovation support, is organized in such a way that regions are the receiving bodies for allocations. With respect to innovation actions such as those animated through DG13, regions have been the focus for Regional Innovation and Technology Transfer Strategies (RITTS) projects while DG16 has, through Article 10 measures, promoted Regional Technology Plans (RTPs), now Regional Innovation Strategies (RIS) and Regional Information Society Initiatives (RISI). Because of the RIS focus on less-favoured regions where regional governance is often less formalized or mobilized, such initiatives can have an effect in helping actors in weakly-defined regions with few competences perceive the importance of regional identity and proactivity more clearly. As this research showed in the least-favoured cases of the Centro region in Portugal, Féjer in Hungary and Lower Silesia in Poland, and even in relatively prosperous but peripheral Friuli in Italy, an audit of regional assets quickly reveals the institutional deficits concerning innovation support, but also highlights the fundamental potential importance of, for example, a regional university as a catalyst for possible future economic impact in addition to its more traditional scholastic functions.

But reference to such limited focal points in the innovation architecture of the region also underlines features which firms in less-favoured regions share with those in more advantaged settings. This is, as our results show, that firms everywhere learn most from other firms. Thus, when asked for the main sources of information concerning innovation opportunities, and the main partners for innovation application and implementation, firms in general cite other firms, especially customer and supplier firms, as their main interlocutors. Hence, as Lundvall and others have argued, innovation is interactive. But our results, which are drawn from less-favoured economies for the most part, suggest strongly that such interaction is limited to a relatively narrow band of other firms and agents. For example, use of the public technology transfer infrastructure tends to be low except in regions like Baden-Württemberg, which is economically advantaged and has a rich infrastructure of specialist research institutes and technology transfer centres; or the Basque Country, which is less-advantaged but relatively autonomous in terms of regional governance, and as a result has a regional science and technology strategy now in its third phase of development and a number of specialist technology centres have been established to meet large- and small-firm innovation needs.

This is, perhaps, one of the more important revisions capable of being made to the model of interactive innovation developed from research conducted within a National Systems of Innovation perspective. At the national scale, with the full panoply of universities, government research establishments, independent research institutions and associations, private research laboratories, government departments, national science foundations and legal or accounting frameworks which constrain and incentivise innovation activities by firms, it can appear that the opportunities for interaction centred upon innovation are massive. This is not to mention interactions that can occur supranationally either through state, market or network linkages. But, in reality, this panoply of research and innovation resources is not used directly by most firms because most firms are small and medium-enterprises (SMEs) and their focus is more circumscribed, indeed our results suggest links are surprisingly regional, and to a roughly equivalent degree also national, and strongly inter-firm focused. Our results also show that, on balance, large firms are more innovative than SMEs, so it is conceivable, indeed likely, that large firms are more intensive users of wider innovation networks, including supranational ones. And of course, there are exceptions, such as high-tech spin-off firms, perhaps originating in a university or corporate research setting, that have global innovation interactions. But these are a minority in the context of the EU, although regionally, where they occur in agglomeration, critical mass may give rise to associative activity and the development of joint innovation actions both locally and globally.

A key question which remained to be answered, even following the forward steps made by national innovation systems research, is what does *systemic* interaction comprise with respect to innovation? Definitions of systemic innovation given by Lundvall (1992) and Nelson (1993) are somewhat limited to institutional elements and relationships that interact in the production, diffusion and use of new and economically useful knowledge. Freeman (1987) makes use of the *network* concept to link public and private institutions whose interactions initiate, import, modify and diffuse new technologies. But this leaves out organizational innovation and is perhaps imprecise in its use of institutions to encompass the more concrete and empirically tractable concept of organizations. Whatever these conceptual difficulties, we do not have a sense of the regularity or intensity of interactions, nor indeed the diversity of the network of actors with whom regular or irregular, intensive or non-intensive, important and non-important interactions occur.

The information contained in Chapter 4 goes at least some way in showing which kinds of innovation partners are the most and least important at which level from regional to global. Following customer and supplier firms, the next most important partner is either a regional or national university followed by consultants, sources of subsidy (usually government departments) and training bodies. Venture capital bodies, research organizations and trade associations are the less important partners of firms engaged in innovation processes. The importance of regional and national universities strengthens by a significant magnitude for firms that are product and process innovators, with regional university links being notable for the latter. Technology transfer and training bodies also increase in importance for innovative firms, the former more for product innovators, the latter for process innovators. Regions in which firms show a higher than average use of the regional innovation support infrastructure in general are Baden-Württemberg, Styria and the Basque Country, each with a rather diverse and well-developed set of innovation support organizations.

In Chapter 5 a conceptualization of an idealized regional innovation system is presented. The two key sub-systems are: the knowledge application and exploitation sub-system; and the knowledge generation and diffusion sub-system. The first is principally occupied by firms with vertical supply-chain networks and lateral co-operation network relationships, each driven by the ultimate goal of competitiveness. This sub-system is well-represented in our findings regarding the relationships between firms concerning innovation and is particularly common systemically in the vertical dimension. However, especially in industrial district regions, horizontal, more collaborative network relationships are also found. The second sub-system is more the province of public organizations concerned with technology transfer, public research, third-level education and workforce training. Systemic linkages between these organizations and firms, and amongst organizations themselves are, as we have seen, weaker. However, innovative firms have stronger than average links with all four sub-system elements. Moreover, as noted, in regions with well-developed and understood innovation support capabilities, more wide-spread systemic interaction between firms and innovation support organizations tends to occur.

Outside the regional innovation system, linkages with national innovation support organizations are also strong, though they are less so at the transnational level, except with respect to EU policy instruments such as Framework Programme funding and other innovation initiatives. It is also of relevance that interactions between regional innovation systems, either within a particular country or interna-tionally, may occur. This possibility is enhanced where there are innovation programmes actively promoting inter-regional linkages as with the Article 10 initiatives, Interreg and voluntary partnerships such as the 'Four Motors for Europe' arrangement which began with Baden-Württemberg, Catalonia, Lombardy and Rhône-Alpes but has extended to include other regions within and beyond the European Union.

3. The research approach

The predominating goal of the research undertaken was future-oriented and sought to identify the key elements for systemic innovation support at the regional level, in the light of anticipated needs expressed by firms and innovation organizations concerning their future capability to innovate and compete in global markets. This devolved, analytically, into a number of research objectives of a scientific and policy-related nature. Scientifically there was the task of integrating insights from, for example, innovation theory, regional science and political science especially regard-ing multi-level governance of innovation. Furthermore, a methodological approach maximizing comparative analysis was a crucial objective. Arising from the develop-ment of an analytical framework for investigating regional innovation system variability was the task of designing survey instruments to capture the nature and extent of innovative activity and its contribution to competitiveness by firms, as well as exploring the innovation support practices of knowledge generation and diffusion organizations. In brief, the research sought to establish the extent to which regional innovation systems could be said to exist in the eleven regions under investigation.

There were also policy-oriented objectives, including generating preliminary information about the innovation capacity of the regions studied, as a baseline information resource for policy-makers in the region, the state and the EU as well as for those conducting the research itself. We set these in the context of globalization and emerging policy requirements for this book, as shown in Chapter 1, but at the level of research reportage, the first, primarily desk-based task was a regional innovation audit, and its results are summarized in Chapter 2. From this survey, a useful analytical device emerged for classifying the regions according to their economic and innovation indicators. Five categorical types of region were shown to exist: high performance engineering regions such as Baden-Württemberg; reconversion regions with pronounced upstream linkages between firms and the knowledge generation and diffusion sub-system e.g. Styria; reconversion regions with stronger downstream links with respect to innovation through more near-market, inter-firm and supply-chain linkages, e.g. Wales; industrial district regions like Friuli and Centro; and transitional regions such as Féjer in Hungary and Lower Silesia in Poland. Analytically, this was modified by reference to the varying governance powers of regions with respect to innovation capability.

Other policy aims were to try to assess whether EU policy in support of innovation was bringing about greater or lesser convergence between diverse regions with respect to their innovation support capability, to stimulate policy learning between regions, either directly through dissemination of comparative research results to regional bodies, or indirectly through communicating findings to higher level bodies with innovation policy competence such as the EU. An auxiliary objective was to identify policy innovations to assist by transfer the improvement of regional innovation potential to meet future challenges of global competitiveness. Much of the content of Chapters 5 and 6 refers to the organizational structure of innovation support and comparative policy stances of the regions, while Chapter 7 draws out the general lessons from the overall analysis for future policy guidance.

To reach these conclusions, and following the first-step audit of regional situations based on analysis of economic and innovation indicators, further methodological steps were taken. The first of these involved conducting questionnaire-based research on firms in key sectors of the regions in question. Thus representative samples of firms in up to six (mainly manufacturing) sectors were drawn and batteries of questions were posed relating to firm competitiveness, innovation activities and achievements, innovation partnerships and information sources, barriers to innovation and relationships with the innovation support infrastructure *inter alia*. The results are presented in detail in Chapters 3 and 4.

The next step was to investigate the organizations in the regions responsible for innovation support. These consisted of universities, research institutes, technology transfer agencies, consultants, venture capital firms or organizations, government ministries, training organizations and various intermediary bodies. These face-to-face interviews of some fifteen or so bodies per region elicited information on their activities in promoting systemic linkage with firms and other organizations, policies pursued in promoting innovation, funding and other resources available, their perceptions of regional firms, barriers to innovation, etc. and, crucially, as a triangulation instrument, their responses to firms' views of their contribution to firm innovation, in particular, and the presence or absence of systemic innovation relationships within the region, in general. The results of this part of the research are found in Chapters 5 and 6.

Finally, armed with the results from the questionnaire survey of regional firms and the interviews with innovation support organizations, researchers returned to a small, but representative sample of some fifteen to twenty firms to explore further, in face-to-face interviews the nature of the innovation process in which they engaged – whether they were engaged in radical or incremental innovation, for example, or what could better be termed adaptation work which could not adequately be considered innovation. Accounts were elicited of typical innovation activities to aid assessment of the kind of innovation conducted. As well as radical or the far more common incremental innovation, a third kind, which we termed 'recombination' innovation was identified. This involved customized producers engaging in a kind of flexible specialization around a key technology which could be systems-integrated to meet the demands of a wide variety of markets. The findings from this stage of the research are embodied in Chapter 4.

Chapter 7 draws out the implications of all that was written and spoken in these surveys and interviews for future regional innovation policy. This stresses the need to facilitate the functioning of interactive innovation by enabling a more systemic flow of information, a more inclusive involvement of SMEs and a better integration of firm needs and organizational capabilities at a regional level. Of some importance, generically, is the wide perception that universities have a strong future role to play in assisting systemic innovation capability within regional innovation systems. Chapter 8 ties together the analysis, empirical findings and policy proposals for improving the future design of regional innovation systems, especially in less-favoured regions.

CHAPTER ONE

Global Asymmetries, Learning Economies and Regional Innovation in Europe

1. Introduction

This chapter sets the scene for the study of innovation practices of European firms in a variety of regional settings by exploring the macro processes in the international political economy in which those practices are, to a greater or lesser extent, embedded. We refer to the widely observed 'European paradox' whereby first-class scientific and technological research performance in the European Union is not matched by the transformation of such results into commercial innovations by European firms. The innovation gap between European innovation performance and that of competitor economies is a weakness that needs to be addressed. Here, we explore key ideas concerning where the origins of such weakness may lie. In order to do that, we consider what most experts agree to be a weakness in European competitiveness in the face of two powerful forces structuring the contemporary economic arena – globalization and innovation, in the context of market liberalization.

Though globalization is by no means complete, its effects are strong in the financial system and in the production practices of multinational firms where competitiveness has been intensified by the interpenetration of ownership, investment, procurement and supply of parts, components and services. Globalization, in a context of market liberalization and deregulation, creates uncertainties and a reluctance on the part of investors in some advanced economies to make long-term investments in research and development (R&D), a key input to the innovation process. In the European Union, where attention has been focused particularly upon macro-economic stabilization, this is thought to be an institutional factor further constraining business expenditure on R&D. Thus, in the first section of this chapter, the nature and extent of globalization and innovation, as drivers of contemporary competitiveness are explored as a prelude to a consideration of the direction European firms are evolving towards in the new international political economy. One key weakness identified here and elsewhere concerns a relative failure to come to terms fully with important aspects of organizational and broader economic *learning* amongst firms and organizations that supply enterprise support. Linkages remain narrow and firms' perspectives on problem-solving and innovation remain, to a degree, introverted, resulting in a lower commercialisation than absolute production of innovative activity. The importance of 'knowledge capital' in a knowledge society remains under-appreciated.

One of Europe's key distinguishing features is its heterogeneity and this is echoed in its regional economic diversity. This can be a strength since regional economic specialization, provided it is not overdone, can enable localized global excellence and interactivity with global business networks. Our view is that the EU is correct to promote regional innovation-building capacities, not only in strong, but also less-favoured regional economic contexts. As this book helps to show, the innovation deficits and policy gaps relating to European business, especially its extensive small and medium-enterprises (SMEs) sector, are better understood and further improvements can, in principle be made. The kinds of policy helpful for EU innovation enhancement, taking advantage of diversity, as well as certain universalities in business perceptions of the challenge ahead, are considered in the last section of this chapter. This then leads to a discussion in Chapter 2 of the *ex ante* state of play in eleven selected regions of the EU and Central and Eastern Europe (CEE). This precedes our in-depth inquiries and findings regarding the reasons for that state, and proposals for improving on it in subsequent chapters of the book.

In general, we think there are good reasons for developing *innovation* policies for implementation at regional, rather than member-state level, where science and technology policies may be more appropriate. We distinguish these below. The linkage between regional and state levels for innovation can be weaker in many cases than that between the regional and European levels. This is because a consensus has built up in many regions that the kind of judicious support provided by the EU through regional policies and regional innovation experiments is well-attuned to regional capabilities in building human, social and knowledge capital through networks in localized settings. The state level can be too cumbersome and insensitive to local nuances for this.

2. What kind of international economy?

International political economy is experiencing a succession of upheavals. Are they the birth pangs of the new, the death throes of the old, or merely business as usual, to misquote Gramsci? A fashionable argument has arisen to the effect that 'globalization' represents the new economic and cultural paradigm. Various events, notably the nanosecond swiftness with which the exchange-rate values of the currencies of significant economic powers can plummet as confidence evaporates in the economic fundamentals of economies like Brazil, South Korea and Russia, bear witness to this new power. Why would such rapid collective judgements be reached around the globe? Because financial indicators such as an overvalued currency or a debt overhang are taken to signify a major weakness in the competitiveness of a given economy. Adjustment will come sooner or later, so it might as well come sooner, cheapening goods for export thereby undermining competitiveness in next door and more distant economies, creating the dreaded 'domino effect'. All this may occur with respect to a real economic performance that is little different from the day before the day after the crash, except that initial panic reactions by beleaguered bosses are likely to have involved 'reducing overheads', i.e. making workers redundant and impoverishing families.

Presented in this way, 'globalization' is indeed powerful. But it is, from this perspective, fundamentally a power of financiers and speculators akin to backing horses based on informed judgement, or even bluff. Interestingly, though, when things do go wrong globalization in this financial sense appears less powerful – indeed panic-stricken in its agents' flight from risk, where even hedge funds, designed to make risk redundant, can no longer be seen as safe havens. So globalization is far from self-regulating and financial markets remain prone to market failure. Recourse is routinely made to national governments, foreign governments and international financial agencies to bail out the losers, something which, in the case of the International Monetary Fund, they recently appeared insufficiently resourced to achieve. So, in the final analysis governments intervene, as they must, as the insurer of last resort. These remarks are a useful corrective to a widespread view that markets had, through the power of global finance, and the distinct but parallel power of multinational enterprises, somehow triumphed over the normal boom-bust cycle over the longer term and even significantly moderated the normal business cycle over the short term. This has also given a moment of thought in the minds of those who have recently been advocating a fashionable view that at this *fin de siècle* a 'New Economy' has come into existence that is more or less capable of continuous growth with minimal fluctuation (for critiques see Krugman, 1995, Hirst and Thompson, 1996).

The New Economy view is more a product of journalistic hype than sober analysis (for examples, see Kelly, 1998 and *Business Week*, August 24–31, 1998) although at least one US government department bought into it in connection with its implications for land and property development (HUD, 1996). One anxiety attached to the New Economy perspective is its reliance on the twin supports of financial globalization and its market moderating capabilities on the one hand (which, as we have seen, was misplaced), and innovation on the other. It is instructive to note how innovation has moved up the policy agenda of late with the discovery that so much of GDP growth is bound up with productivity growth which, in turn, is largely determined by innovation rates, something we comment on further in Chapter 2. A key to the belief in the future growing power of innovation is the 'information revolution' which will spread productivity-enhancing effects ever deeper even into the services economy. Expectations of major technological breakthroughs in biosciences, nanoengineering and so on, in a globalizing context which forces firms to be more competitive as it enlarges markets, will hasten increasing rates of economic growth. To this, critics such as Krugman (1995) not only question the optimism but assert, that by comparison with the effects of electricity and combustion engines, recent gains from technology have been limited and disappointing and there is little reason to anticipate great leaps of progress in the future.

This echoes Krugman's earlier scepticism, which now looks like remarkable prescience, concerning the sustainability of the high economic growth of the Asian 'tigers' or Newly Industrializing Countries (NICs) (Krugman, 1994). Clearly, their past success fuelled the globalization thesis but in a manner closely intertwined with their perceived innovativeness and, given the massive presence of China as an emergent producer and consumer market close by, created the conceivable prospect of a major future shift in the axis of world economic power. The NICs, it is argued, actually grew less than their published GDP growth rates because their spectacular increases in output growth were an effect of huge increase in input costs. Investments in human capital, in particular, were very large and, in consequence, successful in assisting catch-up with the West, but these gains are unrepeatable. Future growth would have to come from the difficult and exacting processes of more efficient use of production factors to enhance productivity. Krugman might have added that the borrowing to enable, for example, large firms in South Korea to become competitive, not least through capital exports in foreign direct investment (FDI), has to be repaid.

But, as Hirst and Thompson (1996) show, Krugman cannot resist going too far by disparaging as old-style deferred gratification the efforts and sacrifices made by the NICs to achieve developed country status. This underestimates the albeit flawed but recoverable government strategy in many such countries, of seeking endogenous growth rather than relying simply upon FDI, especially in the case of Taiwan, or where FDI was attracted, manipulating it, as with Singapore, to fit in with domestic political and economic goals regarding the kind of innovation-based growth through which future productivity gains could be secured. These points raise some important and interesting avenues for exploration and discussion which are taken up more fully in Chapter 2. For the moment, the NICs in Asia followed their own routes to development, influenced to some degree by the model of Japan, but not slavishly following it, except in clearly perceiving a central role for the state in policy guidance (sometimes, unavoidably also, as in Indonesia, the military who physically own segments of that economy). Another fast growing small economy is the Republic of Ireland where the state has also been centrally involved in economic policy guidance. But the reliance on FDI in achieving that growth has been immense while the capability for endogenous business growth had, until the late 1990s, been less so, except for important sectors such as dairying and food processing.

So, globalization and innovation, it can be deduced, are contested but, to a considerable extent, active presences in the new international political economy. But the omnipotence of the one and the omniscience of the other are by no means as pronounced as the advocates of the New Economy would have us believe. If the financial meltdowns of 1998 are a symbol of the imperfections and incompleteness of globalization, especially beyond the redoubts of North America and the European Union, then the retrenchments and closures of the likes of Fujitsu, National Semiconductor, Seagate and Siemens, to name just the most prominent memory chip plants to be closed in the UK during 1998, are symbolic of the volatility and vulnerability of innovative, high technology industries.

Thus it is not a case of saying that neither globalization nor innovation are important processes in the contemporary international political economy, rather they may not be all-important, and though intimately linked they are by no means always as benign as the New Economy optimists like to believe. The negative chain reactions of globalization and innovation were clearly captured by Chesnais (1993). There, conceptually, he showed how globalization's liberalizing tendencies circumscribed the scope for national macroeconomic policies when taxation is also lowered. Lower tax revenues weaken public expenditure but make financial sector investments attractive, a factor which leads to investment capital being assigned to takeovers and mergers with investments concentrated in some regions with strong financial sector attractiveness, government policies becoming more attuned to supporting them, and disinvestments in financially unattractive or uncompetitive regions. These may also, as in the case of the UK in the late 1990s, be further encumbered by loss of export markets caused by high interest rates designed to protect financial not industrial assets.

But if we live in a world where such chain reactions are not only conceivable but actually occur, with varying impacts and degrees of frequency, how can their malign effects be minimalized? Chesnais is perhaps over-gloomily looking at globalization with French eyes which also see the relative weakness of the capabilities of the French state, acting alone, to resist the worldwide tide of 'global monetarism' (Cooke, 1997). Yet, some would argue that state-centralism of the French kind is no longer an answer, if it ever was, in an international political economy dominated by trading blocs, liberalized trade and, in the European case, the referral upwards to the supranational level of many of the key elements of former economic sovereignty which are also the main levers of economic power.

These issues have recently been the subject of reflection in a parallel study to the one reported in this book, commissioned by the Science and Technology directorate (DG12) of the European Union, co-authored by B. Lundvall and S. Borrás (CEC, 1998). The analysis is similar to that of Chesnais but seeks mechanisms and policy stances that enable governance regimes to cope with the compression of space and time entailed by globalization and innovation. In line with previous work of Lundvall and his collaborators, the future political economy is conceived as having to be of necessity a 'learning economy' (Lundvall and Johnson, 1994). This mode of thinking derives ultimately from evolutionary economics; it is not, therefore, tied to the neoclassical reification of markets nor to the Keynesian belief in the virtues of states as economic regulators. It is more of a 'Third Way' theory of business economics and advocacy of specific types of policy practice. It is thus more in tune with the new international political economy than either of its tried, tested and found wanting alternatives (for a fuller appraisal of the approach see Lundvall, 1992; Hodgson, 1993; Cooke and Morgan, 1998).

Globalization and innovation are two key motors of the contemporary international political economy, producing greater integration of economies through commerce, foreign investment, elongated supply chains and seamless financial flows. However, as we have argued above this is by no means a monolith, rather it is a set of relationships, deeply fissured and capable of partial or temporary conditions of collapse. Among its key blocs of North America, European Union and Japan – particularly the first two – there are strong internal and inter-bloc linkages in each direction. From Japan there are strong outward but weak inward linkages with the other Triad economies (Cooke, 1997). What this globalization of some 'georegions' nevertheless means is heightened competition compared to the position when national economies rather than trading blocs were the key arenas of economic governance and practice. In the study reported in this book, especially in Chapters 3 and 4 we show in great detail precisely how innovation is forced upon firms by the twin competitive pressures of rising quality and declining costs, so that even if most firms are not in direct contact with a global final market they are indirectly affected by it through the supply-chain.

However, while globalization predominates in financial markets it does not do so in knowledge markets. The learning economy is a response to the rise to prominence of the information society and the knowledge economy. Information is relatively globally mobile but knowledge is remarkably spatially rooted. Scarcity characterizes this key factor of production that authors such as de Geus (1997) see as becoming more important than relatively abundant capital, especially specific or tacit knowledge or problem identification and collective solution capability. One only has to think of the remarkable information technology capability of firms clustered in Silicon Valley, multimedia capability in Hollywood, and Grand Prix racing car engineering competence around Silverstone, let alone the innovative and creative industrial districts of northern Italy, to see this obvious point. As Lundvall and Borrás put it:

> If all knowledge were readily transformed into information to which everyone had easy access, there would be little incentive for firms, regions and nations to invest in R&D and technology gaps between regions and countries would be minor and temporary. (CEC, 1998, p.33)

That this situation does not prevail is plain, and that it particularly could not in times of rapid technological change is also apparent. Hence, it can be deduced that knowledge capital is largely not codified but tacit and to that extent, relatively geographically fixed. In Chapter 2 we discuss work which designates the process by which the 'stickiness' of knowledge capital occurs as 'asset stock accumulation'. Thus firms will only exchange knowledge capital with 'significant others' who have knowledge capital of their own which is worth accessing. This is a limit to globalization and, except for the privileged few, to innovation too, except insofar as 'leakage' occurs through informal channels or, in time, imitation becomes possible. That leakage occurs is testified; for the north Italian case, in Cooke and Morgan (1998), Silicon Valley by Saxenian (1994) and Silverstone, through rapid employee labour market mobility, by Henry and Pinch (1997). However, in all these cases, leakage occurs most within the cluster, making what Alfred Marshall called the 'industrial atmosphere' of such places yet another locational attraction, reinforcing the externality effects of the agglomeration.

More is said about this and the role not only of monetary exchange but 'untraded interdependencies' in the following chapter but these sketches show just how central learning is to knowledge capital, innovation, competitiveness and, ultimately, globalization, especially in a period when time-economies are being compressed. However, one crucial element of a future international political economy in which neither state planning nor relatively unregulated market competition prevails, is that it will rest increasingly on associational, networked interaction and even team-like relationships within and among firms and between them and key non-firm organizations such as governance bodies, universities and many kinds of intermediaries from venture capitalists to skills-providers. Thus, hand in hand with the exploitation of knowledge capital goes a renewed emphasis on the importance of social capital and trustful inter-personal and inter-organizational relations within the economic sphere (Putnam, 1993; Lazaric and Lorenz 1998; Cooke and Morgan, 1998).

Thus, to summarize, globalization and innovation are two key processes operating within contemporary international political economy. Innovation is affected by globalization because it heightens competition and pressures firms into being more innovative, even permanently innovative to a greater or lesser extent, because of rapid change and the cost-quality pincer-movement that constrains strategic choice. Globalization is not a monolithic process, nor is it necessarily hegemonic, though it approaches that status most with respect to some financial markets and least with respect of knowledge capital. The notion of 'techno-globalisation' (Archibugi and Michie, 1997) may therefore be overstated if meant as a description of fact. Globalization has its negative effects which can lead to a decline in productive investment in, for example R&D, as OECD (see CEC, 1998) statistics have recently registered, but firms and organizations must develop capacities appropriate to a learning economy if they are to cope, through innovation, with globalization.

3. Where does Europe fit in?

We turn now from our review of key tendencies in international political economy to a consideration of how Europe, and more specifically, the European Union affects and is affected by these changes and added pressures. It is clear, as we state elsewhere in this book, that the European Commission perceives an innovation gap between European firms and those from Japan and the USA (CEC, 1996). The first thing to note about the EU, in comparison to the two countries that out-perform it in innovativeness is that it is larger and far more complex culturally, institutionally, politically and economically than either. If the metaphor for America is a melting-pot and that of Japan is homogeneity, then that for Europe is clearly 'diversity'. The EU is a trade bloc and governance structure, indeed uniquely in the world it is a structure of multi-level governance, something we explore in detail in Chapter 5. Thus it is both more than a collection of states and less than a state. It has some state-like powers – supreme court jurisdiction, tariff-setting powers, control of competitiveness, monetary policy, science and technology policy and environmental regulation to name a few. But that does not mean that the traditional nation-states have been hollowed-out since they retain the key state functions relating to taxation of and provision of security for their citizens. As long as they retain these the EU will not have the necessary budgets or 'legitimate means of violence', to allude to Weber, that define state functions at base.

To a very limited extent 'regions' represent more of a marginal erosion of state functions in that some exist with distinctive police forces (Basque Country) if not yet armies, and can vary rates of personal and corporate taxation (Catalonia, Scotland). However, this should not be over-stated even though, as we say later, some 'regions' can represent themselves and even their member-state at EU Councils of Ministers on reserved items, notably culture but also for example, innovation and regional industrial affairs. Basically, what has been evolving in the EU is economic integration, especially in relation to trade and commerce and diverse modes of centralization and decentralization of governance functions, filtering up and down the as yet by no means settled multi-level governance structure of the regions, member-states and the EU itself. A key question is, how does this large and complex structure relate to and influence the international political economy in the context described earlier? Perhaps the first thing to be said is that in terms of financial management it seems less prone to crises than non-members. Of the sixteen biggest fiscal crises occurring between 1977 and 1995, measured in terms of the fiscal cost of bank bail-outs as a percentage of GDP, not one involved an EU member-state, although Spain, Sweden and Finland were hit before joining (Caprio and Klingebiel, 1996). It appears as though macroeconomic stability is one, important, achievement of the member-states of the EU through the pooling of aspects of their economic sovereignty. This cannot be said of the USA during the 1977–95 period where the fiscal cost of its 1984–91 bank bail-out was some 4 per cent of the GDP. Nor can it be said of Japan in the late 1990s, the fiscal cost of whose bank bail-outs may prove to be larger.

Economic integration through European monetary union (EMU), within which the traditionally highly stable DMark is the anchor currency, will, most experts believe, lead to a further strengthening of capabilities to resist large-scale fluctuations, particularly those deriving from too large public indebtedness and too much land and property speculation. These have been intertwined in the debt overhangs of Asian fiscal crises in the 1990s as they were in others elsewhere previously. The difficulties of UK manufacturing in the run-up to the launch of the Euro were explicitly linked by automotive exporters to that country's non-membership of EMU. High associated interest rates and, consequently, currency exchange rates made exports expensive creating the threat of large-scale job losses in manufacturing. Hence, EMU reinforced the macroeconomic stability that EU economies following the EMU criteria of low inflation and low public indebtedness enjoyed through the 1990s. However, this stabilization was achieved at the expense of high and persistent unemployment, particularly in EMU member countries like Germany, France and Spain.

Thus, the EU, faced with the twin pressures of globalization and innovation created a 'fortress' characterized by fiscal rectitude within, but weak competitiveness and job-creation capacity without, particularly in relation to the USA and, until recession caused unemployment to rise, Japan. These problems infused the Green Paper on Innovation (CEC, 1996), where low competitiveness and high unemployment were both thought susceptible to major improvements in innovation capacity by EU industry. The 'European paradox' as the Green Paper put it, was that excellence in scientific performance was not matched in technological and commercial transformation of sufficient scientific knowledge into products, processes or services capable of attracting market demand. Barriers weakening EU industry response to this challenge included insufficient research expenditure and industry involvement in research, insufficient human research capital, lower levels of co-operation among innovation actors, including university–industry linkages, limited venture capital and long-term loan capital, regulatory inefficiencies and a weak enterprise culture.

It is difficult to gauge whether these barriers were identified by the Commission through research or on some other basis. Some of the more measurable indicators like comparisons of research expenditure between countries are well known. However, such statistics are well known also to be measures of inputs to the innovation process rather than outputs from it. Moreover, the majority of firms, not being large enterprises, probably do not have R&D budgets, but may well be innovators, though as the results in Chapters 3 and 4 show, they are likely to be incremental rather than radical innovators. That means they are also likely to be operating in markets where demand for radical innovation is low, such as automotive, electronics or other manufacturing where innovation is orchestrated through supply-chains in relatively mature products. Thus both smaller or medium-sized and larger enterprises in the European economy may be unduly 'locked-in' (Grabher, 1993a) to each other's demands and capabilities. Two things follow from this; first it is likely that large firms in Europe are the greater innovators, given that they are mainly responsible for one of the key inputs to innovation, namely R&D expenditure, but second, they are not themselves sufficiently radical but rather mainly incremental innovators. Breaking this probable 'lock-in' condition by encouraging a weakening of over-strong ties or forging looser coupling may seem perverse in an era when, elsewhere, programmes of support for building 'economic communities' (Henton *et al.*, 1997) by promoting 'networks' and 'clusters' is also advocated. But, as will be seen from the following chapters, particularly 3 and 4, there is evidence from a variety of industries to support this diagnosis.

To return to the concept of the 'learning economy', it seems inescapable that European firms of all sizes have to become more overtly learning organizations if they are to become more innovative. This point is picked up somewhat in the Green Paper on Innovation (CEC, 1996) by reference to 'economic intelligence'. However, what is called for here is far more pervasive than the gathering and dissemination of economic intelligence for firms by public agencies. Firms must become more adept at this for themselves. The role for public agencies and consultants may be to provide 'coaching' to help firms learn how to learn. Here, the work of de Geus (1988, 1997) and others such as Senge (1994) are particularly relevant. The former author was one of the key influences on the work of the latter, through his systemization of the lessons learned at the Shell Oil Company.

The fundamental lesson is that the success and longevity of companies (and conceivably other organizations, too) is closely related to their ability to change rather than remain the same. This immediately resonates with the earlier argument that European firms, especially larger ones with their inordinate influence upon the fate of SMEs through the supply-chain, need to become more learning-oriented towards each other and abroad to improve the innovation capability of whole branches of European industry. Similarly, SMEs need encouragement to become less introverted by increasing involvement in loose SME networks to balance up their more common involvement in supply-chains to a limited range of final customers. Our findings, reported more fully later in this book, suggest that the observation in the Green Paper that 'many public innovation schemes still appear to be tailored to large firms' (CEC, 1996, p.27) is well-founded. While the work of corporate learning advocates such as de Geus focuses on larger firms, some of the lessons are valid for firms of any size.

Thus, in discussions of what makes firms change, the argument that the most effective motivation is the pain of crisis management is rightly dismissed since that course leaves minimal choice from an ever-reducing range of options. Even if decision-making is swift, decisions taken may be poor. Long-lived companies learn from planning towards inevitable change and institutionalizing the learning process. This is a key insight complementary to that in evolutionary theory which is based on the idea that all living systems learn constantly by reference to their relationship to their environment. In a globalizing, competitive and innovative context the issue for firms is not whether to learn and to change but how swiftly can learning be absorbed and change implemented. Making rule-changes, modelling scenarios, and making implicit strategies and assumptions explicit, or presenting strategy models of other real or imaginary companies, are amongst the successful change-management cata- lysts that have been deployed at Shell, a successful, global but EU-domiciled firm.

And the key people at whom such learning has to be successfully directed are that powerful minority – the managers.

There is a great deal in the 'learning corporation' literature that echoes that in the 'learning region' research (see Asheim, 1996; Cooke and Morgan, 1998) which relates to regional economies composed of both large and small or medium-sized enterprises, mainly SMEs. The question of policy-transfer from one region to another, perhaps in a different continent, let alone country, is a much-performed but poorly understood process. For example, economic indicators show that two of the EU's most prosperous and consistently successful regions are found in northern Italy and southern Germany. Because of this, intermediaries ranging from academics like Charles Sabel and Michael Porter, through consultants like Richard Hatch; or Stuart Rosenfeld of Regional Technology Strategies who also organizes study-visits for policy-makers, sought to systematize what were perceived to be the sources of success and transfer those models elsewhere, mainly to the USA.

Because SMEs were key to the success of these regions and they were seen to be engaging in co-operation as well as competition, the concepts of 'networks' and 'clusters', rather than markets or hierarchies, came into vogue. These were then further refined by policy organizations that had absorbed and learnt the lessons of the original setting and wished to implement change in their own. In the process, some relatively expensive programmes to promote 'networks' and 'clusters' among firms of various sizes, but mainly SMEs, were implemented worldwide and some change effects were registered. Amongst the more striking from Australia and Italy were that SMEs in networks rode out the recession of the early 1990s with few job losses and better wages and profitability than equivalent firms not in networks. Elsewhere, in countries such as Denmark and the USA, the most positive finding was that firms with clear objectives about the reasons for working in networks with complementary firms ascribed more of their business performance improvement to their network membership than those with a more unspecified reason for networking. As a consequence of evaluations of network programmes in Denmark, the USA and Australia, policy-makers have become rather less enthusiastic, but for many firms whose first experience of co-operation came through involvement in publicly-funded network-building programmes, the effect has been to change a rule ('only compete') and effect organizational as well as product and process innovations.

Why did policy-makers become sceptical? Primarily because their experiments failed to reproduce the degrees of permanence and stability that seemed to go together in the Italian and German originals. Because firms left networks that were funded by programmes leading to network collapse once the programme funding ended, policy-makers deemed the programme of network-building to be a failure. They discounted the fact that while some firms benefited little from network involvement, others in significant numbers learnt from the experience and voluntarily, at their own cost, entered new network arrangements in order to achieve clearly articulated business objectives. For policy agencies, firms taking ownership of an idea without conforming to the expectations of the policy is a condition they find difficult to deal with because they have 'lost control' of the process and the policy. This means they cannot easily be judged by the performance indicators which are as crucial to their continued existence as the 'bottom-line' is for firms.

Hence, more is now known about the reasons for both success and failure of close inter-firm interaction, especially at regional levels where networks of SMEs have often come together, as well as more globally, where strategic alliances among large enterprises have existed for a decade or more. Common to both kinds of interactive learning context are the possibilities of breach of trust, therefore the importance of implicit or explicit contracts and confidentiality clauses. Complementarity is important to successful partnership since no firm will divulge proprietary information that could lead to it being out-competed by a partner firm. But too great a distance between technologies or even industry cultures, such as the regular failures of partnerships between computing and telecommunications firms, may also be a weakness. The outlines of systemic innovation potential from interactive learning are thus made clearer.

4. What are the challenges to policy?

The key challenges for policy towards the promotion of innovation involve assisting firms to change and to deal with change by enhancing their learning capabilities, becoming more radically innovative than they have been hitherto in a globalizing and highly competitive economic context, but one in which, in the EU, macro-economic conditions appear stable and favourable. Because innovation is increasingly an interactive process involving more demanding users and specialist technological requirements, much more needs to be done to raise the possibilities for firms to engage in co-operative, trustful interaction in pursuit of innovation while improving their powers of competition both within and beyond the EU. Of particular importance here is the process of exploiting 'knowledge capital' for commercial gain. Thus sources of knowledge capital whether public or private must be brought closer to business without compromising the essential, scholastic and critical, functions of public universities and research institutes.

A great deal of attention is devoted in policy and academic literature to creating closer university–industry relations (see, for example, Etkowitz and Leydesdorff, 1997). The argument is basically a good one, and if transformed into practice it might have significant positive effects on firm competitiveness in Europe. But it is important to recognize that, even in the country where such relationships are believed to have spread widest and penetrated deepest, the USA, it is far from ubiquitously the case that university–industry relationship are close and fruitful. In some celebrated cases such as Stanford and MIT (Massachusetts Institute of Technology) such relationships exist, but for most Ivy League universities these relationships are not found. It is certain that the spin-off of new enterprises is more intense from US than from European universities and research institutes, but how long-lasting or fast-growing are the resultant businesses? Some clearly grow to monster size as in the cases of Hewlett-Packard or Microsoft, but clearly the majority does not. One thing is clear about universities and industry and that is that they are even more different functionally and culturally than computer and telecommunications firms.

Not only is the importance of this distinction stressed in CEC (1998) where Lundvall and Borrás draw on the observations of Pavitt (1995) but it shows up clearly in some results from recent research into university–industry relations also funded by the EU-TSER programme (Cooke *et al.*, 1999). Pavitt's argument is that university research occurs in a controlled environment where continuity and special-ization are important, while in firms, problem-solving in a rapidly-changing context is the norm, and flexibility rather than specialization is valued. Organizational, motivational and procedural conventions in knowledge-production thus differ sub-stantially. Even though authors like Gibbons *et al.* (1994) are correct in observing changes to the relationship between these separate worlds such that industry and academia now interact more and the latter operates in a more interdisciplinary style, important barriers still exist. Thus, in the Cooke *et al.* (1999) study, academics' views of university–industry interactions are generally quite cynical in that they see industry mainly as an alternative source of funding helping to replace some of the budget lost by public research cuts. Also the short-term nature of time-scales and contracts was seen as a sign of the lack of depth and lack of interest in 'blue skies' research on the part of industry. Academics, at their most sceptical saw industry seeking only 'testing' work from universities at a price lower than consultants would charge. While academics may be rewarded through publishing original ideas or findings, industry has little or no interest in novel ideas and often seeks to delay or prevent publication. This is true even in the late 1990s after a decade, or more, of encouragement for greater university–industry interaction.

There is a challenge for policy here, deriving from the relative failure in the EU to construct more bridges between the worlds of industry and academia. Policy-makers should recognize the desirability of forging stronger university–industry research links through promoting contexts in which industry understands the competing pressures on academic time, the relative poverty of university research resourcing and the importance of continuity, and in which universities need to understand the time-constraints and problem-solving focus of firms better than they do at present. If the core cultures are less than compatible, a hybrid culture needs to be encouraged, perhaps through varieties of 'campus company' or spin-off firm acting as an inter-mediary, or through something akin to the *Aninstituten* first established in Baden-Württemberg in Germany. This is where basic research institutes establish a consultancy arm working to more exacting time and task constraints than the research colleagues themselves. Industry sometimes funds campus laboratories, it could do the same with campus companies. But, because of 'cherry-picking' there is a role for policy to spread the benefits beyond elite centres.

On a broader scale, there is also a role for policy in helping to increase the prospects for synergy among a variety of organizations, as well as firms, that have good reason to know of each other's needs and expertise. We have seen how in the EU industry has for many decades benefited from supply-chain relationships with flotillas of more or less geographically proximate sub-contractors. Supply-chain management has itself improved dramatically with the systemization of westernized models of industrial organization originating in Japan, such as 'lean production'. More generally, however, it is not necessarily fortunate for innovation capability if such networks become more introverted as they become more elaborated, as seems to be the case with Europe's 'captive' suppliers. Horizontal as well as vertical SME networks are needed, with knowledge centres centrally involved in diffusing usable knowledge capital. Policy for promoting localized or regionalized learning and innovation capability through this 'associational' mode is thus called for (Cooke and Morgan, 1998).

Lastly, what about large firms and what about the loser regions or social groupings that are among the slower learners? With respect to the former, Cooke and Morgan (1998) suggested that there were good reasons for allowing larger firms to deal with their own innovation deficits rather than public bodies pumping in sizeable injections of innovation support funding which comprise only a minuscule portion of firms' overall R&D budgets. Such funding could have greater impact if diverted to SMEs and hybrid organizations of the kind discussed earlier. As we show in subsequent chapters, SMEs in the EU are lesser innovators than large firms despite a prevailing belief to the contrary among those who assume SMEs to be more innovative; but perhaps they focus only on innovator firms rather than firms in general. Moreover, in the EU compared to competitor economies there are innovation deficits in high technology despite the fact that billions of ECUs have been spent by the Commission on precisely those sectors. It seems, as Edquist (1997b) and others have noted, that large European firms are innovators in yesterday's technologies. Policies should aid large firms where they are overtly seeking to overcome these past weaknesses, by working closely with knowledge centres and innovator firms, large or small, in the EU or beyond, in an associational and learning-oriented manner (Boekholt *et al.*, 1998).

Innovation policies cannot directly assist the unemployed back into jobs or backward regions to develop, but in concert with other policies, such as skills-training and infrastructure investment (including softer, knowledge centre investment) it can. Moreover, it should aim at promoting less-favoured areas to develop innovation in industries and skills that are appropriate and meaningful for the region or locality in question. There are strong signs that innovation policy and regional policy are becoming more intertwined in the EU and that, for example, Structural Funds will be more closely linked to both skills-development and business innovation in future (Landabaso, 1997). But it is important not only to see policy as a safety net for the losers. Although innovation policy cannot cover every requirement for economic development, we argue that for clustered, specialized, supply-chain intensive sub-economics it is crucial. Examples are found in many regions of the EU from the electronics complex found near the Arctic Circle at Oulu, Finland to the design-intensive fashion clothing districts of Galicia in northern Spain, not to mention, of course, northern Italy, and from the biotechnology and software cluster at Cambridge, England to the automotive cluster centred on the world-leading, combustion-engine research firm, AVL in Styria, Austria. For each of these, and many others, some discussed in subsequent chapters, innovation is at the heart of economic development.

Recognizing this feature of the new international political economy the EU has initiated a number of experiments and actions in subsidizing regional authorities to develop Regional Innovation Strategies. We say much more about these in Chapters 5, 6 and 7, but it is no coincidence that regional levels are being targeted. In a globalizing economy composed of large and highly competitive multinational firms co-ordinating production, key nodes develop as the specialized production or services complex for particular activities. In the nineteenth century Alfred Marshall first noticed that within national economies there were often localized industrial districts, such as Sheffield or Remscheid for cutlery, Stoke or Limoges for chinaware, Kidderminister or Kortrijk for carpets, nowadays in a more globalized setting the organization of production is on a larger scale too. Thus Baden-Württemberg is a global leader for luxury car production, Silicon Valley and California more generally for computing, software and multimedia and London or New York for financial services of many kinds. The key for regions and their policy animators is to find the local and regional networks that can link to global networks and enhance their learning capacity, innovativeness and competitiveness.

5. Why regional innovation systems and regional innovation policy?

In this book we make a strong case for focusing innovation policy and enterprise support at the regional level, indeed we argue that the world has moved on from the days when regional policy was primarily a spatial version of the redistribution of welfare to needy people in areas hit by deindustrialization or underdevelopment to a position where regional innovation policy is at the heart of economic development. This is because of the already-discussed incomplete or asymmetrical globalization of production and, particularly, financial systems organization that has already occurred, within which global competitiveness is fuelled to a large extent by innovation. In a knowledge society, learning is the means of exploiting the vital resource of implicit or tacit know-how. But this very factor of production is the 'stickiest' or least mobile of all. It is produced at a few points on the globe, surrounded by a rich tissue of inter-firm and inter-organizational linkages at each point and it is in the interests of global, or ambitious, competitive firms to be positioned so as to take the maximum advantage possible of such locations.

What do we mean by a regional innovation system? It is a concept drawn from evolutionary economics which stresses the choice firm managers have of choosing the trajectory of their firm by learning and changing as a consequence of social interaction focused on economic issues. Such interaction moves beyond the business sphere, especially where innovation is the firm-function in question. It reaches the public sphere of universities, research labs, technology transfer and training agencies. Where knowledge flows through networks of innovators, for example, such that an innovation problem may induce a solution or response from others, or a skills deficit may be met by augmentation of training opportunities, 'seamless' interaction is systemic. Where many or all these functions are available and operating in reasonable proximity, backed by judicious regional governance and administration, we can speak of a regional innovation system. Of course, these always exist in interaction with systems at other governance levels. The research in this book seeks to identify such phenomena in Europe. They are rare worldwide but examples do exist, often in traditional as well as advanced industries.

As noted previously we are not only speaking of leading edge, high technologies in this respect, but many traditional industries such as horticulture in the North and South Holland horticultural complex, or pulp and paper machinery in the Tampere region in Finland, or Styria in Austria. All make use of advanced electronics and even biotechnologies, advancing the innovativeness of those technologies through their demands of the producers. This extends the notion of regional innovation systems and policies well beyond the privileged to the less-favoured areas. However, these will have their own specialist economic tendencies which may relate to acquaculture in coastal regions or oenology in wine-producing regions. Regarding the latter, by way of example, the 'region' of South Australia, much of it desert, has developed a world-leading wine production innovation system, the technological products of which are not only being experimented with, but transforming wine production in some of the highest status, most traditionally-minded vineyard regions in the world, namely the Bordeaux and Burgundy producing regions of France.

The Barossa Valley north of Adelaide, South Australia is the epicentre of this complex or innovative production system. The key breakthrough was by the Wolf Blass Company that introduced the stainless steel container to replace the barrel as the main means of storage and maturation of wine. Greater consistency and stability of the product could be ensured with this approach, and production for mass-markets facilitated. But the loss of quality in taste caused by moving from wood to steel containers created a demand for special oakwood chips, the tacit knowledge for the production of which exists only in Barossa. The region itself has become an innovative system, oak veneer is used in barrel manufacture as it is cheaper than solid oak and produces the same effects. Demand for stainless steel containers and valves, control systems and sensors is enormous, new bottling plants and cork importing firms have developed, and special courses in diverse aspects of oenology technology and production culture now exist in the regional university. South Australia now exports more than half the wine shipped abroad from that continent. The region has achieved global competitive advantage and the policy of BREDA (the Barossa Regional Development Authority) assists in whatever ways possible to maintain it.

This is merely a sketch of a particular 'cluster' but one which has, in a relatively short time, moved to the forefront of the international stage for wine production. It is by no means an SME-only region, large firms like Southcorp own many of the wineries such as Orlando or Hardy, but they leave them under local management, conscious of inherited learning, knowledge and social capital that are central to the region's growth trajectory. There is also co-operation as well as competition amongst businesses and there is linkage of a regular, systemic nature between customers and suppliers whether of bottles and corks or specialized viticultural know-how. But above all the scale of the place means that interaction with respect to society and culture or learning and innovation is swift, tacit knowledge exchange and user-producer interaction are regular and activities to ensure continuation of the associational nature of the industry are facilitated and animated by regional intermediaries. This simply could not be achieved with the same degree of success outside a regional setting because the nuances of trustful interaction, the sensibilities and sensitivities of the actors involved, and the prospects for exchanging 'untraded interdependencies' would be far less well understood and capable of being developed.

However, this is not to say that in the new international political economy, the region is somehow a privileged action space. Rather, it rises from being an historically often provincial space on which were inscribed the decisions of metropolitan elites whether in governance or economy and to which resources might be 'redis-tributed', to an active, potentially valued arena of economic and, in consequence, political force in its own right. But it achieves this in the context of its sovereign state (unless, as with the Baltic states, it becomes sovereign itself) and in the EU context, within a complex system of multi-level governance involving state and supra-state levels of governance. We explore this phenomenon in greater detail in Chapter 5.

However, intriguing questions arise about appropriate functions at specific levels in multi-level governance settings such as the EU. While excessive Cartesianism should be resisted, given the divergent and disparate histories and statuses of regions in contemporary Europe, some relatively new lines of inquiry can be suggested or even speculated upon with regard to innovation, but to some extent other functions too. Lundvall and Borrás (CEC, 1997) hint at this by reference to the widespread feature common to EU member-states which is that, through taxation they fund by far the largest amount of science and technology research, and only occasionally do they not also directly fund higher education, notably universities. Accordingly, states govern science policy, choosing democratically where and how to invest in areas of knowledge and human capital that are perceived to be strategic for that state. Hence military R&D expenditure is more pronounced in the UK and France because of historic path dependencies and projected future global and continental market advantages. Civilian R&D expenditure is more pronounced in Germany because it lost the war and was forced to detach its economy from military emphasis, though that situation is changing.

The EU has developed a rather powerful role in technology policy in the sense that nowadays its Framework Programmes increasingly align with, but also induce alignment from, member-states and their priorities. It could be said that this is unsurprising since the member-states through the Council of Ministers control both but in fact it is a rather large achievement aimed at minimizing duplication and encouraging co-operation and learning. The origins of the Framework Programmes are also relevant in describing the technological or applied emphasis they have. Influenced by large European technology firms, the initial programmes were cap-tured by those firms, but although this has changed, the constant message from the Commission is to the effect that technological (and ultimately scientific) research must be made more capable of being exploited for commercial purposes so that Europe can be more innovative and competitive, is easy to understand if not to react to.

So what, if anything, does the regional level of multi-level governance claim as its special area of expertise if science policy is mainly a state-level function and technology policy is increasingly influenced through and by the EU? It is clear from the foregoing that innovation, the more near-market part of the knowledge capital transformation process, is an emergent regional function and one which as we state in Chapters 6 and 7, many regions are presently ill-equipped to fulfil, though others are clearly not. In the globalizing but also regionalizing economy that has been described, where regional systems of innovation may be emergent and, in the EU at least, much innovation support activity is organized to stimulate the development of regional innovation policies, the connection between regions and the innovation support function for SMEs becomes compelling. Of course, the picture is actually dynamic and diverse, but as a broad orientation this division of functions and interaction among them has a degree of realism and logic to it.

As Lundvall and Borrás (CEC, 1998) put it in this respect:

> The EU shows great diversity in the division of tasks between these three levels of government. ... On the one hand, national governments still play a central role in devoting economic resources to basic research by funding research groups. ... On the other hand, there have been important trends towards decentralisation and European-isation of these public actions. The regional governments in some large federal and semi-federal European countries are in charge of the university system ... the EU Framework Programme ... stimulated scientific cooperation across European borders. (p.85)

The picture is thus rather messy and uncertain, but broadly speaking a division of functions and a growth of responsibilities at all levels seems evident, particularly the regional and the EU.

6. Conclusions

We have sought to set the case for a greater focus on the value and importance of the regional level within an EU system of multi-level governance of innovation in the context of what is new in the international political economy. The research findings we report in succeeding chapters were elicited from within a research design which set out to discover how much and in what ways a perceived globalization process was impacting upon firms' competitive strategies, particularly those involving a focus upon innovation. Without jumping the gun with respect to the nature of those findings, it is nevertheless worth commenting now on a number of generic features of the position European (EU and CEC) firms face with respect to business organiza-tion, opportunities and challenges at the *fin de siècle*.

Most firms are not in touch with the final market if that market is global. This also applies to a lesser degree if markets are EU in scope. Most European firms have their direct trading relations, linkages to other firms as customers or suppliers, and innovation relationships with other firms in their region or country. We are speaking here of firms in manufacturing and some services close to manufacturing but we believe this would be even more the case for services firms in general since their markets are normally even more confined. We conclude that globalization for most firms in Europe is mediated by their position in some kind of supply-chain relation-ships which may, in some circumstances, take the form of geographically agglomerated 'clusters'.

We also find the majority of European firms to be quite introverted with respect to problem-solving for innovation, and highly dependent on a few customers or suppliers for ideas and partnerships concerning development of innovations. In association with this, firms engage in innovation activities to a greater extent than they are able to recoup total costs of innovation by getting new products and processes to the market. This may not be a totally unknown phenomenon in other countries but it suggests perhaps a lack of clear objectives regarding innovation and a persistence of a perhaps wasteful 'tinkering' mentality associated with traditional craft production.

More worryingly, given our emphasis on the importance of learning in the new international political economy, we find European firms, as noted, tending towards a strong belief in their own internal resources for problem-solving and innovation, perhaps oblivious to the existence of ready-made solutions on the market whether of European or non-European origin. Reinforcing this introversion regarding innovation is a relatively low use of the enterprise support infrastructure for innovation by all firms but particularly small and medium enterprises. Larger firms are more internally capable of tackling innovation than SMEs, yet large firms are greater users of the support infrastructure than SMEs. This might be predictable for universities but it applies also to other kinds of public or private support such as training or technology transfer too. Learning seems only to occur at the behest of customers, or possibly supplier firms.

This means that the programmes put in place in support of innovation by the EU, member-state and regional governments in Europe are probably quite good programmes which are missing their target. Most are aimed at SMEs, but these are harder to persuade to become regular users because they are not as receptive as larger firms, there are more of them and few are likely to have sufficient 'organizational slack' to devote attention to external learning opportunities. Despite celebrated examples to the contrary, most European SMEs do not operate in network relationships with other SMEs except in so far as they are possibly suppliers to a common customer who meet in the client's supplier development or simultaneous engineering group if it exists.

Firms both large and small are remarkably regionally and nationally focused in Europe, both from the organization and market-orientation angles. This helps convince us of the efficacy of strengthening the capability of firms, especially, but not only SMEs, to engage in collective learning in what others see as a globalizing, learning economy. Where firms have local complementarities and the possibilities of shared learning in a university or other knowledge-centre context, opportunities should be taken to enhance this by the offer of modest incentives. This is beginning to happen in some member-states but could be promoted on a wider basis by the EU. Practically speaking one of the larger EU budgets is for regional policy. Recent consensus among the innovation and regional directorates of the EU on the desirability of a new regional policy with regional innovation systems and strategies at its heart is a welcome recognition of the need to narrow the innovation gap and the 'European paradox' also in less-favoured regions.

These developments and implications should help move the EU closer to its competitors in terms of innovation performance. We noted earlier that, although globalization can be overstated both as a completed process and a universal phenomenon, asymmetrical globalization is a reality, focused on the two-way interactions between North America and the EU on the one hand, and the strong outward but weak inward interaction among Japan and the two major economic markets on the other. As such, a number of implications flowed to which European business had been slow to react. Competitiveness is closely linked to innovativeness and although formerly innovative economies in South East Asia have been condemned to compete on devaluation prices to recover export balances, the EU at present has governance and regulatory institutions in place that seem to dissuade innovativeness for fear of financial instability. Accordingly, the EU is increasingly taking on, through EMU, a role shared with the USA, as anchor of the global finance system. As we saw, the fiscal disciplines associated with this tend to discourage investment in innovation, something which seems to be supported by the comparative innovation statistics.

The most important lesson from recent experience is that EU institutions, other governance levels and firms themselves need to increase their learning capabilities. Learning should not just mean borrowing and adapting from outside but also a kind of internal auditing, benchmarking and excavation of good practices of many kinds, not least those of European scientific research, with a view to learning from experience closer to home.

It is frequently and correctly said that Europe differs in its diversity from the homogeneity of Japanese society and the melting pot of America. In the chapters which follow, strong elements of that diversity will be revealed in the distinctiveness of Europe's regional political economies, something perhaps less pronounced in the EU's main competitors. However, what will also be seen is a quite remarkable level of homogeneity in the perceptions of firms in all regions studied, drawn from eleven countries, of the competitive challenge faced by contemporary businesses, their modes of operation in confronting the challenge, and their posture towards innovation in relation to enhancing their competitiveness. This combination of shared understandings and diversity in regional systems of innovation set in a developing EU structure of multi-level governance, offers some threats but more opportunities for future synergies and improved innovative performance in the new learning economies of Europe.

CHAPTER TWO

Regional Profiles and Trajectories of Change

1. Introduction

We have seen that a powerful and pervasive economic process of the late-twentieth century is globalization. This is welcomed by those who benefit from cheaper goods through free trade but perceived as a threat by producers who lose in the competitive struggle. Some authors, however, see the image of a world economy dominated by a few multinationals, and financial flows under the hegemony of traders not governments, as one that is not borne out empirically (see, for example, Ruigrok and Van Tulder, 1995; Hirst and Thompson, 1996). For these, and other authors, there is also a vertical relationship, from the global to the local or regional levels to be considered, as well as horizontal relationships across space. While, in theory, it may be possible for capital to move easily from one country to another, in practice it is not equally so for all economic functions. Thus currency or stock-market speculation is relatively unhindered, but advanced R&D in computer technology, for example, cannot equally be conducted anywhere on earth. Places develop 'asset stock accumulation' (Dierickx and Cool, 1989) which means they gain and retain competitive advantage from the learning competence, 'absorptive capacity' (Cohen and Levinthal, 1990) and creative capabilities of their expert labour.

It is these aspects of contemporary economic development that this study of regional innovation takes as its central matter of concern. In other words, given that there is at least some quite significant element of globalization going on, how and in what ways do innovation processes interact with regions and their economies? This is especially important bearing in mind that innovation is also significantly influenced by the policies of states and, in the case of the European Union (EU), its member-states as well as the union itself through the European Commission. Why regions? In this chapter, the case for a focus on regions will be made. It will be argued that in this stage of the evolution of capitalistic economic development global competition, and the liberal trading regime which facilitates it, have caused a trend towards *specialization* in the economic activities of countries (Krugman, 1991, 1995). This shows up particularly in time-series data for international trade (e.g. Archibugi and Pianta, 1992; Dalum, 1995; Lundvall and Borrás, 1997). It reinforces competitively advantaged industry sectors and, in consequence tends to lead to a growing regional economic specialization within countries (de Vet, 1993; Malmberg and Maskell, 1997; Storper and Scott, 1995). The processes underpinning regionalization of economic activity include; the necessity for large firms, including multinationals, increasingly to outsource production of goods and services to supply-chains of smaller and medium-sized firms; the consequent re-emergence of external economies where suppliers and customers are co-located; the resultant diminution of transaction costs where industry expertise occurs in regional agglomerations; and the advantages of proximity regarding innovation where tacit knowledge can be readily exchanged, further reducing market uncertainties (Cooke, 1995; Storper, 1995).

As recognition grows of the existence of, or desirability of developing, regional competitive advantage based on knowledge-intensity in specialist industries, so the *governance* structure of the region in question becomes attuned to the needs of regional business and assists in the promotion of the regional economy. Governance consists of more than simply regional government; it includes also private governance organizations such as chambers of commerce, business and trade associations, trade unions, consultancies and private training or technology-transfer organizations. In the public domain, it may include devolved agencies of central government and, in the EU, the activities of the European Commission in promoting regional economic development. While there may be a variety of relationships amongst such organizations, ranging from predominantly vertical, 'top-down' interactions in centralist states, to more lateral, negotiated interactions as in federal states, it is widely argued that many accomplished regional economies operate through 'policy networks' which are inclusive and relatively open in their membership posture towards agencies and actors of consequence to the policy process (Marin and Mayntz, 1991; Rhodes, *et al.* 1997).

Moreover, such policy networks may animate or facilitate network relationships amongst firms in the region, where these do not already exist. Such policies are especially aimed at SMEs which, it is believed, gain obvious benefits from interaction rather than isolation, and co-operation rather than pure competition (OECD, 1996). Such networks are mainly horizontal, bringing SMEs together to engage in joint innovation, production and marketing. Perhaps more common are vertical network-type relationships between larger customer firms and their preferred, or long-term suppliers. Hierarchies of such interactions are increasingly to be found in supply-chains animated by firms themselves or facilitated with the assistance of public development agencies (Semlinger, 1993; Cooke and Morgan, 1994b; 1998; Scott, 1996). Where such lateral and vertical, private and public interactions are relatively pronounced, regional industry may take on the form of the competitively advantaged industry cluster (Porter, 1990; Enright, 1996).

Innovation, as a key factor in competitiveness, is particularly advantaged in such contexts since firms may more readily exchange tacit, creative knowledge with each other and with university research laboratories and public or private research institutes as well as the local or regional innovation support 'infrastructure' (Smith, 1997). As an interactive process, involving this range of actors, innovation can be enhanced by proximity, though localized learning alone is clearly not enough. Where the flow of knowledge and relevant information for innovation is rich and rapid we may speak of the existence of a regional innovation system, complementing and interacting with national and global systems (Edquist, 1997b; Lundvall, 1997). This, possibly ideal, configuration is the stimulus of this research. It seeks to establish the extent to which such arrangements are found to be operating in European regions, to indicate distinctive kinds of regional relationships regarding innovation, and to assess the extent to which there are tendencies towards divergence or convergence towards a European norm in the means by which innovation is conducted at regional level. To repeat, these questions are not limited to a regional focus alone, they recognize the importance of supra-regional interactions and flows of knowledge and information. It is important to establish the division of interactions between regional and other levels to ascertain what is appropriate at each one.

In this chapter attention will be devoted to further elaboration of the role and importance of regions in a globalizing, learning economy (Lundvall and Borrás, 1997). There will also be further brief discussion of innovation, interaction and governance issues. This will then be followed by the main theme of this chapter which is a preliminary indication of the nature of the regions and their political economies of innovation as investigated in this research study. This will be done in relation to certain criteria such as their degree of embeddedness – concerning the nature and extent of interaction for innovation, the kinds of innovation organized regionally, and predominant governance regimes. Thus, at the outset, the nature of, and extent to which, systemic innovation and policies to support it exist in each region can be outlined. In later chapters, hypotheses drawn from this analysis are then tested, based on the results of the research undertaken.

2. Globalization and regionalization of innovation

Whether globalization is perceived to be a pervasive process of the evolving international economic order, or primarily a handy term to capture a broadening of major trade and investment flows from the Atlantic area to include also the Pacific Rim, it seems to be the case that hitherto powerful 'national economies' are less capable of or inclined to erect trade and investment barriers than were once thought necessary or desirable. To be competitive means to be internationally competitive for a larger proportion of firms, including SMEs. Simon (1992) has written persuasively of Germany's 'mid-size giants', *mittelstand* firms that habitually export substantial proportions of their output, and are counted amongst world-leader firms in their particular niches. Recently, evidence has come to light of Spanish, and particularly Catalan firms behaving as 'pocket-sized multinationals' by means of foreign trade and investment, especially, but not only, through foreign direct investment in Latin America (White, 1997). But, of course, it is mainly larger multinationals for whom globalization is both a vehicle for and a result of their activities.

In the early 1980s, one of the first authors to identify globalization conceived it as a process whereby global corporations sought to impose worldwide standards upon consumer markets for mass-consumption goods, enabling them to reap much larger returns to scale (Levitt, 1983). 'World Car' strategies by the likes of the Ford Motor company or, classically, fast-food operations such as McDonald's were the progenitors of this Phase 1 of the globalization process. Phase 2 was initiated by Japanese consumer goods firms who recognized that markets were not and could not be identical worldwide, and professed the aim of achieving 'global localization' whereby the full range of business functions would be duplicated in the European and American, as well as Southeast Asian markets, enabling products to be adapted to local market requirements, even if only superficially (Cooke *et al.*, 1992). This opened up the prospect of innovation activities being conducted not only in the home base but in export markets where production had already been established. However, only some 25 per cent of Japanese R&D units established in the UK and Germany, for example, are free-standing laboratories unattached to factories, signifying that, as yet, most innovation by Japanese firms in Europe is of relatively modest proportions.

Nevertheless, foreign direct investment (FDI) by North American and South East Asian firms into Europe has undoubtedly had effects upon competitiveness of economies and these have often been regionally focused. For example, Wales, one of the regions under investigation has been a major recipient of investment from Japan with some 55 plants having been established since the early 1970s. Other parts of the UK such as northern England and Scotland have also been major recipients of Asian and American investment, often in high-technology sectors such as computing. The Republic of Ireland, too, has been a major beneficiary, especially of American computer and software firms and this has undoubtedly had a major impact upon that small country's remarkable Gross Domestic Product (GDP) growth, averaging 6 per cent 1990–97 (Gray, 1997). Interestingly, it has recently been argued that the Irish experience (and this may, to some extent, be extended to the Scottish and Welsh cases) 'might be viewed as a harbinger of a *new model* or pattern of industrial development, with new possibilities for late-developing peripheral countries ...' (O'Donnell, 1998; emphasis added). It is suggested that this undermines key aspects of Porter's (1990) cluster theory of competitive advantage based on strong domestic rivalry and a robust home base as the centerpiece of competitiveness. If, as further suggested, Ireland's lack of fit with Porterian assumptions is likely to be permanent, this experience of strong transnational innovation linkages, but relatively weak internal linkages or interactions, may have significance for innovation promotion policies more generally. This also testifies to the importance in developmental terms for weaker regional economies of globalization processes more generally, and, especially in peripheral, reconversion and transitional (Central and Eastern European) regions with which this study is mainly concerned.

If externally-induced development of the kind referred to does indeed constitute a 'new model' of economic evolution, then it remains relatively restricted to the rather open economies of the UK and Ireland, on the one hand, and perhaps Poland and Hungary, along with other CEE countries, on the other. While there is evidence of a new awareness of the importance of inward investment in larger continental economies such as France and Germany, especially in regions hit by the decline of older industries, even economies which have a history of attracting it, like Belgium and The Netherlands, scarcely build their developmental strategies upon it. And in some cases, such as Italy, FDI is of relatively minor importance. Nevertheless, the injection of *technological* and *organizational* innovativeness that FDI entails can have significance for the receiving economy, especially where there is a critical mass focused upon specific regions. Thus, as will be seen for the UK case of Wales, the entry of South East Asian firms has led to the development of localized supply-chains, suppliers 'clubs' and training strategies; all of which have sought to upgrade the responsiveness of local firms and labour markets to their exacting demands in terms of quality, delivery and innovativeness.

What, therefore, are some of the key implications and conditions for regional economies that become hosts to FDI? Equally, what are they for those with a lower density of FDI but which are, nevertheless, affected by change in competitiveness conditions implied by globalization? To return to the anatomy of Irish success in relation to FDI, the analysis of one or two highly respected economists should be considered. Both Arrow (1997) and Krugman (1997) place emphasis on the quantity and quality of labour force skills and past investments in both secondary and tertiary-level education, particularly Ireland's heavy investment in improving Information Technology (IT) skills. Krugman also places emphasis on the importance of FDI in a context where fast productivity growth occurred without a comparable increase in wages. The latter, crucially, was a product of the adoption by the Irish state of a 'social partnership' agreement to assist macroeconomic stabilization. Finally, Krugman makes the important generic point that international trade has shifted from being dominated by transportation costs to domination by factors such as delivery time, communication and personal contact. In consequence, he concludes, 'it seems clear that Ireland has developed some more or less classic Marshallian clusters, especially in the electronics and pharmaceutical industries' (Krugman, 1997, p.48).

Clearly, Ireland is a sovereign state and thus has more control over its economic policy than do regional economies within states; yet, Krugman and others see many features of a 'regional economy at European level in the Irish experience'. In those regions less dominated by FDI but possessing industries prone to increased competition due to the impact of globalization, steps have to be taken to seek to retain competitiveness. Enterprise support to help indigenous firms become more innovative, given that innovation accounts for some 80 per cent of productivity growth (Freeman, 1994b), is clearly implied. Ensuring that necessary skills are available to enable firms to increase quality while remaining competitive on price is an imperative. Finally, opening up economies to increased international trading activity, whether in terms of seeking new overseas markets, or identifying cheaper sources of supply, whether of goods and services or labour, is a necessary step. In many of the higher cost locations this means exporting production to cheaper production sites, lowering the share of less-skilled labour and seeking to pursue a 'high road' strategy of higher skills, higher value-added and higher incomes for more knowledge and innovation-intensive workforces. These processes are and have been under way in many EU economies for some time. They entail, for the firm, improvements in management capability and organizational innovation, and for governments, the need to develop innovative solutions to problems of unemployment and social exclusion. There seems to have been more widespread accomplishment of the former than the latter imperative in many EU member-states in recent years. It is likely that the growing importance of the services industries, now increasingly important in export markets in certain sectors such as financial, cultural (including tourism, retail, hotels and restaurants) and communications services will have to become a strong focus of policy attention, as will those more locally-consumed such as health and education.

In light of these changes in competitive conditions, it has become clear that regional authorities have had to become more alert to the requirements of firms for aspects of enterprise support. This is not least because state policies to assist industrial and regional development have tended to diminish even though EU support for regional development had, through the 1980s and 1990s, grown considerably. Some regions and even whole countries such as Ireland and Portugal seem to have benefited noticeably from Structural and Cohesion Fund disbursements. The emergence of multi-level governance (Marks *et al.*, 1996; Hooghe, 1996) of regional development is one of the most interesting and pertinent policy developments of the period during which EU regional policy has grown, particularly following the post-1988 period when the Structural Funds were reformed and their scale doubled. More will be said about this in relation to this research in Chapter 5 but for the present, suffice it to say that regional capacity to engage in formal and informal policy and other networks, to lobby, particularly through having a presence in Brussels in the form of a regional Mission, and to maintain good receptiveness to information on funding opportunities, is now of great significance to regional authorities, particularly less advantaged ones.

3. Theorizing new regionalism

Speaking in theoretical terms, and picking up on points made in the introduction to this chapter concerning regional advantage, a consensus has formed from amongst writers such as Grabher (1993b), Amin and Thrift (1994), Saxenian (1994), Cooke (1995), Florida (1995), Maillat (1995), Storper and Scott (1995), and Cooke and Morgan (1998) that accomplished regional economies tend to display certain common features. Amongst the most important of these are; *agglomeration economies, institutional learning, associative governance, proximity capital*, and *interactive innovation* (see also Johnson, 1992; Amin and Thomas, 1996; Crevoisier, 1997; Edquist, 1997a; Malmberg and Maskell, 1997). Briefly these are explained below.

3.1. Agglomeration economies

Since Marshall, the advantages of co-location by firms in single or complementary industries have been well-understood. Krugman (1997) itemizes these as follows: first, a concentration of producers supports local suppliers of specialized inputs who thus help generate external economies of scale effects; second, agglomerations generate localized skills-pools benefiting workers' and firms' flexible labour market opportunities; third, information spillovers are implied by the existence of agglomeration. In the sphere of regional *innovation* these translate into opportunities for lowering transaction costs from uncertainty due to the possibilities for specialist, tacit-knowledge exchange present in the agglomeration (though always subject to efforts to minimize leakage and maximise equivalence from tacit-knowledge exchange with others) (Saxenian, 1994; Storper and Scott, 1995; Malmberg and Maskell, 1997).

3.2. Institutional learning

This refers to the institutional setting of norms, routines, 'rules of the game' and 'conventions' (after North, 1993) whereby it is widely understood that certain practices are acceptable and promote trustful relationships amongst firms and organizations (which may also help reduce transaction costs). But, among the norms of growing importance for firms and enterprise support organizations is the presumption in a globalizing economy, characterized by turbulence and uncertainty, that openness to learning good practice from others is of special importance. In Lundvall and Johnson's (1994) formulation this is conceived of as the externalized form of the kind of learning more typical of what Argyris and Schon (1978) referred to as the internalized characteristics of the 'learning organization' or firm. It applies equally to organizations that interact with firms, including governance agencies, that must 'learn-by-monitoring' (Sabel, 1996) in respect of the performance of the wider economy, their own goals-achievement and that of competitor agencies. It goes without saying that such learning is global as well as local.

3.3. *Associative governance*

Here, reference is made to a networking propensity whereby key regional governance mechanisms, notably the regional administrative bodies, are interactive and inclusive with respect to other bodies of consequence to regional innovation. This may lead to an organizational setting in which, let us say, the regional administration animates or facilitates associativeness among representative bodies inside or outside public governance, but does not seek to dominate a process of consensus formation with respect to, say a readjustment of regional economic strategy. It may involve a government agency 'letting-go' of, or at least sharing, a function which it may have been responsible for innovating, with legitimate private governance bodies such as chambers of commerce or business associations.

3.4. *Proximity capital*

This can be hard or soft, financial or human and refers to different kinds of infrastructure of relevance to regional innovation. According to Smith (1997) there is a strong association between past investments in a variety of infrastructures and economic performance. Thus, the existence of appropriate communication links such as road, rail, airports and telecommunication services is crucially important in proximity to industrial agglomerations. As Krugman (1997) puts it, quoting US Federal Reserve Chairman, Alan Greenspan 'the gross domestic product is getting *lighter*'. Hence 'for businesses which depend on personal contact and/or rapid shipment of goods, two locations 500 miles apart but close to major airports with frequent direct flights are effectively closer to each other than two locations on opposite sides of the same large metropolitan area' (Krugman, 1997, pp.44–6). This is material capital, but Crevoisier (1997) refers also to the importance in agglomerations (especially of SMEs) of localized, trustful means of raising investment capital, maybe through local entrepreneurs or 'business angels', not necessarily banks. Intellectual capital from previous investments in universities and research institutes in proximity to complementary firms is yet another form of 'proximity capital'.

3.5. *Interactive innovation*

As elaborated in Chapter 1, this concept is very much associated with the 'national systems of innovation' literature (Lundvall, 1992; Nelson, 1993; Freeman, 1994,

1995; Edquist, 1997a) but it is of obvious relevance to the regional level too. Where there is a rich innovation infrastructure, ranging from specialist research institutes, to universities, colleges and technology transfer agencies, and institutional learning is routine, firms have considerable opportunities to access or test knowledge whether internally or externally generated to the region. Clearly, by no means all innovation interactions can or even should occur locally, but the rise of the 'entrepreneurial university' (Smilor *et al.*, 1993) and promotion of the so-called 'triple helix' of interaction between industry, government and universities as a key feature of the knowledge economy (Etkowitz and Leydesdorff, 1997) testifies to the practical evolution of interactive innovation processes.

It is in respect of this 'new regional science' approach to thinking about regional economic development that regional studies and innovation studies *à la* Lundvall, Nelson, Freeman and Edquist themselves begin to interact. The latter tradition is more overtly evolutionary in its theoretical perspective on economics. But all of what has been described in the new regional science approach is compatible with evolutionary economics. Summarizing Edquist's (1997b) presentation of key concerns of contemporary innovation research in light of the interests of new regional science, especially where innovation is under the microscope, we find that both fields envision innovation and learning processes involving knowledge transfer as a key focus, they share an interest in systemic interaction within political economies and are concerned with questions of path dependence, development trajectories and the role of institutions and ways they evolve over time (see also, Cooke *et al.*, 1998).

4. Conditions and criteria for regional innovation systems

In considering the prospects for regional systems of innovation, Cooke *et al.* (1998) have explored theoretically the key organizational and institutional dimensions providing for strong and weak regional innovation systems potential. This is a pioneering attempt to specify desirable criteria upon which systemic innovation at the regional level may occur. These can be divided into infrastructural and superstructural characteristics.

4.1. Infrastructural issues

The first infrastructural issue concerns the degree to which there is regional financial competence. This includes private and public finance. Where there is a regional stock exchange, firms, especially SMEs, may find opportunity in a local capital market. Where regional governments have jurisdiction and competence, a regional credit-based system in which the regional administration can be involved in co-financing or provision of loan guarantees, will be of considerable value, especially for innovation-financing which, typically, the private sector perceives as high risk. Hence, private 'proximity capital' can clearly be of great importance especially as lender-borrower interaction and open communication are seen to be increasingly important features in modern theories of finance. Following on, regional governance for innovation encourages the facilitation of interaction between parties, including, where appropriate and available, the competences of member-state and EU resources. This can help build up capability, reputation, trust and reliability amongst regional partners.

However, regional *public* budgets are also important for mobilizing regional innovation potential. We may consider three kinds of budgetary competence for those situations where at least some kind of regional administration exists. First, regions may have competence to administer *decentralized spending*. This is where the region is the channel through which central government expenditure flows for certain items. Much Italian, Spanish and French regional expenditure is of this kind although there are exceptions, such as the Italian Special Statute regions and for some Spanish regions. A second category applies to cases where regions have *autonomous spending* competence. This occurs where regions determine how to spend a centrally allocated block grant (as in Scotland and Wales in the UK) or where, as in federal systems, they are able to negotiate their expenditure priorities with their central state and, where appropriate, the EU. The third category is where regions have *taxation authority* as well as autonomous spending competence since this allows them extra capacity to design special policies to support, for example, regional innovation. The Basque Country in Spain has this competence as will Scotland, although to a far lesser extent. Wales will not have this facility when its National Assembly is established in 1999. Clearly, the strongest base for the promotion of regional innovation is found where regions have regionalized credit facilities and administrations with autonomous spending and/or taxation authority.

A further infrastructural issue concerns the competence regional authorities have for controlling or influencing investments in hard infrastructures such as transport and telecommunications and softer, knowledge infrastructures such as universities, research institutes, science parks and technology transfer centres. Most regions lack the budgetary capacity for the most strategic of these, but many have competences to design and construct many of them or, if not, to influence decisions ultimately made elsewhere in respect of them. The range of possibilities is enormous in this respect, so we classify broadly into types of infrastructure over which regions may have more or less managerial or influence capacity. Thus regions are likely to have no control regarding strategic investments such as a major international airport, some may have some control and influence over, for example, the provision of local or regional communications, some may be in a position to share control and management, for example, regional science parks or research institutes, and they may have responsibility for the provision of, for example, technology-transfer centres. The greater the scope of competences with respect to the provision of hard and soft infrastructures for innovation, the greater the prospects, in principle, for the animation and facilitation of systemic regional innovation.

4.2. Superstructural issues

Three broad categories of conditions and criteria can be advanced in respect of superstructural issues. These refer, in general, to mentalities amongst regional actors or the 'culture' of the region and can be divided into the *institutional level*, the *organizational level for firms* and the *organizational level for governance*. Together, these help to define the degree of embeddedness of the region, its institutions and organizations. Embeddedness is here defined in terms of the extent to which a social community operates in terms of shared norms of co-operation, trustful interaction and 'untraded interdependencies' (Dosi, 1988) as distinct from competitive, individ-ualistic, 'arm's length exchange' and hierarchical norms. The contention here is that the former set of characteristics is more appropriate to systemic innovation through network or partnership relationships. This does not mean that innovativeness is not also associated with conditions of 'disembeddedness' since certain American cases such as Microsoft and Silicon Valley would appear to conform to that state. However, it should be noted that the work of Saxenian (1994) points strongly to the conclusion that a key reason for Silicon Valley's better long-term innovation performance than that of Route 128 Boston was that Silicon Valley was the region with the greater embeddedness.

Therefore, if we look, first, at the institutional level, the 'atmosphere' of a co-operative culture, associative disposition, learning orientation and quest for consensus would be expected to be stronger in a region displaying characteristics of systemic innovation, whereas a competitive culture, individualism, a 'not invented here' mentality and dissension would be typical of non-systemic, weakly interactive innovation at regional level. Moving to the organizational level of the firm, those with stronger systemic innovation potential will display trustful labour relations, shopfloor co-operation and a worker welfare orientation with emphasis upon helping workers improve through a mentoring system, and an openness to external-izing transactions and knowledge exchange with other firms and organizations with respect to innovation. The weakly systemic firm characteristics would include antagonistic labour relations, workplace division, 'sweating' and a 'teach yourself' attitude to worker improvement. Internalization of business functions would be strongly pronounced and innovativeness might be limited to adaptation. Regarding the organization of governance, the embedded region will display inclusivity, mon-itoring, consultation, delegation and networking propensities among its policy-makers while the disembedded region will have organizations that tend to be exclusive, reactive, authoritarian and hierarchical. In outline these characteristics are summarized in Table 2.1.

Clearly, both sets of conditions are ideal types in the sense that it is unlikely that a single region would conform to all of one or other sets of characteristics. However, it could be expected that regions might display tendencies towards one or the other end of the continuum and, in dynamic terms, it might be possible to identify evolutionary tendencies by regions towards one or the other pole, perhaps signifying an element of convergence influenced either by globalization processes, or the policy effects of state governments or EU programmes. In the next section of this chapter we profile the eleven regions in the Region Innovation Systems: Designing for the Future (REGIS) study in terms of these and other relevant characteristics that indicate their similarities and their distinctiveness. General economic character as well as features concerning governance for innovation come into play here.

5. Analysis and classification of REGIS case regions

The regions under investigation are diverse, being drawn from north, south, east and western parts of Europe, including two from outside the EU, in Poland and Hungary, which, are included in accession negotiations for the next round of EU enlargement. Nevertheless, on initial inspection, and primarily in terms of their

Table 2.1 Conditions for higher and lower regional innovation systems potential

Higher	Lower
Infrastructural Level	
Autonomous taxing and spending	Decentralized spending
Regional private finance	National financial organization
Policy influence on infrastructure	Limited influence on infrastructure
Regional university–industry strategy	Piecemeal innovation projects
Superstructural Level	
Institutional Dimension	
Cooperative culture	Competitive culture
Interactive learning	Individualistic
Associative-consensus	Institutional dissension
Organizational Dimension (Firms)	
Harmonious labour relations	Antagonistic labour relations
Worker mentoring	Self-acquired skills
Externalization	Internalization
Interactive innovation	Stand alone R&D
Organizational Dimension (Policy)	
Inclusive	Exclusive
Monitoring	Reacting
Consultative	Authoritative
Networking	Hierarchical

economic structures and trajectories, they can be located in one of five broad categories. The first of these may be termed regional economies with *high performance engineering* in large, indigenous firms with integrated supply-chains but some problems of competitiveness and possible future reconversion problems. The second category refers to regional economies based on traditional industry in decline (coal, steel, shipbuilding, textiles) but which are engaged in *reconversion with upstream innovation* interactions, in which linkage to universities and research institutes to promote new industry clusters is pronounced. The third category concerns regions displaying *reconversion with downstream innovation* trajectories whereby innovation impulses in developing clusters and/or sectors derive more from firms' roles in the supply-chain to larger customers.

The fourth category concerns regional economies, peripherally located in the EU, with important clusters of SMEs in *industrial districts* contributing to key economic activities, typically in traditional industries such as furniture, leather, and metal products. Finally, the fifth category refers to *transitional economies*, the two Central and Eastern European regions of Lower Silesia in Poland and Székesfehérvár (Féjer region, west of Budapest) in Hungary. These regions are important centres of electrical and mechanical engineering, the Féjer region having major western FDI from the likes of General Electric, IBM, Audi and Opel. The rationale for inclusion of particular regions in specific categories is provided in what follows.

5.1. High performance engineering

Two regions, Baden-Württemberg (BW) in Germany and Brabant in The Netherlands are represented amongst the high performance engineering regions. In the former case this is because a major part of the regional economy is dominated by the automotive industry (Daimler-Benz, Porsche, Audi) and its suppliers, the electronics industry (SEL-Alcatel, IBM, Hewlett-Packard) plus supply-firms, and mechanical engineering (Trumpf, Traub, Heidelberg), especially machine tools and industrial machinery, e.g. printing presses. In the case of Brabant, the regional economy is dominated by Philips and Daf along with numerous SMEs that act as suppliers to them or independently of them. In the REGIS firm survey, Baden-Württemberg's three main sectors were the focus, while a diversified set of Brabant's SMEs were concentrated upon.

The case of Baden-Württemberg is well known (see, for example Cooke and Morgan, 1994a, 1998; Herrigel 1989, 1996; Sabel *et al.*, 1989). It has a population of 10.3 million, an increase of over a million since 1980, a manufacturing labour force of 2.2 million and 2.5 million in services. Unemployment has risen from approximately 2.0 per cent in 1980 to almost 10.0 per cent in the late 1990s but GDP per head almost doubled to DM45,000 between 1980–93. In the same period stocks of FDI in the region trebled to DM32 billion while FDI export from the region quintupled to nearly DM45 billion. Baden-Württemberg has a consistently high level of R&D expenditure at around 3.6 per cent of GDP over the period 1985–93. In 1993 two-thirds of the workforce had vocational training or higher qualification.

With respect to whether or not BW has strong regional innovation systems potential, it can be stated with reasonable confidence that it does, and more than that, the region has one of the strongest cases to be considered to have systemic innovation whether in Europe or more widely. Within the federal state system, BW like all other German *länder*, has relatively high regional autonomy, although negotiated with the upper level in German's system of 'co-operative federalism' (Scharpf, 1976, 1988; Sturm, 1996, 1998). Private and public availability of finance for innovation investment is moderately high and the *land* can bring influence to bear upon infrastructural decisions through co-operative federalism. Because of its associative, co-operative industrial and civic culture there is high social partnership, low antagonism in labour relations and, through substantial initial vocational, then further training, strong mentoring in the workplace. The policy culture tends to be inclusive, consultative and networking-oriented. Innovation infrastructures are rich, with nine universities, 39 *Fachhochschulen* and over 100 research institutes plus over two hundred Steinbeis technology centres. Accordingly, the interactions of governance, industry and knowledge centres within an associative, networking culture and society mean that knowledge flows rather freely among key actors, though perhaps less so to those not close to key nodes of the system. BW has some significant problems relating to its over-dependence on automotive and other engineering and the key test is whether systemic innovation can be adjusted to promote and support new sectors and possible future clusters.

Brabant is much smaller than BW, with 2.1 million people in 1993. Moreover, due to the restructuring of Philips and the near-bankruptcy of Daf, parts of the region already possess EU Objective 2 reconversion region status. The south-eastern corner of the region, centred on Eindhoven, is the main problem area where Philips, especially, has shed 8,000 jobs. Helmond, nearby, has restructuring problems in its textile and metal industries. Hence, unemployment in the early 1990s hovered around the 9–10 per cent mark but GDP per capita remained at 98 per cent of the Dutch average. In 1991 industry constituted 32 per cent of the workforce, services 67 per cent. Firm-size structure reveals 61 per cent of employment to be in small firms (< 50), 29 per cent to be in large firms (> 100) and only 10 per cent in medium-sized firms (50–99). Besides the automotive and electronics 'clusters' in the region, there are other, developing clusters with supply links to firms bordering Brabant. These include agro-food, transport and logistics, electronic equipment (office and medical) and environmental technologies. Research shows that inter-firm networks are crucial for innovation in the clusters of south eastern Brabant. The Philips NatLab is dominant in R&D employment, though this declined to 1,800 from 2,500 between 1980–94. Nevertheless, in terms of overall R&D intensity measured by personnel, 'the region is very well positioned as an innovation system, not only in national but also in European perspectives' (Boekholt, 1996).

The governance structure of the region means the south-eastern industrial belt has low regional autonomy, though this changed in 1997 with the region being assigned the prized 'Province' status. Despite this, public innovation finance support is relatively high though private sources are rather poor. The region does not have the scale to develop a regional innovation policy. At the Province level economic policy is focused on more traditional investment and infrastructure instruments. Since 1994, though, initiatives to organize 'strategic conferences' on specific technologies, actions to improve inter-firm networking, promote clusters and technology transfer as well as corporate and university spin-offs have evolved.

The quality of communications infrastructures of all kinds is high while there are two higher education centres (Eindhoven University and Technical High School), a division of TNO (materials research) and private research and innovation centres. Social partnership is moderate rather than high but there is no Science Park or Technopole, nor venture capital funds locally based. There is no regional innovation policy but there are local networks, support for cluster-building and an innovation infrastructure but 'the region's technology transfer networks are multi-level and funding and initiation comes from many sources' (Boekholt, 1996). Despite this, or perhaps because of it, 'separate projects and initiatives from different actors in the institutional networks gives a fragmented approach. There is no integrated concept how to maintain the innovative edge and upgrade local supplies' (Bockholt, 1996). Clearly the southeast Brabant sub-region is a medium candidate for a regional innovation system, scoring rather higher on inter-firm interaction than more general interactive governance for innovation.

5.2. Reconversion regions – upstream

The two regions falling into this category are the Austrian *land* of Styria and the Finnish region centred upon the city of Tampere in Southern Finland. Both are reconversion regions and receive European Union Structural Funds. There are similarities between these regions in that both are strong in the forest products or pulp and paper processing industries. But, importantly, both have the significant presence of firms manufacturing processing equipment for the pulp and paper industry and are, indeed, two of the world-leading locations for the production of this equipment. Both are also committed to university-industry interaction to stimulate the growth of new firms and sectors. These industry sectors plus metals, electronics and automotives in Styria and metals, electronics, textiles, chemicals and food in Tampere were the focus for the research on regional innovation by firms.

Styria had a population of 1.2 million in 1993, a small rise from 1.18 million in 1980, and a 1993 workforce of 394,000, 10,000 more than in 1980. Industrial employment declined from 47–39 per cent of the workforce while services rose from 51–60 per cent over the period. Unemployment, which was 2.2 per cent in 1980 had risen to 8.4 per cent by 1993. Nevertheless, GDP per capita nearly doubled from 8,000 ECU per head to 15,000. Gross expenditure on R&D as a percentage of GDP rose from 1.4–1.8 per cent, 1980–93. While 42 per cent of the workforce had only elementary school qualifications in 1980, 58 per cent having apprenticeship or higher, by 1993 the equivalent figures were 28 per cent and 72 per cent respectively. The most important industries remained steel, automotive, electronics, leather goods, and pulp and paper over the period. Economically, the *land* is divided between the north where the steel and metals industries contributed to a 20,000 decline in overall manufacturing employment, warranting Objective 2 status when Austria joined the EU in 1995, and the south where Graz is a key centre of electronics and automotive production and research (Sedlacek and Tödtling, 1996).

With respect to regional autonomy, Styria, an Austrian *land* has significant regional economic development and innovation promotion capabilities. Policies are part of the 'social partnership' arrangements involving *associationalism* 'in advance' between the chamber of industry and business associations, chamber of labour and trade unions and the federal and *land* administrations. 'Due to this basic agreement the relevant actors and agencies in general work reasonably smoothly together rather than compete antagonistically' (Sedlacek and Tödtling, 1996). However political tensions do exist between levels and sub-regions. Nevertheless, influence can be exerted over infrastructural decisions and, particularly, over soft network innovation and industrial policies. Thus finance can be focused upon specific development concepts even though grants are allocated to Styria from federally-raised taxation revenues. In 1993 20 million ECU in federal subsidies supported innovation policy in Styria. Styrian *land* grants are less and focused on support for innovative projects (including research institutes), support for firms in crisis, and regional policy projects. The partly-privatised Styrian Development Agency (SFG) now co-ordinates much Styrian technology and economic development policy. The culture of Styria is broadly co-operative, associational and consensus-oriented while firms and policy organizations tend to be interactive and network-minded. 'For Styrian industry there is some indication of regional inter-firm linkages giving certain coherence to the production system ... The Styrian market is important for 57 per cent of firms' output and for inputs, Graz (45 per cent) and Upper Styria (33 per cent) were relevant input markets' (Joanneum Research Institute, 1995).

In Tampere region, while the economic experience is in some ways comparable, the governance system is much weaker. The population is 0.43 million, up from 0.41 between 1980–93. Contrariwise, the labour force declined from 0.19 to 0.16 million in that period. Between 1980–93 industrial employment declined from 44–32 per cent of the workforce while services increased from 46–59 per cent. Unemployment rose dramatically from 6–21 per cent (declining to 17 per cent in 1997), though as elsewhere, and partly in consequence GDP per employee rose by 41 per cent to 212,000 Finnish Marks, though only 20 per cent to 77,000 (or 13,4000 ECU) per capita GDP in general. In 1995 GDP per capita had risen to 15,300 ECU. The region exports more capital in the form of FDI than it imports, though both kinds have increased substantially since 1980 to 500 million marks inward and 800 million outward investment. Gross expenditure on R&D has remained at some 2 per cent of GDP, a relatively high regional figure. Qualifications in the workforce have shifted from 38 per cent with post-primary education to 55 per cent, 1980–93. The predominant industry sectors in the region are pulp and paper, machinery to a great extent related to pulp and paper production and chemicals, textiles now having slipped to relative insignificance, whereas a new industrial cornerstone – Information and Communication Technologies – has emerged during the last 20 years. Otherwise there has been no major change in this sectoral dominance of the regional economy between 1980–93.

In terms of regional autonomy, this region is one of the weaker ones, somewhat comparable to the case of Brabant before it was upgraded. As a small country, Finland is, administratively, relatively centralized, but a new Regional Development Act and decree in 1993 'increased the importance of local government in regional policy by delegating power from the central government to the regions' (Kautonen and Schienstock, 1996). This now complements the state regional administrative authorities but requires co-ordinated action to meet goals set by the Regional Council. The 1996 strategy for Tampere stresses promotion of an information society, utilization of knowledge for innovation, strengthening of basic regional infrastructures and encouraging the development of new clusters, e.g. healthcare, IT and technological services. A new Employment and Economic Development Centre, combining existing offices, has a 170 million ECU budget. Tampere has numerous research centres (eight including universities), training, enterprise and innovation support organizations (ten) and financial institutions (six, mostly public e.g. Sentio Invest Ltd, with 30 million ECU in risk capital) plus seven business associations. Large firms have their own supplier networks, SMEs are only beginning to discover networking opportunities and there are problematic links between the diverse economic development agencies. Systemic innovation in Tampere is rather limited with agencies pursuing either national technology policy goals or local employment and education policies. Links between the Technical University and large as well as spin-off firms in the Science Park are probably the best. The region 'is not big enough to develop its own innovation policy' (Kautonen and Schienstock, 1996). Clearly governance questions and scale questions largely explain the piecemeal nature of innovation, though that is not to say that innovation is low in the region.

5.3. Reconversion regions – downstream

Three regions occupy this category, the Basque Country, Wales and Wallonia. Each suffered significantly from the decline of older heavy industries, notably shipbuilding, steel manufacture and coal mining. Thus each region is a beneficiary of EU

Objective 2 status and with this assistance, efforts have been made to restructure the regional economies towards the development of new sectors or clusters. The sectors studied were, respectively: auto, electronics and machine tools; auto, electronics and healthcare; and food, chemicals and machinery.

The population of the Basque Country is 2.2 million, slightly higher in 1991 than in 1987. Of these 0.87 million are economically active, again an increase from 0.76 million over that period. Industry was in 1981 larger in employment terms; 298,000 versus 275,000 service employees, but by 1991 that was reversed to 256,000 in industry and 274,000 in services. Despite these changes, unemployment rose from 15.6 per cent in 1981 to 19.2 per cent in 1991. Per capita GDP nearly trebled over the period from 0.6–1.6 million pesetas, while GDP per employee rose from 2.0–5.1 million pesetas. Beyond first stage qualification level was displayed by 211,000 employees in 1980 and 235,000 in 1991. Regional R&D as a percentage of GDP reached 1.1 per cent by 1993, higher than the Spanish level of 0.85 per cent but below the EU mean of 1.92 per cent. FDI was very low at 80,000,000 pesetas (480,000 ECU) in 1995 and export of capital was one-sixth of this at 80,000 ECU. The main industries, which are part of a strategic cluster programme designed by Michael Porter's consultancy, Monitor, are metal manufacture, white goods, automotive components and machine tools with emergent industries in telecommunications, new materials and IT.

The Basque government is one of the most regionally powerful, with autonomous spending and taxation authority, ability to influence and be responsible for hard and soft infrastructure policies and consistent in producing regional technology policies since 1981 when the Autonomous Community assembly opened. The region is not characterized by social partnership but locally, especially amongst the Basque language speaking community, there is remarkably high co-operation, learning disposition, innovation, associationism and consensus, most notably represented in the fabric of the Mondragon Co-operative system. This is a regional, and increasingly, supra-regional entity which is, in itself, highly systemic with close links and strong flows from finance to industry to technology transfer and to training closely involving the new Mondragon University. The policy of establishing regional technology centres across the Basque Country has now been supplemented by the 'cluster' policy and the new Regional Technology Plan which, increasingly, seeks to include the three other Basque universities in the regional innovation system. Public rather than private finance for innovation predominates but there is a mixture of strong and weak networking between innovation actors who tend to have strong vertical rather than horizontal links. 'The relations between the technological environment and the industrial environment though in many cases insufficient, are being produced' (Etxebarria *et al.*, 1996).

The case of Wales is different, despite the severe deindustrialization of the 1980s when 75,000 jobs disappeared in coal and steel alone. The population rose from 2.8–2.9 million 1980–93. The labour force also rose from 1.2–1.3 million and industry almost maintained its share, moving from 24 per cent down to 23 per cent compared to services which rose from 65–68 per cent of the total. Over the 1980–93 period GDP per capita rose from 7.1 thousand ECU to 9.7 thousand ECU, but per employee rose from 13,000 ECU to 22,000, reflecting large influxes of capital investment from FDI. This was over 220 million ECU in 1993, rising from 36 million in 1980. R&D expenditure as a proportion of GDP rose from 1.1–1.4 per cent, a modest level compared to the UK (2.2 per cent) and EU (1.9 per cent) averages. Qualifications rose between 1980–93 with a 60 per cent apprenticeship equivalent or higher in 1980 to 75 per cent in that category in 1993. In 1980 coal and steel were important production sectors, by 1993, automotive and electronic engineering had become the more important sectors. These displayed some cluster features such as supply-chains, supplier 'clubs' and associations. Firms and colleges have developed specialized training, and there are emergent innovation links both inter-firm and with respect to university research (Cooke and Schall, 1996; Cooke, 1997).

Governance of innovation and economic development has traditionally been hierarchical. A high level of autonomous spending authority existed in the territorial ministry for Wales in the UK government, the Welsh Office, and its development executive body, the Welsh Development Agency (WDA). While taxation is centralized to the UK, spending on and designing roads policy was a Welsh Office responsibility, building industrial estates and land reclamation have been traditional WDA responsibilities, as has attracting FDI for both bodies, in addition to promoting exports and supporting innovation for SMEs. Training is the responsibility of firms and education institutes mediated by local Training and Enterprise Councils, created as mixed public-private bodies. Innovation finance is either public or privately raised by firms, though venture capital is scare inside Wales, less so in London. Though there was a long history of antagonistic labour relations in the coal and steel industries, this has been replaced by a more consensual approach within firms and between unions, firms and the regional state, especially when representing Wales abroad, on trade missions for example. Associationism around innovation is emerging as cluster-type relationships develop between firms and the development actors animate suppliers clubs and the like. FDI firms tend to encourage a mentoring, partnership and consensus approach, though the dominant governance bodies have tended to moderate their hierarchical approach only a little. In 1997 Wales voted to have its own National Assembly, opened in May 1999 – one key reason for support for this was to moderate the 'democratic deficit' by establishing a more inclusive body and modernize the economy further by building on the success of earlier initiatives such as the EU-funded Regional Technology Plan for Wales.

Wallonia's industrial experience has been quite similar to that of Wales in terms of its loss of heavy industry, but its recovery seems less coherent than, for example, the emergence of automotive and electronics clusters in Wales suggests, despite the fact that Wallonia competes with the Basque Country and the federal *länder* regions to display primacy in terms of regional autonomy. Wallonia's population was 3.2 million in 1993. The labour force increased from 1.25–1.33 million, with a large decline in industrial employment from 356,000–272,000 and a rise in services employment from 666,000–741,000, 1980–93. GDP per head dropped from higher than the EU level of 100, at 103 in 1980 to well below it at 85 by 1993. There is little FDI to Wallonia and a relatively low 1.2 per cent rate of R&D expenditure as a share of GDP.

As stated, Wallonia has a strong regional government with shared jurisdiction for innovation and industrial development with the federal government. Although taxation is a federal matter, revenues are allocated such that spending autonomy is high at regional level. The Walloon government has a Ministry for Technological

Development and Employment, responsible to which is DGTRE (the Directorate for Technologies, Research and Energy) which finances and monitors research projects. It also monitors Walloon participation in EU and international research programmes. This in turn interacts with universities, research centres, federal scientific establishments and business research bodies. Hence it is hierarchical but not necessarily inclusive or associative. Recognizing this, consultative channels were opened with the establishment in 1989 of CIMPS (the Inter-Ministerial Conference on Scientific Policy). Only research for technological application purposes is available at a 1993 allocation of 72.5 million ECU, so 'the instruments developed by the region are already downstream of the move by business in the field of innovation; they provide support for business chiefs to implement their innovation projects, rather than helping them generate them in the first place' (Van Doren, 1996). Wallonia is comparable to the Basque Country and Wales in being structured around vertical networks and channels which do not interact particularly strongly in the horizontal dimension.

5.4. Regions with industrial districts

The two regions in question are located on the eastern and western edges of the EU, respectively Friuli-Venezia Giulia on the Italian-Slovenian border, and Centro region, south of Porto in Portugal. Both are characterized by diffuse SME and micro-firm production systems focused upon traditional industrial sectors. Sector studies were done of food, electromechanical and metals in Friuli and footwear, ceramics, cork, metals and automotive in Centro. Geographical clustering occurs in industrial districts, set in a rural-agricultural background. Centro is a part of Portugal's comprehensive Objective 1 classification as a less advantaged economy, Friuli has only a limited area designated as Objective 5b, echoing its more prosperous socio-economic condition. In the late 1980s, Centro ranked as the eleventh weakest region in the EC with a GDP of 50.2 per cent of the EU mean of 100, with a typically low 'southern' unemployment rate of 36 per cent of the EU norm for its population of 1.8 million. Coincidentally, Friuli-Venezia Giulia was number 143 out of 171 EU-defined NUTS 2 regions in terms of economic 'weakness'. Its GDP per head was 116.1 per cent of the EU norm, and unemployment though double that of Centro, was 72.4 per cent of that of the EU as a whole. Friuli's population is smaller than Centro's at 1.2 million.

Friuli's peripheral location is associated with population decline despite its relative prosperity. In 1980 population was 1.23 million but in 1993 it was 1.19 million; correspondingly the labour force had declined from 463,000–455,000. Industry's share declined from 184,000–152,000 while services rose from 243,000–279,000. The rate of unemployment rose from 4.3 per cent in 1980 to 6.9 per cent in 1993. Nevertheless, GDP per capita doubled from 15 to 30 million lire and per employee quadrupled to 80 million in 1993 compared to 1980. Overall GDP quadrupled from 9.7–36.6 billion lire. Qualifications intensity rose from 283,000 with post-primary level (59 per cent) in 1980 to 405,000 (83 per cent) in 1993, though R&D expenditure declined from 0.64 per cent to 0.57 per cent in the same period.

This region is one of Italy's Special Statute regions, established in 1967. Special Statute regions have greater spending autonomy than Ordinary Statute regions but while both have taxation authority the spending priorities for this are set by central government. Thus Italian regions collect taxes for health expenditure which is determined by the Italian state. Nevertheless, Friuli's share of overall expenditure on items such as economic development and innovation is about twice the level of an ordinary region like Emilia-Romagna at some 12 per cent of the total annual budget. Friuli may thus be considered closer to the Basque Country, Wallonia and the federal *länder* than to the weaker pole of regional autonomy. Finance for innovation is better-provided by the private than the public sector, however. This is in tune with the widespread presence of local and regional banks between whom and SMEs there develops a trustful, reputation-based relationship making for relative ease in accessing credit. Communication infrastructures are a central Italian responsibility where strategic investments are concerned. Industry is concentrated to a noticeable degree in the four key districts of Maranzano (furniture), Magnago (cutlery), San Daniele (prosciutto) and Livenza (furniture). In the Friuli sub-region (Udine and Pordenone) SMEs prevail and the area is characterised by 'endogenous entrepreneurship, spatial diffusion of the development process, ... social cohesion and cultural and linguistic identity, where traditional rural values support industrial modernization' (Grandinetti and Schenkel, 1996). In Venezia Giulia (Trieste and Gorizia) industry is large scale, state-owned and urban in location. Networking, consensus and learning dispositions are pronounced in Friuli, particularly amongst business actors and communities. Local business associations and chambers of commerce are important media of information and knowledge exchange. Innovation is incremental although firms can 'buy' research with subsidies from the region for more radical innovation requirements, especially where firms form consortia. University-industry linkages have traditionally been weak even on the Trieste Science Park, but there are signs that this may be changing as SMEs find local technology centres like CATAS (furniture) cannot fully meet their innovation needs.

Centro has the weakest form of regionalization, a large proportion of employment (36 per cent) in agriculture in the early 1990s compared with 31 per cent in industry and 33 per cent in services. GDP per capita was 4,083 ECU in 1990. The economically active population was 711,000 in 1991 and the main employment sectors (outside construction, wholesaling and retailing) were metal products and transport equipment, wood and cork, ceramics, clothing and food production. Between 1986–92 R&D expenditure rose slightly as a share of GDP from 0.32–0.48 of GDP.

Industrial support is nationally provided, e.g. the PEDIP programme which is EU supported promotes SME development by encouraging knowledge access from scientific and technological sources as well as nurturing entrepreneurship and product and process innovation. Support is given for university and research institute projects through SINFRAPEDIP (technological infrastructures), and related schemes subsidizing consultancy, innovation finance, technology-transfer and training. The national PRAXIS programme supports research and technology transfer to firm consortia. Centro has intermediary rather than governance organizations, thirteen of which are regional or local business associations who work in partnership with the Centro Region Coordination Commission and national research, trade and training bodies which 'have a crucial importance to the economic development of the region, resulting in their almost total control of financial resources coming from the EU' (de Castro *et al.*, 1996, p.35). This organizational co-operation contributes to 'the thickening of institutional relations at local level' (ibid. p.31). Higher education institutes are the main infrastructural supports for innovation in the region; University of Beira, University of Aveiro and University of Coimbra being central. However, 'relations between universities and industry in the Centro Region have low significance to economic performance' (ibid p.33). And, although there is administrative consensus there are clientilistic social relations which make social and commercial interactions locally and sub-regionally rivalrous. Centro's industrial change is characterized by adaptation-modification of products and processes rather than more widespread incremental processes, though some developments may fall into the latter category (development of cork for tiles, shoes, etc.).

5.5. Regions in transitional economies

The Féjer region in Hungary and Lower Silesia in Poland are very different kinds of space, both of which exist in former state-centralized governmental systems in which regions had no meaningful place and innovation was state-directed, often to military ends. Now, there is more awareness of the importance of regional proactivity in a globalizing economy where FDI is seeking new markets and production locations. So these regions, like their countries, are in transition. So much so, that the decision to establish regional governments in Poland was only taken in December 1997 following the general election which ushered in a decentralist-minded government conscious of the modern centralist dilemma about seeking to maintain control without the power to solve economic problems. The solution is to regionalize responsibility and some power, a process entirely in line with the evolution of EU policy and one which, in Poland, coincides with its forthcoming accession to the EU at the next enlargement. Hence, Lower Silesia will move from anonymity to relative regional autonomy in the period leading up to 2000.

First, though, we draw attention to Féjer (Székesféhervár) region, the population of which grew from 422,000 in 1980 to 428,000 in 1993, of which 251,000 and 256,000 were economically active respectively. In 1980, 45 per cent were employed in industry, 34 per cent in services and 21 per cent in agriculture. By 1993, the proportions were 30 per cent, 47 per cent and 13 per cent respectively. In 1993 GDP per capita was 3,734 ECU and FDI 10 million ECU, 51 per cent of the workforce had post-elementary qualifications (up from 48 per cent in 1980) and the most important industrial sectors, also studied in firm survey work, were automotive and electronic engineering and metals. Foreign firms such as Ford, Opel, Audi and Keiper-Recaro (automotive), Philips-Grundig, Nokia, IBM and Videston (electronics) and Alcoa (aluminium) were already established.

Féjer has a Regional Development Council, an Economic Development Marketing Office, a Labour Office and a presence of the National Technological Development Committee charged with co-ordinating research activities and financing technical innovation in both firms and research institutions. There is a branch of the Hungarian Development Bank charged with financing targeted industries and SMEs and there are various training and research or business consultancy firms in the region. But major business linkages work vertically to the national level where most infrastructural and financial power for innovation lies. Amongst the reasons for sub-optimal use of regional centres of technology or innovation are that the 'market, as well as the current industrial structure, are not conducive to co-operation. The multinational firms which have come here use their own (global) development facilities ... local intellectual human resources are left untouched' (Mako *et al.*, 1997). Neither universities, nor governance bodies are in a position to influence the multinationals significantly. There is no systemic innovation other than that which occurs within multinational firms. The regional vision – somewhat similar to post-economic crisis Wales in the 1980s is that 'the region will continue to play its role in industrial development and innovation, largely as the partners of the large, multi-nationals building here' (Makó *et al.*, 1997).

Lower Silesia, centred upon the city of Wroclaw (former Breslau) focuses upon textiles, food and chemicals as its main manufacturing activities, accounting for 60 per cent of the economy, the remainder being services. Sixty-six per cent of firms are private, 27 per cent in public ownership and 4 per cent FDI (UK and Germany). Average employment per firm has declined 1990–95 from 294–206. Most business functions are controlled in the region and there is a high level of inter-firm interaction and even embeddedness (Galar and Kuklinski, 1997). Qualifications above unskilled level are possessed by 79 per cent of employees and some 40 per cent of firms have participated in science and technology, innovation or training projects. Funding for these was shared amongst EU, Polish state and regional sources. Over half of the firms in Lower Silesia claim to have introduced new products or production processes in the 1993–96 period. Given the transformations experienced it is hard to judge the extent to which these claims are exaggerated or, in fact, reasonably accurate estimations.

Before concluding this chapter it is important to present these regional profiles in terms which take account of the theory and analytical frameworks presented in the first half of the chapter. We shall, at this early stage provide a relatively simple statement of the extent to which regions conform to strong or weak regional innovation systems potential by use of a scattergram which positions regions in relation to the four axes drawn from Table 2.1 (p. 37), namely *infrastructural, institutional, organizational (firms)* and *organizational (policy)* for systemic innova-tion potential at regional level. The results of this are represented in Figure 2.1.

6. Conclusions

Figure 2.1 summarizes the profiles of all eleven REGIS regions in terms of their current and near-future projected Regional Innovation Systems potential in relation to four theoretically and analytically-derived axes of performance; these are their infrastructural and financial capacities, their institutional capacities for systemic interaction, the organizational capacities of firms for consensual workplace and inter-firm relations and the organizational capacity for policy inclusiveness, associa-tionism and networking *inter alia*. These axes act as dimensions operationalizing the five key regional mechanisms enabling regions to gain advantage from strong tendencies in the globalization of economic co-ordination. The five were, it will be recalled, agglomeration economies, institutional learning, associative governance, proximity capital and interactive innovation.

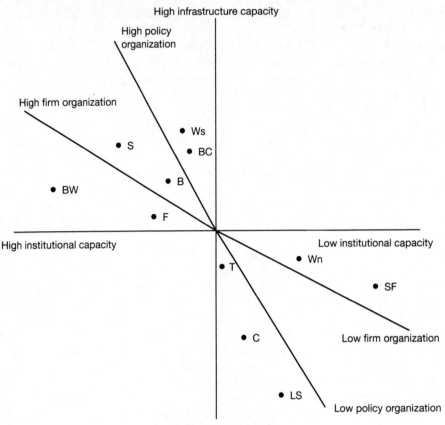

High infrastructure capacity

High policy organization

High firm organization

High institutional capacity

Low institutional capacity

Low firm organization

Low policy organization

Low infrastructure capacity

• Ws
• BC
• S
• B
• BW
• F
• Wn
• T
• SF
• C
• LS

Figure 2.1 Scattergram of regional innovation systems potential

Following this theoretical and analytical logic Figure 2.1 locates regions above or below the mid-point and in terms of which of the four axes they are strongest and weakest, again in terms of systemic innovation. Thus, to interpret the scattergram, regions are located first above or below the institutional capacity line, then the precise quadrant in which they are located represents their particular strengths in terms of innovation systems potential. Thus Baden-Württemberg is both the strongest candidate for being designated already close to the condition of having systemic regional innovation, mainly because of very strong interactive firm organization and high institutional capacity for co-operation. Styria comes next, some way behind, with strong firm and policy organization. The Basque Country and Wales are next because of high infrastructural and policy capacity. Brabant and Friuli-Venezia Giulia follow based on firm/policy and firm/institutional strengths respectively. Tampere and Wallonia have low systemic innovation potential at the regional level because of weak infrastructure/policy and institutional/firm organization capacity respectively. Centro is particularly weak on policy and infrastructure as, even more so is Lower Silesia, while Féjer has particularly low institutional capacity and little regional firm organization presently.

CHAPTER THREE

Competitive Strategies and Innovation

1. Introduction

The previous chapter highlighted the fact that companies and regions in Europe are facing new challenges due to globalization. It refers to the fact that not just goods and services but also companies, finance capital as well as labour and knowledge have become increasingly mobile on a global scale in the 1980s and 1990s (Oman, 1996). In addition, there are severe changes within Europe. Here, we observe an ongoing integration within the Western European Union (internal market, move towards a monetary union, inclusion of new members) as well as a rapid transformation and an opening of Central and Eastern Europe in the 1990s. All these changes have strongly reinforced competition for firms in most regions of Europe (Lundvall and Borrás, 1997).

In this situation firms can rely on various strategies in order to stay competitive (Porter, 1990; Ruigrok and van Tulder, 1995; Tödtling, 1995). First, they can try to lower their costs through relocations, more efficient production technologies or through an increasing pressure on labour. Due to the often negative effects on employment and the respective regions Pyke and Sengenberger (1992) have called this a 'low road strategy' of restructuring. Second, firms can try to become more flexible and faster through organizational rearrangements such as flat hierarchies, outsourcing and a change of supplier relations. Such 'flexibility strategies' are at the core of concepts such as flexible specialization or 'post-fordist' production (Benko and Dunford 1991; Storper and Scott 1992). Third, firms can try to rely on high quality and on innovation, i.e. they constantly have to improve their products as well as to introduce new ones. Such a strategy has been the main direction of innovation policies and of innovation systems approaches at the national (Lundvall, 1992; Nelson, 1993; Edquist, 1997a) and regional levels (Lundvall and Borrás 1997; Braczyk *et al.*, 1998).

In this context the present chapter investigates the following questions: How do firms compete in certain regions of Europe and which are their competitive advantages? To what extent are they oriented towards 'high road strategies' based on innovation and quality of products as against 'low road strategies' based on low cost and low wages? How strongly are firms engaging in innovation and technological change and what are the outcomes? Which competitive challenges are the firms facing and how do they respond to them?[1]

These questions will be analysed in this chapter before we look more deeply into

---

[1] This chapter has benefited from a working paper by Schienstock and Ropoonen (1998) which has a wider scope than the present analysis. Schienstock and Ropoonen focused more on the competitiveness of firms and also included aspects of firms' growth.

the interactive nature of the innovation process in Chapter 4. We will mainly use the common data base from the firm survey for answering these questions. First we will look at the overall data set (with answers from 833 firms) and investigate differences with respect to company size and innovation type. Then, we will analyse differences between the REGIS regions concerning these aspects.

2. Overall pattern and types of firms

2.1. Competitive advantages

What advantages do European firms have *vis-à-vis* their competitors? From Table 3.1 we can see that quality of products and innovation rank high from the perspectives of the firms. 'Quality' was most important and stated by 75 per cent of firms[2] as an advantage. Technical standards and innovativeness were indicated by 55 per cent of firms as an advantage. Flexibility and fast response to customer demand is another important aspect of competitiveness in the modern economy. Being able to deliver fast and promptly was stated by 57 per cent of firms to be a competitive advantage. An additional element of competitiveness nowadays refers not just to the

Table 3.1 Competitive advantages of firms (figures show % of firms indicating the listed items)

	Total	Firm size			Innovation type	
		Small < 50	Medium 50–200	Large > 200	Product innovation	Process innovation
n =	833	379	258	157	323	385
Competitive advantages						
Quality	75.4	74.9	75.6	80.9	79.9	82.1
Delivery time	57.3	57.8	57.4	59.2	56.0	61.6
Innovativeness	55.1	52.5	51.6	72.0	71.2	63.1
Services	39.7	36.9	41.1	46.5	49.2	41.8
Price	29.3	34.6	24.4	26.8	24.1	27.8
User friendliness	23.9	26.4	20.2	25.5	31.9	25.2
Ecological aspects	17.4	15.3	17.4	24.2	21.1	18.7
How do firms sustain competitive advantages?						
Skills/knowledge	63.4	68.3	56.2	66.2	67.8	64.4
Internal R&D	49.6	44.1	50.0	68.8	66.9	58.7
Patents/licences	11.5	7.7	12.0	20.4	20.1	15.3
Organization of production	47.8	39.3	57.4	58.6	54.2	54.5
Marketing	37.5	31.7	41.5	50.3	50.8	41.8
Co-operation – regional	19.0	22.2	16.7	14.6	19.8	20.8
Co-operation – national	16.8	17.9	14.7	17.8	20.7	19.0
Co-operation – european	16.6	13.5	15.5	25.5	21.1	19.5
Co-operation – global	10.0	7.7	8.1	20.4	14.9	11.7

Importance > 3 in % of all observations of this set

[2] This and the following percentages include those firms which indicated that the respective advantage, or factor, is more important than 3 on a scale from 1–5.

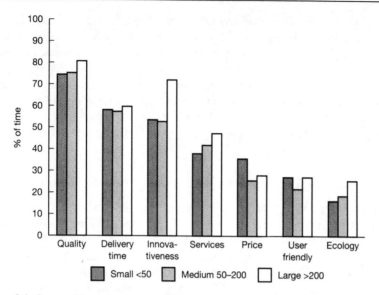

Figure 3.1 Competitive advantages of firms

products but to the complementary services coming with them (e.g. after sales service). For 40 per cent of firms these services constituted specific competitive advantages. This underlines the move towards a service economy also within the manufacturing sector (Moulaert and Tödtling, 1995).

A low price is only rarely seen as a competitive advantage. It was stated by less than 30 per cent of firms as an advantage. This is not surprising for high-cost locations which most of the investigated regions are. It indicates that most of the firms aim at 'high road' competition strategies. The question arises, however, whether considerations of price and cost have been given too little attention by the firms so that they have become vulnerable in a situation of reinforced global competition. The least important factors are the user friendliness of products as well as ecological aspects. Obviously, customer orientation and the respect of environmental standards is not high on the agenda of the investigated firms. In the long run the neglect of ecological aspects may turn out as short sighted, not just from a broader societal perspective but also from the perspective of the firms' competitiveness.

With respect to firm size we can observe that large firms (i.e. those with more than 200 employees) indicate clearly more competitive advantages (see Figure 3.1). They stress in particular technical standards and innovativeness more (72 per cent) than smaller companies. Also product quality, complementary services and ecological aspects are considered by them to a higher degree in their competition strategies. For small firms (below 50 employees) price and user friendliness are more important competitive advantages in comparison.

There is a distinctive pattern of competitive advantages for product and process innovators (see Table 3.1).[3] Obviously, innovation strategies correlate with other

---

[3] 'Product innovators' are firms which introduced products that were new to the respective market within the past three years (1993–6). 'Process innovators' are those that have introduced new production technologies similarly.

competitive advantages. For product innovators, besides technical standards, the quality of products (80 per cent of firms), complementary services (49 per cent) and user friendliness (32 per cent) are important competitive advantages. For process innovators, quality is even more important (82 per cent) but also delivery time (63 per cent). The introduction of new technologies seems to support fast delivery and Just In Time (JIT) concepts. This demonstrates that certain competitive strategies are not exclusive and may go together. Innovation is often part of a more comprehensive strategic orientation of firms and it cannot really be separated from those broader aspects.

2.2. How do firms sustain their competitive advantage?

The skills and the knowledge of the labour force are the most important factors to sustain competitive advantage as stated by 63 per cent of firms (Table 3.1). This supports the view of the evolutionary innovation model that tacit knowledge embodied in the labour force is an important source of advantage for firms. Internal R&D comes second and was indicated by 50 per cent of the firms. Other important factors are the organization of production, as well as marketing. Therefore, for most of the firms advantages arise from internal factors. Only for less than 20 per cent of firms do co-operation with other firms or organizations at regional, national and higher levels have relevance.

As is to be expected, large firms draw competitive advantage more clearly from internal R&D (69 per cent of firms), also from patents and licenses, than is the case with smaller firms. Moreover, marketing is more important to them and they co-operate more frequently at the European and global scale (Figure 3.2). For small firms the skills of the labour force are most important (68 per cent of firms) while R&D, organization of production and marketing are clearly of lower relevance. This

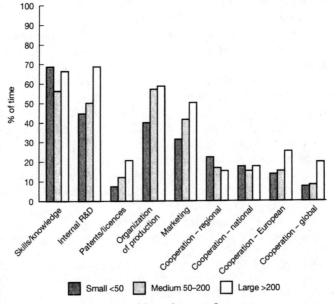

Figure 3.2 How do firms sustain competitive advantage?

reflects the fact that small firms often simply do not have R&D and marketing departments on which they could rely. With respect to co-operation we observe that spatial proximity is more important for small firms. Co-operation at the regional level is relatively more frequent for them (22 per cent of firms) than at higher spatial scales.

There is again a distinct pattern for innovating firms (Table 3.1). In particular, product innovators base their advantage more often on internal R&D, patents/licenses, skills and knowledge of the labour force, production organization and marketing. This indicates that they have better internal preconditions than the average firm for 'high road strategies'. It also shows that product innovation requires not only R&D but also a qualified labour force, an adequate production organization and marketing efforts. In addition, product innovators are co-operating more frequently with other firms. They are better networkers at national, European and global scales than non-innovative firms and they can be regarded as leaders not just regarding technology but also with respect to the introduction of new organizational models in their economies.

2.3. Competitive challenges and responses

We mentioned in the introduction that competitive pressure has been increasing for many firms recently due to globalization and changes in Europe (internal market, opening of Central and Eastern Europe). What challenges do these changes

Table 3.2 Challenges to companies (figures show % of firms indicating the listed items)

| | Total | Firm size | | | Innovation type | |
| | | Small < 50 | Medium 50–200 | Large > 200 | Product innovation | Process innovation |
n =	833	379	258	157	323	385
Challenges to companies						
Price competition	61.3	49.3	68.6	83.4	67.2	64.9
Quality requirement	56.4	53.6	60.1	62.4	59.8	63.4
Personnel costs	44.9	37.5	51.2	52.2	46.7	47.8
Demand change	40.2	34.8	48.4	42.0	42.7	45.2
Technology change	40.1	39.1	39.9	45.9	50.8	47.8
Product development cost	38.7	35.6	40.3	47.8	50.2	43.9
New competitors	30.1	28.8	32.6	31.2	35.6	34.0
Responses to challenges						
Cutting costs	53.2	42.2	56.6	77.1	58.8	56.6
Organization restructuring	43.9	30.9	53.5	65.6	52.9	51.9
Speed of product development	43.0	35.9	45.7	61.1	62.8	53.5
Intensify internal R&D	41.8	36.7	44.2	53.5	56.3	49.9
Subcontracting	18.6	16.6	23.6	17.2	20.4	21.8
Outsourcing	17.6	14.2	21.3	21.7	22.9	19.7
Co-operation – technology	15.1	15.8	10.9	22.9	19.2	16.1
Co-operation – marketing	14.0	14.8	13.6	14.6	14.9	13.5

Importance > 3 in % of all observations of this set

bring about for companies in the REGIS regions and how do they respond to them?

Table 3.2 demonstrates that, overall, firms feel the pressure of price competition most strongly (stated by 61 per cent of firms). Partly, this has to do with high personnel costs (stated by 45 per cent of firms). Both challenges reflect to a large extent the new global and European conditions. In addition, it is a consequence of the rather low price competitiveness of firms which was indicated above.

Other challenges relate to the rapid change of technologies and demand: for 56 per cent of firms the requirement of increasing product quality is an important challenge. Forty per cent consider the speed of change in demand and technology as problems. Firms respond to these changes partly through faster product development. As a consequence 39 per cent of companies are facing the problem of high development costs.

Interestingly, medium sized and large companies identify challenges to a higher degree than small ones (Figure 3.3). This may partly be an awareness problem in the case of small firms, partly it may have to do with the fact that larger firms are in more competitive markets. Large companies are challenged in particular by price competition (83 per cent) confirming the low price competitiveness identified above. In line with this is the frequent statement of cost pressures such as personnel cost and product development cost.

Somewhat unexpected is the finding that innovative firms face more challenges than non-innovative firms (Table 3.2). Product innovators, in particular, find rapid technological change as well as high costs of product development to be problems. Process innovators are also challenged by fast technology change and demand changes. Innovation seems to be related to these challenges in two ways: on the one hand, specific competitive challenges lead to innovative responses of companies; on

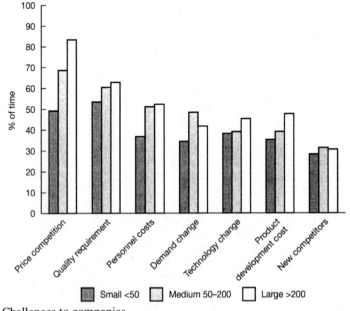

Figure 3.3 Challenges to companies

the other innovation leads to new challenges such as the mounting costs of product development.

2.4. *How do companies respond to these challenges?*

From Table 3.2 it can be seen that the most frequent response to competitive challenges is the cutting of costs (53 per cent of firms). This is supported by organizational restructuring (44 per cent) such as e.g. the introduction of lean production. This reaction is not surprising given the fact that price competition and high costs are the most prominent challenges to firms. But it seems that restructuring does not simply follow the old Fordist route, since it goes along with quality production and innovation: 43 per cent of firms have been speeding up product development and 42 per cent have been intensifying internal R&D. External strategies have a clearly lower relevance: subcontracting (19 per cent) and out-sourcing (18 per cent) are somewhat more frequent than technology and marketing co-operation (15 per cent). Obviously, modern production and management con-cepts based on networks and new supplier relations are not as frequent in the investigated regions of Europe as may have been emphasized in the literature.

Reflecting the stronger challenges of large firms we find that they respond much more frequently through cost cutting (77 per cent of firms) and organizational restructuring (66 per cent) than smaller ones (Figure 3.4). Also the speeding up of product development (61 per cent), the intensification of R&D (54 per cent) and technology co-operation (23 per cent) are more common reactions for large, rather than for smaller, firms.

As expected, product innovators respond more often through the speeding up of product development (63 per cent) as well as by an intensification of R&D (56 per cent; Table 3.2). Also relevant to them are cost cutting (59 per cent) and technology co-operation (23 per cent). Innovators, thus, stick in principle to the 'high road

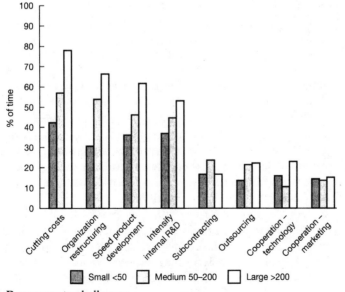

Figure 3.4 Responses to challenges

Table 3.3 Product and process innovation (figures show % of firms having introduced the listed types of innovation)

	Total	Firm size			Innovation type	
		Small <50	Medium 50–200	Large >200	Product innovation	Process innovation
n =	*833*	*379*	*258*	*157*	*323*	*385*
New products	66.5	55.7	74.8	88.5	100.0	80.3
Products new to the market	38.8	31.1	41.5	58.6	100.0	49.9
New processes	46.2	35.6	53.5	64.3	59.4	100.0
Processes new to the market	16.8	13.5	17.4	26.8	24.5	35.8

strategy', but they have to take the cost side into account. Technology co-operation is probably one way of keeping the cost of R&D within reasonable limits.

2.5. Innovation activities

We have already seen that innovation plays a prominent role in the overall competitive strategies of firms. Which kind of innovation activities can we observe for the survey firms in the investigated regions of Europe? In the firm survey we looked at indicators for innovation inputs (R&D budgets and R&D employment) as well as for innovation outputs (new products and processes introduced in the past three years). In addition, we asked for the introduction of new organizational practices in order to cover the organisational side of the innovation process. R&D indicators usually have the problem that they do not reach the full spectrum of the innovation process and particularly the innovation activities of small firms. The indication of product and process innovations on the other hand depends strongly on the respective industry and is also a rather subjective indicator.

Table 3.3 demonstrates that, overall, *product innovations* are more frequent than process innovations. Two-thirds of firms indicated the introduction of new products in the past three years. To a large extent these are smaller modifications or mere imitations as subsequent firm interviews have shown. Only 39 per cent of companies have indicated that these new products were more than imitations in the sense that they were new not just to the respective firm but also to the market. More radical innovations (i.e. those entering new trajectories) were rare events, however, as the firm interviews have shown. *New technologies (process innovations)* were introduced by 46 per cent of firms. Again, most of these are adoptions of available technologies, only 17 per cent of firms indicated that process innovations were also new to the respective market (including own developments).

In our sample innovativeness increases with firm size as can be seen from Figure 3.5. Medium and large companies are more often product- and process-innovators than small companies. But we cannot conclude from this that small firms are not innovative in general. From the analysis of *innovation inputs* (R&D budgets in per cent of sales, R&D personnel in per cent of employment) we can observe a segmented structure (Table 3.4). More than half of the small firms do not report any

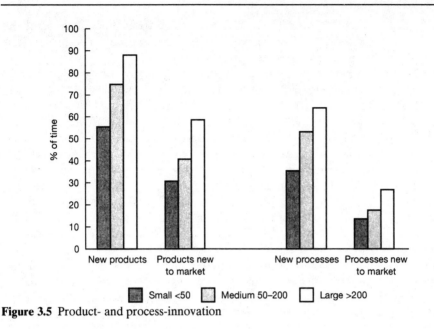

Figure 3.5 Product- and process-innovation

R&D activities (either zero or missing values). However, about a quarter of all small firms have high innovation inputs in relative terms. The surprisingly high share of small firms in the R&D intensive categories probably has to do with certain indivisibilities of R&D activities. Another factor may be the importance of customer specific production of small firms leading to frequent 'development' activities but usually not to 'research'. Concerning large firms, a clear majority report R&D activities, but these are in most cases only on low or medium levels in relative terms (per cent of sales; per cent of employment).

Innovation, however, according to the evolutionary model, covers more than technology changes, (Dosi *et al.*, 1988; Edquist, 1997a, Lundvall and Borrás, 1997). Often, organizational and management changes may be more relevant for the competitiveness of firms than product or process innovations. This has been stressed in particular in the flexible specialization concept (Benko and Dunford, 1991) and in the lean production/management approach (Womack *et al.*, 1990). Table 3.5 shows *new organizational practices* introduced by the firms in the past three years. Quality improvement obviously is the strongest concern to the companies: quality standards such as ISO 9000 (certification) were introduced by 52 per cent of firms, the broader and more far reaching total quality management by 46 per cent. Organizational decentralization is another prominent goal as demonstrated by the frequent intro- duction of group work (48 per cent of firms), flat hierarchies (40 per cent) and profit centres (33 per cent). Information technology has been introduced by 45 per cent of firms and 'just in time' concepts by 38 per cent, both are thus important dimensions of organizational change. We find a rather low indication, however, for outsourcing, networking and systems supplying (between 26–22 per cent of firms). Internal organizational changes are obviously much more frequent than changes in the external relations of firms. Obviously, there are more barriers to engage in network types of relations or to reorganize the supply chain (system suppliers) than to change organizations internally. This supports the impression from other findings of the REGIS project that firms in European regions are rather introverted regarding their competitive strategies and their innovation activities.

In line with the above findings we can observe that large firms are much more active concerning organizational changes. All mentioned practices are introduced much more frequently by large firms than by the smaller ones. This is not really surprising, since some of these practices are simply devices to deal with the organizational complexity which large firms face more often than small ones. Medium sized companies are also quite active with respect to new organizational practices. They show above average adoption rates for measures of quality improvement (ISO 9000, Total Quality Management (TQM)), organizational decentralization (group work, profit centres) as well as for the introduction of information technology. Small firms are clearly less active with respect to quality standards (only 31 per cent of companies), but also with respect to networking or new supplier relations (11 per cent).

Overall, we get the impression from Tables 3.3 and 3.5 that technological and organizational changes are strongly linked. First, product and process innovations are correlated quite strongly, i.e. firms having introduced product innovations are also found to be more active with respect to process innovations (and vice versa).

Table 3.4 R&D budgets and staff (figures show % of firms belonging to certain classes of relative budget and staff)

			Firm size			Innovation type	
	Total	Small < 50	Medium 50–200	Large > 200		Product innovation	Process innovation
n =	833	379	258	157		323	385
R&D budget in % of sales 1995							
Top third (1)	16.3	22.7	10.5	14.0		23.2	19.7
Middle third (2)	16.2	11.1	20.2	24.2		23.2	16.6
Lowest third (3)	16.3	10.0	20.9	25.5		19.2	17.4
No budget	12.7	13.7	16.3	6.4		7.1	10.6
Missing values	38.4	42.5	32.2	29.9		27.2	35.6
R&D staff in % of employment 1995							
Top third (4)	16.8	29.0	8.1	5.7		20.1	16.4
Middle third (5)	16.6	10.8	24.0	22.3		23.5	20.8
Lowest third (6)	16.7	2.9	24.4	41.4		19.2	20.3
No staff	13.0	15.6	14.3	6.4		6.5	10.9
Missing values	37.0	41.7	29.1	24.2		30.7	31.7

Categories:
(1) relative R&D budget > 5.41
(2) relative R&D budget < = 5.41 and > 1.85
(3) relative R&D budget < = 1.85 and > 0
(4) relative R&D staff > 11.11
(5) relative R&D staff < = 11.11 and > 3.59
(6) relative R&D staff < = 3.59 and > 0

Table 3.5 New organizational practices (figures show % of firms having introduced the listed practices)

	Total	Firm size			Innovation type	
		Small < 50	Medium 50–200	Large > 200	Product innovation	Process innovation
n =	833	379	258	157	323	385
ISO 9000	52.0	31.1	65.9	84.1	65.0	62.3
Group work	47.8	36.4	51.6	71.3	55.1	56.4
Total quality managment	46.3	31.1	57.4	72.0	54.5	57.1
Information technology	44.5	32.5	51.2	66.2	52.9	56.1
Flat hierarchies	39.5	26.6	45.3	63.7	49.8	46.5
Just in time	37.7	30.1	40.3	55.4	44.9	46.8
Profit centres	32.7	17.2	41.9	58.6	42.7	42.3
Benchmarking	24.7	13.2	29.5	49.0	32.2	32.5
Outsourcing	22.1	16.4	23.3	36.9	28.5	24.2
Interdisciplinary design teams	22.1	12.7	26.0	40.8	33.4	29.4
Networking	20.0	16.1	20.9	31.8	23.5	26.0
System suppliers	15.5	11.3	19.8	29.3	26.9	24.4

Second, both types of innovators (product and process innovators) also have higher adoption rates of new organizational practices. Generally, this supports the argument of the evolutionary innovation model that different kinds of technological innovations are inter-related and that they also have to be complemented by organizational change in order to become effective.

3. Differences between REGIS regions

How do the REGIS regions differ with respect to competitive strategies, challenges and innovation activities? We have mainly used the common data base of the firm survey in order to answer this question. The Hungarian and the Polish cases are not part of this data base, so they are not included in the common set of tables. Some aspects of competitive strategies and challenges of firms in Central and Eastern Europe have been included, however, on the basis of available reports.[4]

3.1. Competitive advantages of firms

From Table 3.6 we can see that firms in Baden-Württemberg, Wales, Styria and Centro indicate competitive advantages more frequently than firms in the other regions. Competitive advantages were stated less in Brabant, the Basque Country and in Wallonia.

In Baden-Württemberg technical standards and innovativeness are the most important advantages (stated by 86 per cent of firms). High scores were also registered for after sales service, quality and user friendliness. This pattern fits the

---

[4] Makó *et al.*, (1997) for the Shékesfehérvár region in Hungary, and Galar *et al.* (1997) for the region of Lower Silesia (Poland).

Table 3.6 Competitive advantages by region (figures show % of firms indicating the following items)

	High performance			Reconversion-upstream		Reconversion-downstream		Industrial district		Total
n =	Ba-Wü 81	Brabant 98	Styria 107	Tampere 142	Wales 103	Basque 80	Wallonia 91	Centro 56	Friuli 75	833
Competitive advantages of firms										
Quality	84	63	82	77	84	45	71	86	87	75.3
Delivery time	49	51	66	64	65	50	44	63	57	57.3
Innovativeness	86	30	75	45	68	29	53	59	56	55.1
Services	52	24	63	28	43	19	36	59	44	39.7
Price	19	35	21	35	51	23	18	27	27	29.3
User friendliness	41	15	25	32	31	11	8	27	21	23.9
Ecology	21	7	25	20	15	10	9	27	27	17.4
How do firms sustain competitive advantages?										
Skills/knowledge	67	61	68	83	70	25	64	41	67	63.4
R&D	68	29	50	65	49	39	43	39	57	49.6
Patents/licences	21	3	12	3	18	11	18	7	15	11.5
Org.production	49	20	38	49	58	36	58	66	65	47.8
Marketing	42	18	36	64	39	18	30	41	35	37.5
Co-operation – regional	17	14	18	27	31	15	2	9	29	19.0
Co-operation – national	14	8	18	28	33	6	14	4	11	16.8
Co-operation – European	15	7	28	21	20	14	16	7	11	16.6
Co-operation – global	9	2	14	13	16	3	11	5	12	10.0

well-known image of a region of technologically advanced quality producers. Price is clearly less of a competitive advantage for the firms (only for 19 per cent). What might be reflected here is a problem of over-engineering of products (Cooke and Morgan, 1994b; REGIS report on firm interviews by Bechtle *et al.*, 1997). Firms in Baden-Württemberg might have given too much attention to technical standards of their products in the past and they might have neglected the cost side of these standards too much. As a consequence some important sectors (e.g. the machinery industry) face strong competition and suffered a crisis in the early 1990s. This pattern of competitive advantage is clearly different from the other high performing engineering region, Brabant. Here, firms seem to have given more attention to price competitiveness but innovativeness is obviously less of an advantage. Most probably, these differences reflect to a considerable extent the differences of firm size in the samples. In Baden-Württemberg large firms are strongly represented while in Brabant small firms dominate.

In Styria the pattern of competitive advantage is similar to the one of Baden-Württemberg. Technical standards and innovativeness as well as complementary services and quality are high ranking. In addition, firms have advantages from fast and timely delivery. Price competitiveness is, as in Baden-Württemberg and Wallonia, rather low. This reflects the situation of an old industrial region with a strongly organized labour force and rather high labour costs. Competitive advantages in Wales are broadly similar to Styria with the difference that innovation and services are less important but price competitiveness ranks clearly higher. In fact, Wales is the region with the highest price competitiveness of all regions according to the responses of the firms. This might result from a combination of high productivity and moderate wages. In Tampere, innovation is stated less frequently as an advantage. Firms see their advantages instead more often in product quality and in prompt delivery. Also price and user friendliness are considered as advantages.

In the reconversion regions of the Basque Country and Wallonia firms indicate generally fewer competitive advantages. It seems as if firms are still struggling with restructuring and have not yet found specific competitive advantages. In contrast to this, the firms in Centro and in Friuli indicate more competitive advantages. In both regions the quality of products is clearly most important. In addition, the offer of after sales service provides advantage *vis-à-vis* competitors. Particularly for Centro, it is surprising to find that price is not regarded as a competitive advantage given the low labour cost of the region. Obviously, there are only few regions in Europe nowadays where firms can rely mainly on price competitiveness, neglecting other aspects of competition such as product quality or delivery time.

The regions in Central and Eastern Europe (Féjer region in Hungary, and Lower Silesia in Poland) differ from those of Western Europe in various aspects (Table 3.7). Quality is regarded as the most frequent competitive advantage (70–81 per cent of companies), but low prices are much more important as a factor of competition than in the West. In the Polish region low price is the second most important advantage indicated by 67 per cent of companies. This reflects the much lower labour costs in this part of Europe compared to the West. The Hungarian Féjer region is situated in between the Polish and the Western regions in terms of price competitiveness. Table 3.7 also shows that timely delivery is also seen as a relevant advantage (58–70 per cent of firms). Interestingly, the firms in Eastern Europe have stated more frequently than those in the West environmental aspects as an advantage (30–32 per cent of companies). Most probably this refers to the lower environmental standards rather than to ecologically superior production processes. Less frequent than in regions of Western Europe we find after-sales-service as an advantage reflecting the tradition of a low service and customer orientation of those economies inherited from the past.

3.2. How do firms sustain competitive advantage?

In Baden-Württemberg firms strongly rely on their internal competences and on their boundary spanning functions, i.e. those functions linking the firms with their technological and market environments. Most important are R&D as well as skills and knowledge of the labour force, relevant factors are also marketing and the organization of production (Table 3.6). Their R&D activities lead more frequently than in other regions to patents and licenses from which firms derive competitive advantage. Technological innovation, thus, is the main instrument to achieve competitive advantage in Baden-Württemberg, a finding which is supported by the pattern of innovation activities below.

In Brabant the skills and knowledge of the labour force are the most important factors for sustaining competitive advantage. Reflecting the high share of small firms in the sample, factors like R&D play a smaller role.

Table 3.7 Competitiveness in regions of Eastern Europe (% of firms indicating the listed items)

		Fejér (Hungary)	Lower Silesia (Poland)	Other REGIS regions
	$n =$	75	90	833
Competitive advantages of firms				
Quality		70	81	75.3
Delivery time		68	58	57.3
Innovativeness		54	52	55.1
Services		34	22	39.7
Price		47	67	29.3
User friendliness		29	25	23.9
Ecology		30	32	17.4
How do firms sustain competitive advantages?				
Skills/knowledge		68	94	63.4
R&D		21	26	49.6
Pat./licences		24	14	11.5
Org.production		65	49	47.8
Marketing		38	52	37.5
Co-operation – regional		24	48	19.0
Co-operation – national		29	36	16.8
Co-operation – European		18	21	16.6
Co-operation – global		–	10	10.0

Similarly, in Styria, Tampere and Wales the skills and knowledge of the labour force are most important for sustaining competitiveness. In Tampere this applies also to internal R&D and marketing (strong boundary spanning functions as in Baden-Württemberg). In Wales firms draw advantage to a high degree from the organization of production. This supports the finding of Schall and Cooke (1997b) that Welsh firms try to improve their competitive position by becoming quality and system suppliers to large, often foreign, firms. In all three of these reconverting regions co-operations with other firms are regarded more often as a source of competitive advantage than in the other regions. Co-operation exists in principle on all levels. In Tampere and Wales, however, regional and national co-operation predominate, while in Styria European co-operation is more important in comparison.

In the other Western regions the factors for sustaining competitive advantage are less clear. In Wallonia and Centro the organization of production is relatively important; in Friuli in addition the skills of the labour force, R&D activities and regional co-operation are also important.

In the Hungarian and Polish regions firms rely, apart from lower labour costs, to a high degree on the skills of their labour forces (68–94 per cent of companies; see Table 3.7). This supports the above finding of quality as a competitive advantage and indicates that firms in those regions have moved beyond simple and low cost production. As a contrast, internal R&D and technological innovation are clearly less relevant as factors to sustain competitiveness than in the West (stated only by 21–26 per cent of companies).

3.3. *Competitive challenges and responses*

Competitive challenges are more strongly perceived by the firms in Baden-Württemberg, Styria, Wales and Wallonia (Table 3.8). For the three reconverting regions this could be related to the longrun restructuring process. For Baden-Württemberg the strong competitive challenge is probably a more recent phenomenon, and it is an indication of the crisis in the 1990s (Cooke and Morgan, 1994b).

In Baden-Württemberg companies were able to achieve high technological standards in the past but now they have difficulties in keeping this standard in a time of fast technological change. In addition, they are facing a high-cost environment. As a consequence firms are particularly challenged by price competition (77 per cent of firms) as well as by high personnel costs (64 per cent). Other major concerns for the firms are increasing quality requirements of products (65 per cent of firms) and a high speed of technological change (62 per cent). Both result in high costs for product development being another major challenge (64 per cent of firms). Firms respond to this situation first of all through the cutting of costs (74 per cent), partly through organizational restructuring (52 per cent) and outsourcing (32 per cent). However, they also want to maintain their technological level through an intensification of R&D and the speeding up of product development.

In Styria, the strongest challenge also results from price competition (76 per cent of companies). Here, too, this is related to high personnel costs (74 per cent) but also to the appearance of new competitors (40 per cent). This reflects the situation of a

Table 3.8 Challenges to companies by region (figures show % of firms indicating the listed items)

	High performance			Reconversion-upstream		Reconversion-downstream		Industrial district		Total
n =	Ba-Wü 81	Brabant 98	Styria 107	Tampere 142	Wales 103	Basque 80	Wallonia 91	Centro 56	Friuli 75	833
Challenges to companies										
Price competition	77	18	76	52	71	63	69	61	75	61.3
Quality requirement	65	40	57	59	54	55	59	75	49	56.4
Personnel costs	64	15	74	42	35	44	56	38	35	44.9
Demand change	31	30	59	39	48	33	32	41	47	40.2
Technological change	62	26	49	37	50	31	35	41	29	40.1
Development costs	64	22	49	20	41	36	40	52	41	38.7
New competitors	31	13	40	15	37	40	47	34	21	30.1
Responses to challenges										
Cutting costs	74	26	62	44	57	58	67	59	40	56.6
Org. restructuring	52	16	56	34	55	45	38	50	48	42.5
Speed of product development	57	8	47	30	61	49	64	36	53	43.0
Intensify R&D	47	18	50	56	38	33	35	45	49	41.8
Subcontract	17	19	27	16	19	21	12	13	20	18.6
Outsourcing	32	17	23	10	19	5	9	39	15	17.6
Co-operation – technology	11	5	28	20	17	9	18	9	9	15.1
Co-operation – marketing	5	7	27	15	19	10	4	11	23	14.0

high-cost industrial region which is facing the challenges of European integration (Austria became a full member of the EU in 1995) as well as the opening of Eastern Europe (Slovenia and Hungary are bordering countries to Styria). Other major challenges are the rapid changes of demand (59 per cent) and of technology (49 per cent). As in Baden-Württemberg firms react by a combination of organizational change and an intensification of R&D; most important are the cutting of costs (62 per cent), organizational restructuring (56 per cent) and a rearrangement of relations to suppliers and customers (outsourcing and subcontracting). More frequent than in other regions is co-operation in the fields of technology (28 per cent) and marketing (27 per cent).

We find in Wales a similar pattern of challenges and responses as in Styria, albeit with lower frequencies. Also in Wales price competition is the strongest challenge, despite the fact that price was considered to be a competitive advantage by 51 per cent of firms. Welsh firms try to escape competition more through the speeding up of product development than through cutting costs. Also organizational restructuring, outsourcing and interfirm co-operation are relatively frequent responses.

In Wallonia the most important challenge results from strong price competition (69 per cent of firms). Both the high cost of personnel (56 per cent) and the appearance of new competitors seem to be responsible for this. Another challenge is increasing quality requirements. Firms react to stronger competition mainly by cutting costs (67 per cent), and to higher quality standards by a faster product development (64 per cent).

By comparison firms in Tampere and Centro are less concerned with price competition. The most frequent challenges are increasing quality requirements and

Table 3.9 Challenges to companies in regions of Eastern Europe (figures show % of firms indicating the listed items)

		Fejér (Hungary)	Lower Silesia (Poland)	Other REGIS regions
	n =	*75*	*90*	*833*
Challenges to companies:				
Price competition		78	71	61.3
Quality requirement		71	41	56.4
Personnel costs		37	47	44.9
Demand change		29	44	40.2
Technological change		27	27	40.1
Development cost		32	27	38.7
New competitors		49	67	30.1
Responses to challenges				
Cutting costs		73	79	56.6
Organizational restrueturing		54	60	42.5
Speed of product development		22	31	43.0
Intensify R&D		15	17	41.8
Subcontract		11	42	18.6
Outsourcing		11	47	17.6
Co-operation – technology		11	27	15.1
Co-operation – marketing		27	25	14.0

in Centro the cost of product development. Firms in both regions react through an intensification of R&D. In Tampere, in addition, technology co-operation is a relatively frequent response, and in Centro it is organizational restructuring and outsourcing. In the Basque Country and Friuli competitive challenges and responses do not differ strongly from the overall pattern which was presented above.

Despite being more price competitive (see Table 3.7, p. 62), firms in Hungary and Poland are strongly challenged by price competition (71–78 per cent of companies; see Table 3.9). This seems to be a paradox at first sight, but it can be explained by the fact that those firms are in very price-competitive markets and are constantly threatened by other low-cost producers (e.g. in more peripheral countries and regions of Eastern Europe or in South East Asia). In fact, they indicate new competitors more frequently as a challenge than the firms in Western Europe. How do the Hungarian and Polish firms respond to these challenges? Most important is the cutting of costs (undertaken by 73–79 per cent of companies). It is complemented by organizational restructuring (stated by 54–60 per cent). The companies in the Polish region are in addition engaging in subcontracting and outsourcing (42–47 per cent). A clearly lower incidence is found though for technology-related strategies such as an intensification of R&D and a speeding up of product development.

3.4. Innovation activities

With respect to innovation differences between the regions we do not find a totally clear and consistent picture. There are different patterns, in particular with respect to output-indicators of innovation (product and process innovations; Table 3.10) and input (R&D budgets and staff; See Table 3.11).

New products in a broad sense (including imitations and smaller changes) have been introduced frequently in Friuli (80 per cent of firms), Baden-Württemberg (79 per cent) and in Centro (77 per cent). Looking only at products which were new to the market, Baden-Württemberg clearly is leading (64 per cent of companies). High scores can also be found in Centro, Styria, Wales and Wallonia (Table 3.10).

New production technologies (process innovations) were introduced to a high degree in the peripheral regions Friuli (67 per cent of firms) and Centro (66 per cent). In addition, the reconverting Basque Country, Wales and Tampere have strongly introduced new technologies. In these regions the innovation focus is on the modernization of production technologies. Most of these are adoptions of available technologies, only in a minority of cases does it imply the creation of new technologies.

To what extent are these innovations backed by respective innovation inputs? Looking at the R&D budgets (for 1995 in per cent of sales) and at R&D personnel (as per cent of total employment) we find that Baden-Württemberg, Styria, Tampere and Wales have relatively high levels of R&D activities (Table 3.11). In Friuli many firms are participating in R&D but generally at a low and medium level. In Wales we find a polarized situation. A high share of companies (about 40 per cent) indicate no R&D. But those which are engaging in R&D do it at a relatively intensive level (20–26 per cent of companies are in the respective top classes). This contrasts with Brabant, the Basque Country, Wallonia and Centro where we find low response

Table 3.10 Product and process innovation by region (figures show % of firms having introduced the listed types of innovation)

	High performance		Reconversion-upstream			Reconversion-downstream		Industrial district		Total
n =	Ba-Wü 81	Brabant 98	Styria 107	Tampere 142	Wales 103	Basque 80	Wallonia 91	Centro 56	Friuli 75	833
New products	79	31	65	74	63	66	71	77	80	67
Products new to the market	64	17	47	29	45	26	43	48	40	39
New processes	38	24	41	49	52	53	39	66	67	46
Processes new to the market	12	7	20	21	19	13	18	23	17	17

Table 3.11 R&D budgets and staff (figures shows % of firms belonging to certain classes of relative budget and staff)

	High performance		Reconversion-upstream			Reconversion-downstream		Industrial district		Total
n =	Ba-Wü 81	Brabant 98	Styria 107	Tampere 142	Wales 103	Basque 80	Wallonia 91	Centro 56	Friuli 75	833
R&D budget in % of sales 1995										
Top third (1)	28.4	6.1	26.2	16.9	20.4	11.3	15.4	3.6	12.0	16.3
Middle third (2)	40.7	2.0	28.0	17.6	12.6	6.3	8.8	8.9	18.7	16.2
Lowest third (3)	6.2	7.1	15.9	23.9	8.7	10.0	29.7	14.3	28.0	16.3
No budget	8.6	11.2	10.3	4.2	39.8	10.0	3.3	12.5	16.0	12.7
Missing values	16.0	73.5	19.6	37.3	18.4	62.5	42.9	60.7	25.3	38.4
R&D staff in % of employment 1995										
Top third (4)	18.5	16.3	22.4	21.8	26.2	5.0	7.7	10.7	13.3	16.8
Middle third (5)	37.0	5.1	14.0	18.3	16.5	10.0	11.0	8.9	29.3	16.6
Lowest third (6)	17.3	4.1	20.6	16.9	8.7	12.5	16.5	35.7	28.0	16.7
No staff	3.7	10.2	8.4	7.7	40.8	11.3	5.5	10.7	17.3	13.0
Missing values	23.5	64.3	34.6	35.2	7.8	61.3	59.3	33.9	12.0	37.0

Categories:
(1) relative R&D budget > 5.41
(2) relative R&D budget < = 5.41 and > 1.85
(3) relative R&D budget < = 1.85 and > 0
(4) relative R&D staff > 11.11
(5) relative R&D staff < = 11.11 and > 3.59
(6) relative R&D staff < = 3.59 and > 0

rates with respect to R&D inputs. Most probably this is an indication of low levels of R&D activities.

Taking into account all these indicators we can conclude that innovation activities are quite strong in Baden-Württemberg, in Styria and in Tampere. There is a different emphasis, however, in Baden-Württemberg where the focus is more on product innovation, in Tampere on process innovation and in Styria on a combination of both. In all three regions innovation outputs are also backed by respective inputs (R&D budgets and staff) so that the pattern looks robust.

Wales, Wallonia and Friuli have a medium level of innovation activities. Wales and Wallonia have relatively high shares of product innovators and this is backed also by some R&D activities. In Friuli, many firms indicate new products and new processes, but most of these are imitations or smaller modifications (see the report on firm interviews by Boffo and Pugliese, 1997). Consistent with this rather incremental approach of innovation are low to medium levels of R&D inputs.

In Centro the output indicators for innovation are quite impressive, but they are not really backed by respective R&D and qualification inputs. This can be explained by the high share of consumer goods in the sample (such as textiles and shoes). These are industries where product changes are frequent, depending, for example, on fashion cycles, but these changes are usually small (incremental change, modifications) requiring design inputs or fast imitation rather than R&D. In addition, firms adopt new production technologies which are available on the market and do not require much R&D.

In the Basque Country and in Brabant innovation activities seem to be at a low level. In both regions only a minority of firms report any R&D activities. In the Basque Country firms indicate new products and processes but these are, as in Friuli, mainly imitations (new only to the firm). In Brabant we find, probably due to a bias towards small firms in the sample, a very low response rate to these questions.

How do organizational changes fit into this picture? Overall, we find that technological innovations and organizational changes often go together (Table 3.12). In Baden-Württemberg quality improvement (ISO 9000, total quality management) and organizational decentralization (flat hierarchies, group work) have a high priority and are frequently indicated. This is complemented through rearrangements along the value chain (outsourcing, systems supplying).

Styria and Tampere have, overall, similar patterns but with lower frequencies. Tampere also differs from Styria as firms are more active with respect to information technology (a specific strength of the Finnish innovation system). In addition, Tampere firms are more inclined to form interdisciplinary design teams.

In Wales and the Basque Country, firms are also quite active with respect to organizational change. Most important are quality improvements (ISO 9000, Total Quality Management). Also, firms frequently have been introducing information technologies and 'just in time' concepts. Welsh firms are more active with respect to new organizational practices since they have additionally high scores with respect to profit centres, benchmarking and design teams.

The firms in the regions of Hungary and Poland indicate product and process innovations to a similar extent as the Western firms. However, this is not backed by respective R&D inputs (budgets and staff). From this, and the interviews, we can

Table 3.12 New organizational practices by region (figures show % of firms introducing the listed practices)

	High performance			Reconversion-upstream		Reconversion-downstream		Industrial district		Total
n =	Ba-Wü 81	Brabant 98	Styria 107	Tampere 142	Wales 103	Basque 80	Wallonia 91	Centro 56	Friuli 75	833
ISO 9000	68	15	55	52	70	69	50	48	41	52.0
Group work	49	39	54	54	28	54	48	43	60	47.8
Total quality management	51	31	33	39	51	59	54	59	57	46.3
Information technology	25	15	46	67	59	60	23	29	61	44.5
Flat hierarchies	73	35	65	45	32	11	10	27	48	39.5
Just in time	24	27	34	28	45	43	62	34	52	37.7
Profit centres	28	20	23	29	44	19	33	52	59	32.7
Benchmarking	9	6	26	20	31	25	48	46	20	24.7
Outsourcing	41	32	31	14	21	14	12	13	21	22.1
Interdisciplinary design team	20	4	13	42	24	13	15	21	39	22.1
Networking	11	18	22	28	15	9	13	16	31	20.0

conclude that innovations are mainly adoptions and imitations of (often Western) technology or incremental innovations. Subsidiaries of foreign companies are playing an ambivalent role. On the one hand they have been setting up new and modern plants in greenfield locations providing company-wide technology and know-how access (see Makó *et al.*, 1997); on the other hand they do not have much R&D on the spot nor do they have many links to the respective regional economies. New organizational practices are indicated quite frequently in the Hungarian and Polish regions, but this is not surprising given the turbulent changes in the past years. A lower incidence than for Western firms is found for certification (ISO 9000) as well as for the more comprehensive Total Quality Management.

4. Conclusions

European firms are facing new challenges due to reinforced global competition, the process of economic integration and the opening of borders to Central and Eastern Europe. How do companies compete under these new conditions in the investigated regions of Europe? Which are their major challenges and how do they respond to them? How strongly are they pursuing innovation ('high road') strategies as against mere cost cutting ('low road') strategies? The following are the main conclusions from the REGIS firm survey and the interviews with respect to these questions.

1.   Most of the investigated European firms (three out of four) compete through the quality of their products. Innovation and high technical standards are important as a complementary strategy in this respect constituting competitive advantages for more than half of the firms. In addition, the ability to deliver promptly as well as provide aftersales service are relevant advantages underlining a move towards new production models and towards the service economy. But less than 30 per cent of the companies claim to be competitive through low prices.

   The investigated firms sustain their competitive advantage mainly through internal factors, such as skills and knowledge of the labour force, R&D, marketing and production organization. Co-operation with other firms can also be observed at regional, national and European levels, but they are clearly not so frequent as to constitute a dominant new organizational model.

2.   Overall, price competition is the strongest challenge to the firms. This can be explained by stronger competition through globalization and the changes in Europe, but it is also due to the low price competitiveness of many firms. Big challenges are, however, also coming from changes of demand, increasing quality requirements and the high speed of technological change. Firms respond to these challenges on the one hand through the cutting of costs and through organizational restructuring, and on the other hand through more innovation (intensified R&D and faster product development). Competitive strategies, thus, in most cases go beyond pure Fordist cost cutting and include elements of innovation as the second most important strategy.

3.   Innovation activities are most frequently oriented to product innovation. Overall, two out of three companies have been introducing new products in a broad sense in the past three years. Most of these imply just smaller and incremental changes or modifications of products. Products which were new not just to the

company but also to the respective market were less frequent (less than 40 per cent of firms). More radical innovations (those involving major technological steps) were rare events as the subsequent firm interviews have shown. The vast majority of companies, thus, follow existing technological trajectories; entering new trajectories is rare. In the long run this may create problems of lock-in for many firms and regions.

In many cases product innovation is tied to changes in production technology (process innovation) as well as to organizational changes. New organizational practices most frequently have to do with quality improvement. Certification (e.g. ISO 9000) as well as the more comprehensive Total Quality Management are quite common. Other practices refer to organizational decentralization (group work, flat hierarchies, profit centres) which are supposed to lead to higher flexibility as well as to a better innovative performance. Most of these changes were internal ones. We found networking strategies (co-operation with other firms) or the move towards new supplier relations (e.g. systems supplying) less frequently than implied in the literature.

4. Large firms are generally more engaged in innovation than small companies. Both product and process innovations as well as new organizational practices are introduced more frequently by comparison in large firms than in small ones. However, most large firms are in more contested markets being strongly exposed to price competition where they are often confronted with cost disadvantages.

    Small companies rely more on the skills of their work force than on internal R&D. Good quality of products and high flexibility are typical advantages. Also, small companies compete more often through low prices than larger firms. However, not all small firms are non-innovative. A certain segment of them has high R&D intensities (often far higher than those of large firms), and these firms are also doing well with respect to product innovation.

5. There are considerable differences regarding competitive strategies and innovation between the REGIS regions, but they do not always give a clear and consistent picture. According to expectations is the finding that innovation strategies and activities are obviously more frequent in high performing Baden-Württemberg than in other REGIS regions. Here we find a high share of technologically advanced quality producers. They rely strongly on their internal competences (knowledge of the work force, R&D, marketing) but surprisingly little on external co-operation. In the past, the firms in Baden-Württemberg may have followed too much the strategy of the high-quality producer, however, some of them have been facing problems of 'over-engineering' and a loss of price competitiveness more recently.

There are also intensive innovation activities in some of the reconversion regions such as Styria, Tampere and Wales. In all of these regions there seem to exist specific trajectories which are followed by the firms. In Styria product innovations were comparatively more important, and most of them were incremental changes in traditional mechanical engineering industries. Tampere firms were more focused on the introduction of new technologies, in particular of new information technology. This is backed by a specific strength of the Finnish innovation system in this respect.

In Wales, innovation is often the result of an upgrading of supplier relations. In particular large foreign firms as customers exert a pressure on Welsh suppliers to improve their products and to innovate.

The high indication of product innovations in the case of Centro was rather unexpected. This is a region where the preconditions for innovation are weak. A closer look revealed that in Centro much of this product change is in labour intensive consumer industries such as shoes and textiles, where we find frequent fashion changes. Friuli is a similar case in this respect. Innovation is important but not in an R&D intensive manner. Firms innovate rather through small incremental and design changes (e.g. in the furniture industry), not strongly based on internal or external R&D activities.

The companies in the Féjer region of Hungary and in the Polish region of Lower Silesia compete to a higher degree on the basis of low cost than the firms in the West. Technological innovation is clearly less frequently a competitive advantage, although it is not irrelevant. Innovation mainly takes place in the form of technology adoption, imitation and incremental change and it supports the upgrading and quality improvement of the production process. Foreign firms play an ambivalent role in this respect. They usually do not have much R&D on the spot, but they provide access to company-wide technology and know how, helping to modernize the respective regional economies.

In the following chapter we will look more closely at the interdependencies of firms in the innovation process asking to what extent innovation is systemic in the REGIS regions.

CHAPTER FOUR

The Innovation Process and Interactions of Firms: The Role of the Region

1. Introduction

The view of the innovation process has changed considerably in the past years. For a long time innovation was regarded as a process driven by individual entrepreneurs or by dominant firms. It was seen as a linear process starting with R&D and ending on the market (see Malecki, 1991). More recently, it has been argued that, on the contrary, it is a highly interactive process in which many functions, firms as well as organizations are involved (Hakansson, 1987; DeBresson and Walker, 1991; Edquist, 1997a). There are several approaches along these lines.

One stream of literature argues that firms are not only inserted into their respective sectoral environments but also that national conditions and institutions play an important role. Lundvall (1992) and Nelson (1993) have investigated national innovation systems in this context pointing out that national economic specializations, research strengths, educational systems and financial structures shape the innovation process to a high degree. There is also the argument that through the process of economic integration and globalization innovation systems reach further and further beyond national boundaries. In Europe, for example, the possible formation of a 'European innovation system' has been discussed (Edquist, 1997b; Lundvall and Borrás, 1997).

From these works we might conclude that the level of the region becomes more and more irrelevant for the firms' innovation process. A closer look, however, reveals that this is not necessarily the case. There are arguments that the innovation process to some extent also becomes regionally embedded (Tödtling, 1994a; Storper, 1995; Asheim, 1996). The following factors and processes might be responsible for this:

- Important preconditions and factors for innovation such as highly qualified labour and non-codified knowledge are not very mobile (Malecki, 1991; Tödtling, 1992).
- There are spatial concentrations of R&D which often lead to local and regional knowledge spillovers (Castells and Hall 1994).
- Innovation and technology based firms are often brought forward through regional networks of firms and actors (Cooke and Morgan, 1993; Saxenian, 1994; Tödtling, 1994b; Simmie, 1997).
- Regional innovation policies and institutions play an important role (Hassink, 1996).

- Local and regional production systems may lead to a common understanding between relevant actors ('culture') and a specific milieu favouring innovation (Aydalot and Keeble, 1988; Camagni, 1991; Maillat, 1991).

It seems that the question whether the regional, national or the European level is more important in the innovation process of firms is wrongly posed. These levels may not just be substitutes but they might depend on each other and they may be complementary. Innovative firms might rely on the region as well as on national, European or even global networks in the innovation process. In fact Camagni (1991), Edquist (1997b) and Lundvall and Borrás (1997) have been arguing along these lines.

This chapter investigates these aspects, i.e. the interactions of firms in the innovation process and the partners they use. We are interested in the types of partners as well as in the spatial scale of networks. Although we look at these relations from a comprehensive perspective, we are particularly interested in the role of the region in this respect. The following questions are dealt with:

- How important are interactions within the region for the innovation process of firms and which are the relevant partners?
- Which types of firms are more integrated into a regional innovation system?
- How do the investigated regions compare? Are there similar and common patterns of innovation or can we identify specific regional models?

These questions will be analysed using the common database of the REGIS firm survey as well as the firm interviews. This implies that the Hungarian and the Polish cases will not be included in this analysis. The data for Friuli are also not in the database and have been added subsequently into the respective tables. Concerning the interviews we rely on the respective papers of the research teams (based on the fourth interim report of the REGIS project). We have to consider that this comparison is not a straightforward task, since the papers often chose different approaches and they stress different aspects. The analysis, thus, is necessarily a subjective one, reflecting the views not just of the research teams but also of the authors.

2. Results of the firm survey

2.1. Partners in the innovation process

Which partners do firms interact with in the innovation process, how important are these and where are they located? Our survey data probably underestimate the linkages to partners in the innovation process since the respective question in the survey required some attention by the firms in order to answer it properly. Presumably, some were not willing to spend the time and effort, and did not answer in full detail.

We can see from Table 4.1 that clearly the most important partners for all REGIS regions in the data set are along the value chain, namely first of all the customers and second the suppliers. This supports the findings of the literature (e.g. Hakansson, 1987; von Hippel, 1988; Lundvall, 1992) that innovation often takes place interactively along the value chain. Customers frequently provide the first ideas for product modifications as well as for new products and they also may contribute

Table 4.1 Innovation partners (% of firms having partners; $n = 652$, missing 14%)

	Regional	National	European	Global
Customers	**44**	**61**	**48**	**25**
Suppliers	**35**	**52**	**37**	14
Consultants	16	**20**	10	4
Research organizations	13	17	6	3
Universities	**24**	**22**	8	3
Technology transfer	11	9	3	2
Venture capital	9	7	2	1
Subsidies	17	16	6	1
Government	14	10	3	0
Trade associations	12	17	4	1
Training institutions	17	14	3	1

Emboldened figures indicate the share of firms with partners $\geq$ 20%

substantially to the design and development process. Suppliers also may trigger innovation, e.g. through the provision of better performing components or new materials and they often contribute to the required process technology. Frequently these relations are not of the market type (short term) but interactive and more durable ('networks').

Generally, customers and suppliers as innovation partners are not confined to the region but for our sample more frequently located at the national and European level. This is not surprising because it reflects the distribution of the firms' input/output markets. Still, customers and suppliers of the region are also relevant innovation partners for 44 per cent and 35 per cent of the firms, respectively. In fact, they are, at the level of the region, more important than any other type of partner in the innovation process.

Overall, the third most important innovation partner to the firms are the universities. They have a multiple function as source and interface for new ideas, partners in the R&D process, and as a source for highly qualified labour. Universities are relatively more important at the level of the region (24 per cent of firms have relations to them) and the respective country (22 per cent). This is probably due to their character as public infrastructures as well as to the often tacit nature of knowledge and the importance of proximity for these relations.

Consultants also play a vital role in the innovation process. They provide know-how in various relevant fields, from legal aspects of patenting and licensing to consulting with respect to technology-access, innovation management and marketing/distribution (Moulaert and Tödtling, 1995). Due to the specialized nature of the required knowledge, they are not only drawn from the region (16 per cent of firms) but more frequently from the national (20 per cent) and also the European (10 per cent) levels.

From the other potential partners only providers of subsidies and training institutions seem to have a notable relevance. For these, the level of the region is the most important, followed by the respective country. Rarely used as partners in the innovation process are organizations for venture capital and for technology transfer. It was rather surprising to find that technology transfer and training were mentioned

Table 4.2 Innovation partners of small firms (< 50 employees) (deviation from total (Table 4.1) in % points; n = 302, missing 15%)

	Regional	National	European	Global
Customers	**4**	−7	−13	−7
Suppliers	−1	−6	−14	−6
Consultants	1	−7	−5	−2
Research organizations	−3	−7	−2	−1
Universities	−7	−9	−2	−1
Technology transfer	−5	−4	−1	−1
Venture capital	2	−2	0	0
Subsidies	0	−4	−2	0
Government	−3	−4	−2	0
Trade associations	−1	−7	−1	0
Training institutions	−4	−6	−1	0

Emboldened figures indicate positive deviation from total ≥ 3

rather little as innovation partners. Partly this may be due to the fact that the services of these institutions are regarded more as an 'externality' rather than as a specific and identifiable contribution to the innovation process.

There are some remarkable differences by firm size, organizational status and innovativeness with respect to the innovation partners. For small companies (i.e. those with less than 50 employees) we observe generally less interactions in the innovation process (Table 4.2). This is somewhat contrary to expectations, because in principle their limited resources should make complementary assets of partners more relevant to them. A possible reason for their fewer network-links might be the smaller scale innovation activities (e.g. only small modifications instead of real innovations) which can be done more or less internally. Another reason might be that there may be more barriers to entering into co-operation in the innovation process. Small firms often are not well informed about potential partners, they do not know the supply of innovation support well enough and they do not spend many resources or manpower on search activities either (Malecki, 1991; Tödtling, 1992).

From the pattern of deviations (compared to the total sample in Table 4.1) we can see that small firms have in particular fewer relations to customers and suppliers at larger spatial scales, while the only type of partner to which they relate more frequently than the average are the customers in the region. They have clearly fewer links to universities, research organizations, technology transfer and training. With respect to universities and research organizations this is to be expected and has to do with a lower demand for co-operation with science as well as with differences in language and culture between these types of organizations (Lundvall and Borrás, 1997). With respect to technology transfer, this finding is rather surprising, however, since small firms are often the very targets of transfer activities. From our results it appears that these activities do not reach sufficiently well an important group of clients.

Medium-sized companies (50–200 employees) have more partners in the innovation process, as do small firms. In comparison to the total sample medium-sized firms are better integrated into the respective national and regional innovation systems (Table 4.3). Nationally, they maintain more links both to other firms (customers,

Table 4.3 Innovation partners of medium-sized firms (50–200 employees) (deviation from total (Table 4.1) in % points; n = 193, missing 12%)

	Regional	National	European	Global
Customers	−2	**8**	−3	2
Suppliers	1	**7**	**11**	0
Consultants	2	**8**	3	2
Research organizations	0	1	2	1
Universities	0	0	−1	0
Technology transfer	**3**	**3**	0	0
Venture capital	0	−1	0	0
Subsidies	0	−1	−1	1
Government	**4**	**4**	−1	1
Trade associations	**3**	**8**	3	1
Training instiutions	**4**	**7**	0	2

Emboldened figures indicate positive deviation from total ≥ 3

suppliers, consultants) and to support institutions. Regionally they interact more with support organisations such as government, training institutions and technology transfer.

Large companies (> 200 employees) clearly have most linkages to partners in the innovation process (Table 4.4). This is probably due to more frequent and larger innovation projects as well as to better preconditions for co-operation. The latter has to do with better developed 'boundary spanning functions' (Tödtling, 1992) as well as more assets to offer for potential partners. Not surprisingly, customers and suppliers as innovation partners are more frequently on a European and global scale, reflecting also the larger spatial scale of input and output markets. Consultants and funding agencies are also used more frequently from outside the region (national and European levels). With respect to universities, research organizations, technology transfer and training we observe, however, that large firms are linked more intensively to the region than the smaller firms. Large companies, thus, seem to

Table 4.4 Innovation partners of large firms (> 200 employees) (deviation from total (Table 4.1) in % points; n = 135, missing 14%)

	Regional	National	European	Global
Customers	−5	**4**	**23**	**14**
Suppliers	1	**4**	**17**	**13**
Consultants	−2	**6**	**9**	**3**
Research organizations	**11**	**13**	**4**	1
Universities	**17**	**19**	**4**	**3**
Technology transfer	**9**	**5**	2	0
Venture capital	−2	2	2	2
Subsidies	1	**12**	**6**	1
Government	2	**7**	**3**	0
Trade associations	2	1	0	0
Training institutions	**5**	**8**	**4**	1

Emboldened figures indicate positive deviation from total ≥ 3

Table 4.5 Innovation partners of subsidiaries/branch plants (deviation from total Table 4.1) in % points; $n = 155$, missing 16%)

	Regional	National	European	Global
Customers	−9	−2	**5**	2
Suppliers	−3	0	2	**4**
Consultants	−3	**8**	**3**	1
Research organizations	0	**7**	**4**	−1
Universities	**6**	**8**	**3**	0
Technology transfer	−2	**5**	−1	−1
Venture capital	−3	**4**	0	0
Subsidies	−2	**3**	1	0
Government	**5**	**4**	1	0
Trade associations	0	**4**	0	0
Training instutions	**6**	**8**	1	1

Emboldened figures indicate positive deviation from total ≥ 3

be key actors in innovation networks on all levels, reaching from the region to the global level.

The pattern of interactions in the innovation process also depends on the status and ownership of plants. A clearly lower integration into the region occurs with dependent branch plants and subsidiaries (Table 4.5). These types of plants have, probably due to their integration into a wider enterprise network, innovation partners if more at a national and European level. Only with respect to universities, government institutions and training do they also maintain links to the region.

Foreign firms are even less embedded into the region and they have fewer links also at the national level (Table 4.6). Customers, suppliers, consultants as innovation partners are mainly European or global. The only stronger innovation link to the region concerns universities. On the national level they maintain, in addition, links to government as well as relations to training institutions. Branch plants as well as international companies, thus, have only selective links to the region, and they do

Table 4.6 Innovation partners of foreign firms (deviation from total (Table 4.1) in % points; $n = 67$, missing 16%)

	Regional	National	European	Global
Customers	−14	−9	**27**	**5**
Suppliers	−4	−1	**32**	**14**
Consultants	−1	**4**	**9**	**5**
Research organizations	−1	−1	2	0
Universities	**6**	**5**	2	0
Technology transfer	1	0	−2	0
Venture capital	−6	−4	−1	−1
Subsidies	−5	−4	0	0
Government	1	**6**	2	0
Trade associations	−2	1	2	0
Training institutions	−1	**7**	−1	0

Emboldened figures indicate positive deviation from total ≥ 3

Table 4.7 Innovation partners of product innovators (products new to the market) (deviation from total (Table 4.1) in % points; $n = 269$, missing 8%)

	Regional	National	European	Global
Customers	−1	**3**	**6**	**10**
Suppliers	2	0	**6**	**6**
Consultants	**3**	**5**	**5**	**3**
Research organizations	0	**3**	1	0
Universities	**7**	**7**	**3**	2
Technology transfer	**5**	**4**	0	0
Venture capital	0	2	0	0
Subsidies	2	**6**	1	1
Government	−2	2	0	0
Trade associations	−1	−1	1	1
Training institutions	−2	**3**	0	0

Emboldened figures indicate positive deviation from total ≥ 3

not seem to stimulate interfirm links to a major extent. They do use the universities and training organizations of the respective regions and countries, however, and in fact they do so to a higher degree than, for example, the small indigenous companies analysed above.

As is to be expected, innovative firms have more links to other firms and organizations in the innovation process than the average. This applies both to product and process innovators. Product innovators maintain more relations with European and global customers as well as suppliers (Table 4.7). Services of consultants are used more on all spatial levels, including the regional one. Relations to universities and technology transfer are relatively more frequent at the level of the region and the country. Product innovators, thus, are generally more embedded into networks, both distant and close. In fact these findings demonstrate that regional and large-scale networks are complementary rather than substitutes. Firms which have learned to work with partners at the level of the region also seem to find it easier to engage in national, European or even global links. There may also be an interdependence between innovation and networking: on the one hand product innovators require complementary assets to a higher degree (know-how, technology, finance, market access), so they are looking more intensively for partners and on the other hand they might be stimulated to further innovations by some of these relationships.

For process innovators (Table 4.8), the basic pattern is not too different from the product innovators. Interestingly, process innovators are not less but relatively more embedded into the region. They maintain more links to universities and research organizations, to training institutions and technology transfer as well as to subsidy providers. This supports the argument of the interdependent innovation model (Dosi *et al.*, 1988; Lundvall, 1992) that innovation is a non-linear process where we cannot clearly separate different stages or product from process innovation. From our findings it appears that process innovations often go beyond mere adoptions of given technologies which can be readily bought on the market, but they also require certain development activities as well as links to relevant institutions.

Table 4.8 Innovation partners of process innovators (deviation from total (Table 4.1) in % points; n = 308, missing 8%)

	Regional	National	European	Global
Customers	−3	2	**7**	**4**
Suppliers	0	**10**	**9**	2
Consultants	−1	1	1	0
Research organizations	**3**	**3**	1	−1
Universities	**10**	**4**	**3**	−1
Technology transfer	**4**	**3**	0	0
Venture capital	0	0	0	0
Subsidies	**3**	**5**	0	0
Government	2	**3**	0	0
Trade associations	−1	0	1	0
Training institutions	**5**	**4**	0	0

Emboldened figures indicate positive deviation from total ≥ 3

2.2. Innovation partners – differences between REGIS regions

How do the regions of the REGIS project compare with respect to interactions and partners in the innovation process? Tables 4.9–4.11 show that there is a considerable variation between the regions in the data set. Not included here, because they are not in the common database, are the Hungarian and Polish cases.

From the survey data it appears that the firms in Styria, the Basque Country and in Baden-Württemberg are generally innovating more in interaction with external partners than those in the other regions. Also with respect to the spatial levels and the dominant partners there are interesting differences.

In Baden-Württemberg interfirm linkages at the regional and national levels are clearly more important than in other REGIS regions. This pattern has probably to do partly with the size of the economies of Baden-Württemberg (larger than Austria) and of Germany. Links to customers and suppliers are by far more important than in other regions. The innovation system can therefore be characterized as firm-based. Between 89–93 per cent of companies have regional and national customers as innovation partners, in the case of suppliers it is 80 per cent and 75 per cent respectively. The services of consultants are used by 33 per cent of companies in the region, and by 25 per cent at the national level. Other partners, but of lower importance, are universities (25 per cent in the region), research organisations (18 per cent) and technology transfer (18 per cent). Concerning the support organizations, the firms in Baden-Württemberg certainly can or could benefit from one of the most sophisticated networks of relevant institutions (Steinbeis, Fraunhofer, *Fachhochschulen*, and other institutions). Considering the dense support structure, the actual use of public or other support organizations through firms in the sample is in fact surprisingly low.

Styrian firms are co-operating quite strongly in comparison to most other regions. For them the region is an important co-operation and support space, but they are also strongly oriented to the national as well as the European level. This is probably due to both the higher share of larger companies and the relatively small size of the

Table 4.9 Innovation partners at the regional level (% of firms having partners in the innovation process)

	High performance		Reconversion-upstream			Reconversion-downstream		Industrial districts		Total
	Ba-Wü	Brabant	Styria	Tampere	Wales	Basque	Wallonia	Centro	Friuli*	Total
n =	73	66	93	138	98	68	86	52	74	652
missing %	10	32	13	3	5	32	14	7	–	14
Customers	**89**	**50**	**54**	38	28	**56**	14	35	19	44
Suppliers	**80**	23	**42**	22	22	**56**	18	35	28	35
Consultants	**33**	9	**25**	5	11	**46**	9	8	**24**	16
Research organizations	**18**	0	**28**	**16**	1	**37**	3	6	11	13
Universities	**25**	9	**40**	23	**25**	**30**	**19**	15	12	24
Technology transfer	**18**	5	**15**	4	1	**63**	4	2	5	11
Venture capital	8	**12**	**21**	8	5	**11**	3	2	4	9
Subsidies	12	12	**35**	**20**	16	0	**22**	4	4	17
Government	7	4	**16**	3	**29**	11	**15**	4	1	14
Trade associations	**14**	3	**34**	6	4	**17**	6	**19**	**20**	12
Training institutions	6	8	**29**	6	**20**	**44**	1	**31**	11	17

Emboldened figures indicate share of firms with partners in a region > total

*Not included in the common database. Numbers were taken from the survey report.

Table 4.10 Innovation partners at the national level (% of firms having partners in the innovation process)

	High performance		Reconversion-upstream			Reconversion-downstream		Industrial district		Total
	Ba-Wü	Brabant	Styria	Tampere	Wales	Basque	Wallonia	Centro	Friuli*	
n =	73	66	93	138	98	68	86	52	74	652
missing %	10	32	13	3	5	32	14	7	–	14
Customers	93	49	72	65	56	59	30	58	26	61
Suppliers	75	42	62	35	51	54	46	63	35	52
Consultants	25	6	33	12	27	17	13	31	22	20
Research organizations	19	3	31	20	14	15	4	23	5	17
Universities	19	9	40	15	25	9	26	27	4	22
Technology transfer	12	8	16	2	10	15	5	15	3	9
Venture capital	6	6	24	4	4	6	0	4	0	7
Subsidies	14	17	44	15	5	0	6	23	7	16
Government	6	8	19	2	11	7	12	25	3	10
Trade associations	7	20	37	2	20	11	14	31	3	17
Training instutions	6	12	26	6	11	20	9	40	1	14

Emboldened figures indicate share of firms with partners in a region > total

*Not included in the common database. Numbers were taken from the survey report.

Table 4.11 Innovation partners at the European level (% of firms having partners in the innovation process)

	High performance		Reconversion-upstream			Reconversion-downstream		Industrial district		Total
	Ba-Wü	Brabant	Styria	Tampere	Wales	Basque	Wallonia	Centro	Friuli*	
n =	73	66	93	138	98	68	86	52	74	652
missing %	10	32	13	3	5	32	14	7	–	14
Customers	73	24	71	38	22	68	50	58	23	48
Suppliers	36	14	47	26	26	48	42	60	7	37
Consultants	12	2	28	3	3	13	12	14	3	10
Research organizations	0	0	23	4	3	9	5	6	3	6
Universities	4	2	31	1	3	15	8	4	0	8
Technology transfer	1	0	11	0	2	9	0	2	0	9
Venture capital	0	3	12	0	1	0	0	0	0	2
Subsidies	1	5	27	3	0	2	4	2	0	6
Government	1	2	9	0	1	2	5	0	0	3
Trade associations	1	0	15	1	4	7	5	0	0	4
Training institutions	0	0	7	1	0	2	1	6	1	3

Emboldened figures indicate share of firms with partners in a region > total

*Not included in the common database. Numbers were taken from the survey report.

region. Relevant types of partners are the customers, suppliers, universities, consultants and the providers of subsidies. Compared to other REGIS regions, universities and research organizations in Styria and the rest of Austria play a strong role, and the regional innovation system can be characterized somewhat schematically as university-based. This pattern may be due to a certain bias in the sample towards larger and innovative firms. Both types of firms generally have more innovation projects and related interactions to report on than smaller and less innovative firms (see Section 2.1).

For the Basque firms the region is clearly the most important co-operation and support space for innovation. Apart from the region, Basque firms are relatively more oriented to Europe than to the rest of Spain. This is probably due to cultural and historical reasons such as the long-enduring effort for more autonomy. With respect to innovation partners from the region we find that besides customers, suppliers and consultants, technology transfer organisations (63 per cent of firms), training (44 per cent) and research organizations (37 per cent) are strong partners and much more used than in other regions. This pattern can be explained partly by the strong role of technology centres and related policy programmes as well as to a history of co-operation in the region's Mondragon Co-operative system. We can characterize the Basque innovation system, like the one in Wales, therefore as 'policy-based'.

Due to the relatively strong and proactive role of respective organizations in Wales innovation partners are by comparison more frequently public or semi-public support organizations (government institutions, training organizations, universities). Links to other firms (customer, suppliers, consultants) are relatively rare in the region. This can partly be explained by the relatively high share of externally controlled plants in Wales and a certain lack of innovation-relevant functions and competences. The results furthermore indicate that the cluster-oriented policy approach of Wales has not yet really translated into dense interfirm relations in the region.

Compared to Baden-Württemberg, Styria or the Basque Country, the firms in the Tampere region report generally fewer innovation partners. Besides Finnish customers, research organizations from the region and the rest of Finland as well as providers of subsidies have some relevance. This pattern reflects the relatively strong role of respective institutions (e.g. TEKES) in the Finnish innovation system.

In the other regions of the data set, i.e. Brabant, Wallonia, Centro and Friuli, innovation partners were reported less frequently. In Brabant this is probably due in part to the small firm bias of the sample (all firms below 200 employees). In addition, firms seem to rely more on their own competence rather than co-operating or using external support. In Wallonia there is also a rather individualistic behaviour of firms (see RIDER, 1997a) leading to few links with other firms and organizations with the exception of regional funding and national universities. This low use contrasts with a rather dense support structure in the region (see Chapter 5). There seems to be a considerable gap between the support structure and the firms. In the Centro case the situation is different. Here, the region in a policy sense and as support space does not really exist, most interactions (except training) are therefore at a national level (see Table 4.10). As a consequence, the innovation system in this case is clearly more national than regional. The firms in Friuli use consultants relatively frequently both at regional and national level. From the support organizations only trade associations have a higher relevance.

Summing up we find that firms in the investigated regions of Europe do interact with various partners in the innovation process although co-operation is generally not their top priority. Regarding the relevance of the different actors and spatial levels there are strong differences between the REGIS regions, depending on the structure of firms, their behavioural pattern, the institutional setting and policy approaches. Firms in Baden-Württemberg, the Basque Country and in Styria are relatively more integrated into the region. In Baden-Württemberg, these are mostly firm-based interactions, in the Basque Country institutional networks predominate. In Styria, the region is important in particular for 'upstream' interactions in the innovation process (university, research) and for financial support. In addition, the firms here are strongly linked to national (customers, suppliers, funding) and European partners (customers, suppliers). The firms in Tampere and Wales have rather selective relations to regional and national research organizations, universities and government institutions. Due to a lack of institutional elements at the level of regions (except training), the firms in Centro are clearly more oriented to the national level (Lisbon, Porto) where those elements exist. In Brabant and Wallonia we find only few interactions in the innovation process and a rather individualistic approach by the firms.

In many of the regions we find that innovations are at least to some extent carried out interactively rather than by isolated firms. Yet we must also be aware that the firms did not evaluate many of those relations to be of 'key importance' and they regarded innovation generally as a rather more internal process. We are left in a somewhat ambivalent situation. It seems that many of the above stated relations have a latent character, i.e. they become relevant for innovation occasionally, providing firms with complementary assets or other resources helping them to overcome bottlenecks when they show up. Only in a smaller share of firms are these relations of a more enduring and a really interactive nature.

2.3. Use of support services

To what extent do firms rely on support services in their innovation activities and which kind of support do they use? What is the role of the region in this respect, compared to the national and European levels? To this second question the survey data does not give a reliable answer, since only 41 per cent of firms responded to this question. Still, the data show some interesting results in this respect.

In line with the results on innovation partners (see Section 2.1), the companies most frequently use the services of universities. Universities in the region are a widely accepted support organization, they are used by 56 per cent of the responding firms, representing 23 per cent of all firms in the sample (see Table 4.12). Also universities in the respective member-states are frequently contacted by 38 per cent of responding firms and by 16 per cent of all firms.

Due to their more specialized nature, research organizations are somewhat more important at the national level (33 per cent of responding firms, 14 per cent of total

Table 4.12 Use of support services (% of firms using them)

	Regional	National	European	Global
n = 314, missing 59%				
Technology transfer	**29**	14	10	2
Finance	**32**	**27**	13	3
Universities	**56**	**38**	13	7
Research organizations	**28**	**33**	9	4
Total *n* = 758				
Technology transfer	12	7	4	1
Finance	13	11	5	1
Universities	23	16	6	3
Research organizations	12	14	4	2

Emboldened figures indicate share of firms using support ≥ 20%)

firms). Still, they are also relevant partners in the region (28 per cent of responding firms, 12 per cent of total). These results demonstrate that support organizations which are able directly to provide know-how competences in R&D are highly relevant to firms. Although there are links to higher spatial levels, the most important relations are within the region (universities) and the respective country (research organizations). In particular university–industry interactions seem to be facilitated and eased by spatial proximity.

Financial support has about the same overall importance as research organizations have: 32 per cent of responding firms use financial support in the region, and 27 per cent at the national level. The use of European financial support was indicated only by a small segment of firms, 13 per cent of respondents. As has been indicated in Section 2.1, the services of technology transfer are used relatively little, and if so most often in the region (29 per cent of respondents, 12 per cent of total firms). From these results it appears that most firms get into contact with relevant technology providers directly and that only few of them require intermediaries. As follow-up interview analysis has shown, this finding is certainly true for larger and more innovative firms, but not so for smaller and low-tech firms. The latter group typically has awareness problems and does not really know the supply infrastructure well enough to make use of these support organizations.

2.4. *Regional variations*

What differences can we find in the use of support services between the regions in the data set? Since response rates differ quite strongly between the regions (from only 17 per cent in Brabant to 56 per cent in Tampere region) we use the per cent of total firms as an indicator for service use. Overall, this underestimates the use of services, but makes it easier to compare the regions in a sensible way.

As we have seen for the innovation partners, the firms in the Basque Country as well as those in Styria use support services to a higher degree than do firms in other regions (see Table 4.13). In the Basque Country technology transfer organizations in the regions are used by almost half of all firms in the sample, followed by financial support (29 per cent). Also, universities and research organizations in the region are

Table 4.13 Use of support services by region (% of total firms using support services)

	High performance			Reconversion-upstream		Reconversion-downstream		Industrial districts		Total
total n =	Ba-Wü 81	Brabant 98	Styria 107	Tampere 142	Wales 103	Basque 80	Wallonia 91	Centro 56	Friuli* 74	758
In the region										
Technology transfer	**15**	9	**17**	2	8	**49**	1	4	8	12
Finance	7	1	**29**	6	**14**	**29**	**18**	2	8	13
Universities	14	8	**30**	**30**	**31**	25	22	5	12	23
Research organizations	11	2	**21**	**19**	6	20	3	2	**18**	12
In the country										
Technology transfer	5	1	**19**	4	5	**10**	1	7	4	6
Finance	7	2	**31**	7	5	**16**	7	**16**	**16**	11
Universities	**20**	1	**28**	15	**17**	11	**19**	13	7	16
Research organizations	7	3	**23**	**29**	13	9	1	13	5	14
In Europe										
Technology transfer	1	0	**13**	3	**5**	**5**	1	**5**	1	4
Finance	1	0	**20**	1	3	**11**	3	2	**8**	5
Universities	3	1	**18**	1	7	4	**9**	0	1	6
Research organizations	0	0	**17**	4	1	4	1	2	3	4

Emboldened figures indicate the share of firms using support in a region > total
*Not included in the common database. Numbers were taken from the survey report.

widely used, namely by 25 per cent and by 20 per cent of all firms. The region is clearly the most important support space for Basque firms, confirming the above finding of a policy-based innovation system.

In Styria the services of universities are used most frequently (30 per cent of all firms in the sample), confirming the finding of a university-based regional innovation system above. But also financial support of the *land* is widely accepted (29 per cent of total firms). As was demonstrated for innovation partners above, the national and European level is clearly of more importance to Styrian firms than to those in other REGIS regions. Although support organizations of the region are relevant to the firms, Austria as a supportive environment is even more important for most categories of services. The services of European institutions are used less but still by 13–20 per cent of all firms. Styrian firms, thus, seem to be relatively well integrated into a regional and national innovation system, while a smaller segment of firms maintains relations to European support organizations. An explanation for this pattern is the higher share of large firms in the Styrian sample as well as the relatively small size of the region and the country, making it necessary for firms to look for external support. But the results also indicate that regional, national and European support organizations are not substitutes, but rather complementary and interlinked structures.

While in the Basque Country and Styria all kinds of support services are used, in the other regions only certain types have relevance to the firms. In Tampere it is universities and research organizations, both at the regional and national level, which are widely used. This supports, as in Styria, the picture of an upstream-oriented pattern of co-operation in the innovation process. In Wales and in Wallonia, besides universities, financial support has relevance to the firms. Due to a lack of support organizations at the level of the region, the firms in Centro are clearly more oriented to the national level as a support space, the region has almost no relevance to them. The firms in Friuli use support organizations only selectively. At the level of the region it is research organizations and at the national level financial support.

As stated in Section 2.2, firms in Baden-Württemberg clearly rely more on their own competences or on relations to other firms in the innovation process. Support organizations seem to play a minor role, with the exception of regional technology transfer and universities. This is somewhat surprising given the dense supply infrastructure (Pyke and Sengenberger, 1992; Cooke and Morgan, 1994a) and the 'institutional thickness' (Amin and Thrift, 1994) of the region. We have to consider, that in Baden-Württemberg, as well as in Brabant and Centro, the low use of services is partly due to a low response rate with respect to this question.

Summing up, we find that, overall, the region is the most important support space for the firms. The national level comes second, while the use of European support organizations is still rare. This spatially more confined pattern of support links contrasts to the pattern of interfirm links which are clearly stronger at the higher spatial levels. Concerning the type of services, accessed R&D related organizations and knowledge providers are most important, followed by financial support, while the mediating services of technology transfer are used relatively little. In general, this pattern confirms the analysis of innovation partners above.

From the use of support services we can furthermore conclude that firms are institutionally more embedded into a regional innovation system in the Basque country and in Styria. For Styrian firms not only regional support organizations, but also national and European ones are relevant. In Baden-Württemberg, Tampere, Wales and Wallonia, the support organizations are used in a selective way on both regional and national levels. In Brabant and in Centro, partly due to the low response rate, the use of support services turns out to be very low.

3. Results of the company interviews

Complementary to the surveys, interviews with firm representatives were conducted in order to investigate in more qualitative detail the nature of the innovation process, sources and barriers for innovation as well as relations to other firms and support organizations. In the following we concentrate on the latter aspect of interactions of firms in the innovation process. About fifteen interviews were carried out in each region, the intention was to cover relevant sectors and size classes of firms in each of the REGIS regions. The interviews generally support the findings of the survey discussed above but they reveal new insights due to a better understanding of the overall innovation process of specific firms as well as of the qualities of the respective links.

In Baden-Württemberg the interviews cover innovative firms (the 'innovation avant-garde') from the electronics and information technologies, machine engineering and automobiles sectors. Middle and large firms are better represented in the sample than small ones. According to Bechtle *et al.* (1997) the firms in the innovation process principally face a dilemma between complexity and concreteness. Complexity implies a diversity of knowledge, interests, as well as a temporal and spatial variation. It opens up new opportunities but involves high risks. Concreteness implies proximity to markets, customer needs and production. It guarantees easier implementation of innovation projects but often leads to incremental change only and to path dependency.

How does the innovation avant-garde master this dilemma? Both internal and external conditions have to be met. Internally, a high interdependence of functions is required, e.g. between marketing, distribution, R&D, design and production. Externally, a specific quality of relations to other firms and organizations is needed. For the most innovative firms a radical change in their relations to customers can be observed. While the firms in the past had a strong technology focus, leading partly to over engineering of products and high prices, more recently a stronger orientation on the overall benefits for the customer is occurring. This implies a stronger connection and interface of products and services as well as a stronger involvement of customers in the development process itself. Highly important is a free circulation of know-how (based on trust), and a common understanding in spite of situations of diversity. Spatial proximity of co-operation partners is considered crucial in this respect. The innovation avant-garde also uses the support infrastructure to a higher degree. The more innovative firms establish and maintain direct links, e.g. to research organizations and universities. Intermediating institutions such as Steinbeis have more relevance to the smaller and less innovative firms. An important finding is that regional embeddedness is ambivalent from an innovation perspective; it often leads to closed circles of insiders and to lock-ins. In the case of the most innovative firms, however, embeddedness goes together with social or spatial boundary-crossing.

Interfirm relations also have some relevance for the innovation process in Friuli (Boffo and Pugliese, 1997). Here, from seventeen interviewed firms ten are in 'districts' (chair, knife, furniture, home appliances). In contrast to Baden-Württemberg the firms are all SMEs and they innovate mainly in an incremental way. Sources of innovation are generally suppliers and customers who are sometimes situated within the region. But innovative impulses also come from outside the region, often through return migrants. Co-operation among firms does exist but it does reach beyond the region. Most of the co-operation is vertical (with customers and suppliers). In contrast to other industrial districts of the Third Italy (Pyke and Sengenberger, 1992; Asheim, 1996) we rarely find in Friuli horizontal co-operation with competitors, mainly due to a fear of know-how loss and a more individualistic culture of firms. Also, companies only rarely make use of innovation support. Relations are weak with universities and technology centres as well as to the finance system. Overall, there is only 'light systemness' with respect to the innovation process in the region. 'Systemness' in this case has two aspects: it provides an industrial and social context for entrepreneurship and a socialization of skills and know-how.

In the Basque Country, Wales, Styria and Tampere relations to support organizations are comparatively more important. In the Basque Country (Basque Team, 1997a) companies from the machine tools, automotive, telecommunication and white goods sectors were interviewed, covering both small and large companies (from 5–2500 employees). There are all types of innovators represented, including two radical ones. For incremental innovators and modifiers, customers, suppliers as well as technology centres serve as sources for innovation. Radical innovators and 'recombiners' in contrast rely for their source more on their internal R&D departments. This contrasts with the overall innovation process where we find that radical innovators and recombiners have more co-operation both with other firms as well as with support organizations. They are more strongly integrated into regional clusters which are supported in part by the Basque government. Due to a long-standing co-operative tradition in the region (Mondragon Co-operative), there are both vertical and horizontal links, as well as well-established links to support organizations. Confirming the survey results we find that the firms in the Basque Country use, to a considerable extent, the services of technology centres, innovation and training programmes, universities and regional agencies. Overall, through the institutional support of clusters, there is a strong role of government in the regional innovation system. As in many other regions, and confirming the arguments of Camagni (1991), we see that the more innovative firms are embedded not only into the region but are, at the same time, well integrated into networks at higher spatial scales (in particular Europe).

In Wales mostly small and medium sized firms from the automotive, electronics and health care cluster have been interviewed (Schall and Cooke, 1997a). Incremental innovations and modifications are most frequent, but also recombinations and radical innovations can be observed. A major impulse for innovation in the region comes from foreign firms, so forcing Welsh suppliers to continuously improve their performance in terms of product quality, accuracy of delivery and price. Lead customers and users are, therefore, the most frequent sources of innovation. But also the work force of the companies (for process innovations), informal contacts in the region (for indigenous firms) as well as universities (for radical innovations and spin-offs) are sources of innovation. Interfirm co-operation is mainly with customers, and often outside Wales. Firms with minor product changes (modifiers) also have relations to customers in the region. Support organizations are relatively well used by the firms, except the dependent ones (subsidiaries and branch plants). Frequent interactions occur with Training and Enterprise Councils (TECs), the Welsh Development Agency (WDA), university departments and the Welsh Office. A low use was found in the case of bridging organizations such as Innovation Wales and for general business support, such as Business Connect.

In Styria the interviewed firms are from the metal/steel, machinery, engineering and automobile sectors and there is a certain bias towards the larger firms in the sample (Kaufmann and Tödtling, 1997). Incremental innovations along existing trajectories are the dominant pattern, but there are also cases of recombinations. At the high end we find only one radical innovator. At the low end there are three non-innovating firms which lack innovation competence due to their dependent status. Customer specification is the most important source and mechanism for innovation for Styrian firms. This has the advantage of bringing innovation close to the customer needs ('concreteness') but it also keeps firms tightly on existing trajectories. In addition, firms rely on their internal capacities as well as on their links to universities as innovation sources. Customers are also the most important co-operation partners in the innovation process and they are mostly located outside the region (Austria and Europe). Occasionally there is co-operation with suppliers, but only rarely with consultants or competitors. In comparison with other REGIS regions, universities as well as a Styrian research organization, Joanneum Research, are quite important innovation partners for the firms. These relations are mostly in the region, of a direct type (not via intermediaries) and they involve mainly know-how exchange. Also of some relevance to the firms are providers of funding and innovation programmes at regional, national and EU levels.

In the region of Tampere 21 firms in the information technology, metal, chemical, food and textiles sectors were interviewed (Kautonen and Schienstock, 1997b). They are mostly SMEs. As in most other regions, incremental innovation is most frequent (50 per cent of the firms), followed by recombination and modification. The motives for innovation are often intertwined: increase of product quality, cost reduction, reduction of time to market and market leadership are the most important. Interfirm co-operations are not very frequent but becoming more important. They occur vertically with customers and suppliers, horizontally in the form of technology pooling, benchmarking and joint supply. Most frequently these are with national and international partners, horizontal co-operation being more common within the region. Firms in the Tampere region make quite strong use of the support infra-structure both on the regional and national levels (TEKES, VTT, TUT). The services they use are technology development and transfer, finance, as well as consulting for R&D and internationalization. Not explicitly mentioned were education and training nor industry associations. Some elements were considered as missing in the region, namely institutions which could support the firms' service, marketing, exporting and internationalization activities.

A fairly low level of embeddedness of firms into the regions was found in Centro, Wallonia and Brabant. But these are in fact quite different types of regions. Centro is rather weakly developed and peripheral, Wallonia is an old industrialized reconverting region, while Brabant is considered to be highly developed and innovative (see Chapter 2).

Centro's interviewed firms are in the metallic, ceramic and automotive industries and most of them are SMEs (Esteves *et al.*, 1997). One half of them are incremental innovators, another third technology adopters or modifiers. Innovation occurs as reactive behaviour towards customer requirements, to product or fashion cycles or to technology problems on the shop floor. As a consequence the shop floor (learning by doing or using) and customer needs are the most important sources of innovations. R&D has more the function of observing and monitoring technologies and markets rather than developing technologies themselves. The firms are weakly embedded in the region; a regional innovation system does not exist. There are neither interfirm relations nor significant relations to support organizations. Reasons for this are highly individualistic behaviour of firms, corporate links, as well as deficits with respect to support organizations. Due to a lack of political and financial autonomy in the region, support institutions are organized rather nationally than regionally. The region does not really exist as a support space.

Wallonia differs from Centro in many respects (RIDER, 1997b). The interviewed firms are in agrofood, machine tools, chemicals/pharmaceuticals, and they are quite innovative. From the fifteen firms six were classified as radical innovators, five had recombined or incremental types of innovations and another four were predominantly process innovators. Market leadership and the increase of market shares were frequent motives as well as the qualitative improvement of products and processes. Customer needs and the observation of technological opportunities are the most frequent external sources of innovation, they are internally matched by marketing and R&D departments. The firms rarely co-operate in the innovation process with the exception of some co-operation with suppliers and customers mostly outside the region. Reasons are fear of know-how loss or simply 'no interest'. Also support infrastructure is only rarely used, and in general the support structure works in favour of larger and firms already established as more innovative. There seems to be a 'fracture between public and private components of the regional innovation system' (RIDER, 1997a).

Brabant firms are also only weakly embedded in the region. The interviewed firms are biased towards small firms (all below 200 employees). This is reflected in the innovation pattern where client-driven incremental innovations are dominant as well as product innovations in market niches. Also, customizing of purchased technology and organizational innovations are frequent. As in the above cases, interfirm co-operation is a rare phenomenon, partly due to the fear of losing know-how. Firms with networks are the rare cases of radical innovators, which are looking for complementary expertise. Despite the fact that only SMEs are in the sample, the support infrastructure is only rarely used. Reasons from the firms' perspective are a lack of familiarity with and the fragmented nature of the support system as well as too much effort required to use it.

4. Conclusions

The following shows the main findings and conclusions that can be derived from our analysis:

1. In the investigated regions innovation is still very much an internal process for the firms, depending on the nature of products, the competitive strategies of firms, their internal competences (knowledge base, skills) and their 'boundary spanning functions' (R&D, marketing). Despite this fact, there is evidence that interactions are highly relevant for the innovation process of certain types of firms and regions.
    *   Most important are the relations along the value chain (customers and suppliers), supporting the findings of von Hippel (1988) and others. As the interviews have shown, these relations typically go beyond market relations and are of a network type, i.e. they are usually more durable and also interactive.
    *   Other relevant interactions are with consultants, universities and research organizations. From these, the universities, in particular ranked surprisingly high, indicating a significant strengthening of university-industry relationships in recent years.
    *   Surprisingly little evidence was found of horizontal co-operation among firms, or for the role of technology transfer and other support organizations (venture capital, funding, training, industry associations). It seems that, even if these intermediaries and public support organizations are useful interfaces, they are not recognized as institutions providing important contributions.
2. Networks are relevant at various spatial scales: regional, national and European. For a small segment of firms global links can be observed. The national and the regional levels are clearly the most important for most types of firms.
    *   At regional levels firms interact relatively more with universities, support organizations and training institutions.
    *   Most of the interfirm links take place at national and European levels and co-operation with funding institutions and research organizations is also important here.
    *   We can conclude from this that regional, national and European networks are complementary rather than substitutes. Most of the firms maintain networks at more than one of these levels making use of different types of partner.
3. There are quite strong differences between types of firms with respect to innovation networks.
    *   Large and intermediate firms have more complex networks. This is probably due to their higher innovation activity as well as being better preconditioned for networking. Obviously they are a better able to identify relevant partners and they also have something to offer for innovation networks.
    *   Small firms should have, in principle, more need for partners but at the same time they have more barriers against networking.

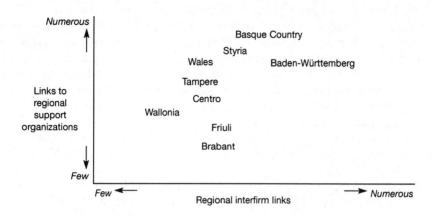

Figure 4.1 Regional networks of innovation

- Companies belonging to larger and foreign corporations are, due to their corporate links, generally more integrated into European and global networks. With the region they often have only selective links to funding and training institutions.
- Not surprisingly, we found that the innovative firms (the innovation avantgrade) are better integrated into networks than the non-innovative firms. Interestingly there were few differences between product and process innovators, supporting the view of the interactive innovation model.

4. The investigated regions of the REGIS project differ quite strongly with respect to the kinds and importance of innovation networks, and the regional embeddedness of firms (see Figure 4.1).

- In Baden-Württemberg interfirm relations are important in comparison, we could speak here of a firm-based innovation system. Vertical relations are dominant (customers, suppliers and consultants), while horizontal cooperation is rare. Support organizations (universities and research institutions, technology transfer) also play a role, although at a lower level than in some of the other regions.
- In comparison, the firms in the Basque Country, Wales, Styria and Tampere have more intensive relations with support organizations. Again there are differences: in Styria and Tampere these are mostly with universities or research organizations (university- or science-based innovation systems), in the Basque Country and Wales they are more often with technology centres, innovation support or regional agencies (policy-based innovation systems).
- A rather low level of embeddedness within the respective regions is displayed by firms in Wallonia, Brabant, Centro and Friuli. The situation in Brabant and Wallonia is different from Centro in the sense that many elements of the support infrastructure are present, but clearly underused due to the individualistic culture of firms. Centro, in contrast, is simply lacking many elements of an innovation system on the regional level and depends rather more on national ones.

5. We need to be aware, and this was indicated for several regions, that networks are not just beneficial for innovation but may create also problems (Grabher, 1993a). There are examples of 'lock-ins' such as the case of Styria where customer-dependent innovation keeps firms tightly on existing trajectories, preventing more radical steps. In Baden-Württemberg the problem of over engineering is also an indication of 'lock-in'. In addition, in the case of strong networks there are often problems for outsiders to get access to the relevant information and resources.

6. Policy conclusions of a general nature are hard to derive since regional pre-conditions and situation are so different. The following might have an overall relevance:

    - The complementarity of regional, national and EU networks and support structures should be recognized and stressed. The services of universities, technology transfer and training are often easiest to access at the level of the region. The national level often has most of the relevant funds for innovation support, also specialized research organizations and training institutions are there. The EU level might focus on generic research activities, on international networking between firms and organizations, as well as on the provision of risk capital or loans.

    - Small and less innovative firms are not well reached by support organizations. In particular, technology transfer institutions often prefer to deal with innovative and/or larger firms. But these do not require intermediaries to such an extent as the smaller and less innovative firms.

    - Although we have found some evidence for networking, many firms rely on traditional and individual strategies. There is often little awareness of the potential advantages of networks, also support organizations are relatively little-used. Innovation support has to address more explicitly and more actively existing barriers for innovation and networking. Partly these are on the side of the firms (conservative and individualistic attitude, low trust towards external partners), partly the problems are on the side of the support organizations (passive behaviour, lack of visibility, difficult access, high cost of use, unco-ordinated service supply). Cluster strategies might be a useful tool to co-ordinate relevant firms and organizations but not the only one.

    - Networks seem to have a natural tendency towards closure and 'lock-in'. It seems an important task for public organizations to explicitly keep networks open. Partly this can be done by interlinking regional, national and international networks. Also, the specific mix of actors (small and large firms, consultants and universities etc.) might help. Then, an explicit focus of public policy on technology diversification (building bridges to new trajectories) might be a helpful solution.

CHAPTER FIVE

Multi-level Governance and the Regional Organization of Innovation Support

1. Introduction

The organization of innovation support occurs horizontally within regions and vertically between regions, member-states, and the European Union. It may also, of course, occur between regions where there are regional partnerships with an innovation focus, such as the 'Four Motors for Europe' partnership involving Baden-Württemberg, Catalonia, Lombardy and Rhône-Alpes, with Wales as an associate, or through Regional Innovation and Technology Transfer Strategies (RITTS) Regional Technology Plan-Regional Innovation Strategy (RTP-RIS) and Regional Information Society Initiative (RISI) initiatives as promoted by the European Commission. Such activities involve, in the main, public organizations such as regional government departments, development agencies, local authorities, research institutes, universities, technology transfer centres and science parks.

In this research, an important area of inquiry has been the institutional or, more accurately, organizational set-up for supporting innovation by firms and other actors at the regional level. This means exploring the nature and functioning of these organizations and, where they are national or beyond, the nature of interactions towards the region as well as those occurring within regions. Clearly, the organizational or 'soft' infrastructure, carries out actions intended to support regional business innovation. These are usually the result of policies whose origins may lie within or outside the region. Current policies are the subject of Chapter 6, but some reference is also made to exemplary cases in this chapter. The main aim here is to present, as far as possible, the diversity of approaches to organizational support for innovation by enterprises, partly to illustrate their nature and extent, partly to assess whether they are converging towards or diverging from some possible EU norm.

It is clear that the role of the EU in promoting innovation support at the regional level is significant and it could be anticipated that regions which have been recipients of, for example, Structural Funds, may have established, with EU support, comparable elements of an innovation infrastructure. However, national and regional innovation support policies may, at the same time, reflect different priorities or resourcing capabilities. So there is a tension in the multi-level governance of innovation between, for some regions, a 'Europeanization' dimension and a national or regional dimension. Of course, a few of the regions focused upon will either not be major recipients of Structural Funds or other EU innovation support measures because they are not Less Favoured Regions (LFRs) or because they are not yet member-states. So it may be anticipated that there will be different models of organizational support for innovation. We have seen already, from earlier chapters that certain kinds of economic region tend to have high or low infrastructure, policy, firm and institutional capacity for soft infrastructure organization even though in economic terms they appear to have comparable experiences.

Thus, we need to explore the ways in which organizational interactions occur both internal to the region and between the region and higher levels of governance. The most important new analytical approach to understanding this is the theory of 'multi-level governance' (MLG). Authors such as Marks *et al.* (1996) and Hooghe (1996) give good presentations of the basic theses concerning MLG, and in the first main section of this chapter this will be explored and its superiority over the older 'state-centric' approach to analysing the formation of European institutions and organizations will be demonstrated. There will then be a brief section on the development of innovation intervention in relation to MLG before the final main section which seeks to analyse the eleven regions under study here in terms of the relationships between levels of governance of innovation in an MLG system.

2. Multi-level governance: theory and analysis

The state-centric view of the development of the European Union (e.g. Moravscik, 1993) was that it is an institutional framework to facilitate collaboration among member-states. It has little or nothing to say about regions despite the fact that one of the principal achievements of the EU has been to give legitimacy and resources to the sub-national level of governance. Thus states are the fundamental elements of the EU system due to their control, in particular, of the Council of Ministers, the key policy-making body of the EU. Other organizations such as the EU Parliament, Judiciary and Commission are presented either as agents of member-states or less powerful than states. Political and lobby pressure for change in EU policy must come up through the member-states and these negotiate with each other about policy which the EU shall promote.

At a fundamental level it is still the case that member-states are powerful within the EU and conceivably remain, in principle, the most powerful actors, though elements of their sovereignty have become pooled and thus less available for exertion at individual member-state level than once might have been the case. But it is this fact of diminution of individual member-state scope of action that nowadays counts as a key weakness of the state-centric approach. For it fails to take account of the influence pooled sovereignty allows supranational organizations to exert, and it completely ignores the much lesser, but not by any means negligible, influence that may be exerted by sub-national authorities directly upon EU organizations. It is this latter dimension that has become of theoretical interest to those who propose an MLG model and prefer to conceptualize the EU as an integrated but multi-level political system.

The MLG approach accepts the greater complexity of overlapping competences displayed by different governances and the emergent and innovative role of new kinds of policy actor, operating through policy networks which may cross the supranational, national and regional levels. In other words, interactions between policy actors are not, as the state-centric model presumes, only filtered through the member-states. Political control is thus not monolithic or homogeneous but variable, according to policy interests, expertise and the appropriateness of involvement by certain kinds of actors according to the policy issue in question. Regional policy is a particularly important instance of this and, as some degree of overlap develops at its edges with other policy spheres like innovation or environmental questions, so these become more important items on the regional as well as national and EU policy agendas. Of course, regional policy is a large budget heading in EU allocations, now accounting for 28 per cent of the budget, and where resources flow so the rationale for developing organizations of policy delivery also grows and with them political influence. Thus MLG theorists hold that in cases such as regional policy and possibly, it may be added, the future development of innovation policy, no single level has exclusive competence over policy.

The capacity of regional polities to engage in multi-level policy networks on issues such as those mentioned depends crucially on the relative degrees of legitimacy, power and administrative authority possessed at the sub-national level in constitutional terms. Although the EU is positively disposed to the evolution of regional administration, there is no EU model of regional competences. This remains a matter for the regionalization actions of states where they define administrative regions in accordance with their own decentralization programmes, or their response to regionalism as expressed by regional communities demanding greater autonomy to manage their own internal affairs (Cooke *et al.*, 1997). Hence, regions within the EU have different competences. Some, as in Belgium, have substantial constitutional rights, including regional representation at EU Council of Ministers meetings, others like German or Austrian *länder* operate in systems of 'co-operative federalism', yet others may manage decentralized budgets. With respect to regional governance links to Brussels on EU matters, MLG theorists tend to agree that these operate in three main ways: regional 'missions' or representation offices in Brussels; inter-regional co-operation agreements or networks; and the Committee of the Regions (Borrás 1998). These are formal arrangements, but of course surrounding them may be more informal actions involving communication, regional meetings or lobbying with EU officials and involvement in informal initiatives such as workshops, seminars, contributions to reports etc., at the behest of the Commission.

In the work of Marks *et al.* (1996) on regional representation in Brussels, they conclude that regions are more likely to be actively involved in MLG the more there is overlap between the competences of subnational and supranational government. Such regional governments, notably Belgian regions and *länder*, have the strongest need for information concerning possible regulatory and legislative policy developments. Yet they are also a useful source of information for the Commission, providing a third-party view other than that of the member-states and the EU itself. Innovation policy is one such area since, it seems, the aims of the Commission to enhance competitiveness and reduce social exclusion have a particular resonance for LFRs who may, correctly, perceive most member-state innovation intervention to be overly centralized in metropolitan locations, thus denying an important instrument of development policy, namely the enhancement of regional innovation capacity, to the regions. Of course, as the EU programming process for Structural Funds requires non-regionalized recipient states to establish regional representation bodies, and as Structural Funds budgets increasingly encourage regional programming bids to contain more innovation-related projects than before, the EU can be seen to be a key driver of multi-level decision processes.

As Hooghe (1996) argues, such partnership arrangements link the three main MLG organizational levels in a direct rather than a hierarchical way. That is, member-states do not act as perfect gatekeepers, filtering through only that information they consider important for regional authorities, the latter are, in some spheres, directly involved in negotiations with Brussels and may access policy instruments that the member-state representatives do not entirely approve. An example of that was the way that strong lobbying by elements of the innovation governance community in Wales both assisted the Commission to promote the Article 10 Regional Technology Plan idea and led to Wales being a pilot region against, initially, the Euro-sceptic and neo-liberal political position of the UK government administration in Wales.

3. Operationalizing MLG in the context of regional innovation

Because, under conditions of globalization and liberal trading as discussed in Chapter 2, the EU is conscious of the relative weakness of the European economy in competing with Japan and the USA on the commercialization of the fruits of research, a great effort has been made to support and promote the improvement of innovation amongst firms of all sizes. While the Framework Programme was at first strongly influenced by and mainly directed towards Europe's largest multinationals (the 'Big Twelve'), the focus has more recently been extended to encompass the interests of SMEs and regional innovation as the Green Paper on Innovation (European Commission, 1996) makes clear. The fact that promoting regional innovation also targets LFRs and thus helps the Commission to meet its cohesion obligations, strengthens this disposition. Moreover, the emergence of innovation promotion as an element in the programming documents of the Structural Funds underlines the commitment to regional innovation policy, and the experimentation under Article 10 with Regional Technology Plans, Regional Innovation Strategies and Regional Information Society initiatives testifies to the growing importance of capacity-building for innovation at regional level.

However, as has been stated, the absorptive capacity and organizational competences in a context of multi-level power relations within different member-states means that building the capability for regional firms to engage in interactive or even systemic innovation varies considerably. It is well-known, for example, that while the wealth disparity within the EU ranges from 1:5, that for R&D expenditure ranges from 1:11, meaning that there is far less basic innovation activity away from the main metropolitan centres in the larger and more northerly member-states. Moreover, the capability of regional administrations in the southern member-states in multi-level lobbying and influence to access regional innovation funding can be affected by decision-making structures that remain centralized for some functions even when a wide-ranging programme of regional decentralization may have been implemented.

If we attempt to present the general picture of the MLG of regional innovation policy in the EU then it looks like the pattern presented in Figure 5.1. Thus, the key

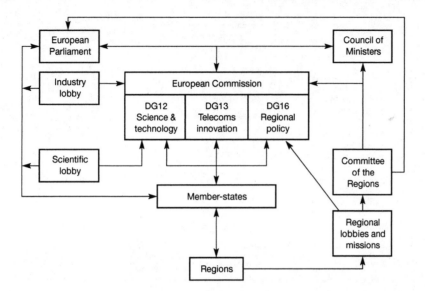

Figure 5.1 Multi-level governance of Regional Innovation Policy in the European Union

DGs, 12, 13 and 16 (see Figure 5.1) sit at the heart of the process and propose policies which are agreed or modified by the Council of Ministers and European Parliament. But the DGs and the parliament will have interacted through lobbying and requests for opinions from the industry and scientific lobbies and the member-states themselves. At regional level, the regional lobbies and missions will interact mainly with DG16 if they are LFRs but with other DGs with innovation competence if they are not. LFRs may also do this. Similarly, the Committee of the Regions will interact with appropriate DGs, giving opinions on regional development and innovation matters as they see fit. And, finally, the regional administrations will interact with their member-states, the Commission and their own missions and representatives on the Committee of the Regions in order to maximize incoming information, express views and provide information of consequence to innovation.

If we look at how this translates into use made of the MLG system at regional level to try to identify how deep the inclusion process goes and how transparent it is, it is worth considering different cases of regions seeking to develop regional innovation capacity by means of their Single Programming Document (SPD) bids to the EU Structural Funds. As our two examples, not taken from cases studied in the REGIS project, it is important to take one northern and one southern case, looking particularly at relations and influences between the region, its localities, its member-state and the Commission, and in this way seek to establish the manner in which policy is absorbed and developed. The examples are based on accounts of the cases of Lower Saxony in Germany and the Valencia region in Spain presented in Heinelt and Smith (1996). We will first outline briefly the case of Lower Saxony, then Valencia.

In Lower Saxony, parts of which have Objective 2 status, the process by which SPDs are formed fits well with the culture of co-operative federalism. Amongst the measures that have been funded are: the establishment on an Institute for Logistics

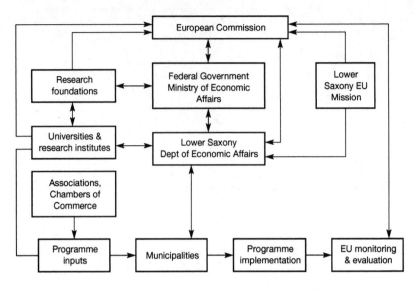

Figure 5.2 Multi-level governance of regional innovation in Lower Saxony

and Expert Systems; a Nuclear Waste Disposal organization; training in modern technologies and advanced scientific training. Under the 1993 reform which required regional involvement in drawing up SPDs, the *land* was charged with producing a regional development plan. This was done by the *land* department of Economic Affairs in consultation with other departments and conveyed to the federal Ministry for Economic Affairs for co-ordination of all *land* submissions. The *land* received relevant information from its mission in Brussels based on their discussions with EU officials and the main sources of project ideas were the municipalities. Hence, there is a policy network within the *land* based on innovation and other relevant regional development organizations and clear interaction channels from the municipalities upwards from *land* to federal and EU levels. This enables a continuing learning process concerning eligible projects. The model is quite bottom-up in character, as Figure 5.2 indicates.

Of some significance to the functioning of MLG in Lower Saxony is the relatively high density of innovation organizations such as Germany's oldest Technical University at Braunschweig, the German Aerospace Research Institute, Agricultural and Biological Centres as well as various industry associations, chambers of commerce and municipal innovation strategies such as a Technology Oriented complex. Thus there is a rather high receptivity to and capacity to take advantage of innovation policy opportunities by regional organizations and those at local levels.

The case of Valencia is interesting because, although it has Objective 1 status, the regional administration has been very active in developing a network of technology centres to support innovation in traditional industries like ceramics, shoes and toy manufacture. Also a policy of building competitiveness amongst SMEs by means of an innovation networking programme which raises interaction between firms, government and technology centres in the region has been pursued. However, the

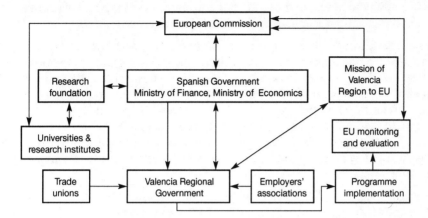

Figure 5.3 Multi-level governance of regional innovation in Valencia

governance process for accessing funding to support projects is dominated by Madrid.

Although regional development plans are required from the regions these differ from the national plan produced by the Spanish government in co-ordinating each regional plan. These are not integrated into the national plan but sent as attachments and it seems that bids are submitted to win funds as a priority over producing co-ordinated projects. For the 1994–99 period Valencia's plan from Madrid was rejected by the Commission because it proposed an increase over the previous programming period for basic infrastructures but not for enterprise and innovation support. EU pressure on Madrid brought about a shift in the allocation of funding towards innovation support. In the resulting financing process Valencia, like other Spanish regions, receives pooled funding allocation, including EU funding, from Madrid. While municipalities and other local actors can be recipients of this funding, they are not directly involved in proposing projects to go forward to the Commission. The MLG process in Spain is thus a top-down one which fails, initially, to build on the learning experiences of the region from the three main regional MLG activities concerning transnational networks, missions and the Committee of the Regions. The model is presented in Figure 5.3.

These illustrations are merely meant to show in as convincing a way as possible how MLG relationships differ because of member-state constitutional and practical political traditions and conventions. What points emerge that may help reinforce our analysis of the regions studied in this project?

1. MLG is highly dependent on the presence of strong and established regional governance organizations.
2. MLG for innovation is significantly assisted where the region has a substantial number and diversity of regional and local innovation organizations.
3. Regional and external innovation interaction among firms and other innovation organizations is important for regional innovation potential.
4. The existence of regional scientific, technological and innovation policies and programmes, assisted by the EU and nationally, is important

5.   The ability to access and use funding for innovation support for regional firms and organizations is crucial for regional innovation promotion.

We shall seek to use these analytical propositions in discussing the organizational capability of the regions under investigation in the following section. In doing this we will seek to show, wherever possible, the vertical and horizontal aspects of inter-actions by regional organizations responsible for assisting innovation. In this process we shall seek to refine the specifications for successful systemic innovation, but in order to do that, it is clearly necessary to say more about the kinds of organizations that may be expected to be found comprising the organizational innovation support infrastructure in a given region. The two key sub-systems in any functioning regional innovation system are, following Autio (1998):

- The knowledge application and exploitation sub-system
- The knowledge generation and diffusion sub-system

The first is principally, but not only, concerned with firms while the second is mainly concerned with public organizations like universities, research institutes, technology transfer agencies, and regional and local governance bodies responsible for innova-tion support practices and policies. In reality there may be some overlaps since firms conduct knowledge creation activities, especially where they have formalized R&D laboratories, and universities and public or private research institutes conduct knowledge application activities. But the latter is mainly the domain of firms, especially with respect to exploitation of knowledge for commercial return. Firms have vertical and horizontal network linkages; vertical relationships are mainly supplier linkages whereas horizontal linkages are found typically amongst SMEs who may, on occasion, also be competitors. Many innovation network policies seek to build horizontal linkages but some also aim to assist the elaboration of vertical

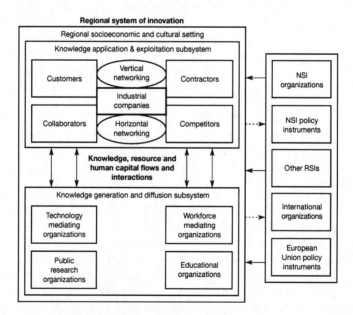

Figure 5.4 Schematic illustration of the structuring of RSIs (after Autio, 1998)

supply-chain relationships. In the knowledge generation and diffusion sub-system are technology mediating organizations; those which mediate with respect to vocational training and workforce skill-provision; public research institutes; and educational organizations. Each of these sub-system organizations interacts with the others and with national innovation organizations or the National System of Innovation of their member-state as well as international policy and knowledge generating organizations such as the EU, on the one hand, and non-European universities, research institutes and firms, on the other. Figure 5.4 is an attempt, based on the work of Autio (1998), to present the structure of a regional innovation system in the abstract.

This model captures the main features and relationships of a functioning regional innovation system operating in an MLG environment. But it only indicates the linkages in a neutral fashion. Empirical research is necessary to capture the variety of degrees of influence and decision-making authority, the presence or absence, or weaker and stronger relationships amongst the diverse possible kinds of application, exploitation, generation and diffusion elements of specific regions and their degrees of 'systemness'.

4. Regional innovation organization in specific cases: towards a typology

It will be recalled from Chapter 2 that our original starting typology of five categories defined in terms of their economic structures (high performance engineering, reconversion with upstream innovation, reconversion with downstream innovation, industrial districts, and transitional) was moderated by the subsequent analysis. This moderation occurred in relation to the four axes of performance; infrastructure capacity, policy organization, firm organization and institutional capacity. Thus, Baden-Württemberg was characterized as having the highest regional system of innovation potential, especially because of its high institutional capacity and high firm, or rather interfirm organizational capacity. Brabant, also for reasons of economic structure, in the high performance engineering category, showed less high regional innovation systems potential because of its lower regional infrastructure and institutional capability.

Styria retained a high potential because of its policy and firm organization capacities set in an already relatively strong regional infrastructural position. Wales and the Basque Country come lower than Styria, but higher than Tampere because they displayed stronger regional infrastructural and policy organizational capacities than weakly regionalized Tampere, which had lower capability in infrastructural and regionalised policy promotion than those reconversion regions. Fruili was positioned relatively well in terms of regional innovation systems potential because of its highly interactive firms and the high institutional, cultural capacity for interaction in its industrial districts coupled with its relatively strong regionalization competence. Centro, an otherwise comparable region, was placed low in regional innovation systems potential because of very weak regionalized infrastructural and policy capacity. Wallonia, a reconversion region with stronger than average infrastructural and policy capacity was placed lower than other reconversion regions because much of this capacity was under-activated. The two transition regions were placed low in regional innovation systems potential because of their general absence or weakness of institutional, firm organization, policy organizational and infrastructural capacities for innovation support at regional level.

In what follows, we shall explore, in particular, the evidence from our regional research of organizational accomplishment or lack of it. This includes the horizontal dimension concerning activities and interactions within the knowledge generation and diffusion sub-system within the region, and the vertical MLG dimension. Both make partial reference to the interactions with the knowledge application and exploitation sub-system, although firm interactions themselves are the subject of Chapters 3 and 4, as we have seen. For the purposes of presentation we shall analyse the regional cases in three broad categories derived from the performance potential analysis just described. These categories are as follows:

1. Regions with high infrastructure and policy organization capacity – Baden-Württemberg, Styria, Wales and the Basque Country.
2. Regions with medium regional innovation systems potential but which have characteristics of limited regional infrastructural or policy organizational capacity, or weak realization of it – Brabant, Tampere, Wallonia and Friuli.
3. Regions with low infrastructural and policy organizational capacity – Centro, Féjer and Lower Silesia.

The aim in conducting this analysis is to try to move closer to a specification of the kinds of organizational good practices, but also deficiencies that may usefully be understood as a means of promoting greater regional innovation systems potential in regions of diverse economic character and stage of organizational development for innovation support.

4.1. Regions with high capacity for developing regional innovation systems potential

4.1.1. Knowledge generation and diffusion

Each of the four regions in this category has a developed organizational infrastructure of mediating organizations for technology and vocational training and a presence of public research and educational organizations. However, Baden-Württemberg has the most fully-developed set of such organizations with a high level of interaction amongst them. Styria probably has the next most developed organizational capacity though lacks the density of organizations and has more reliance on local interactions than Baden-Württemberg. Wales is well-provided with Training and Enterprise Councils mediating training and skills formation, has a variable quality of technology mediating organizations, but its research-based universities contribute strongly to public research and education. The Basque Country has strong technology mediation through its dedicated technology centres, reasonably good labour market mediation but lacks public research institutes (other than the technology centres which conduct mainly applied research) and has universities which, until very recently, were not strong in research but good in education. The new Mondragon University is small but has high expertise in professional higher education and research applications for industry.

Baden-Württemberg demonstrates good practice through its ministry-led 'vision-oriented' innovation approach, a main role of which is to help SMEs adjust to new technologies and innovate around them. A post of government Commissioner for Technology Transfer was created in 1982 with responsibility for promoting the Steinbeis Foundation, a 200 strong network of technology centres for SMEs based in the technical colleges (*Fachhochschulen*) and universities. The *land* has nine universities, thirteen Fraunhofer and Max Planck institutes each, 39 colleges and over 100 industrial research institutes. These are known to be organizationally interactive and to have contributed, in many cases, to the discourse concerning the *land's* 'Future Commission 2000' which in 1993 explored innovation and competitiveness needs of the regional economy. A weakness identified by the Commission is lock-in to established engineering competences but lack of competitiveness in new electronics, multimedia and biotechnologies. Venture capital is now abundant but local banks are risk-averse (Kaufmann *et al.*, 1997).

Styria is less than one-fifth the size of Baden-Württemberg in demographic terms but its social partnership model produces 'a stable institutional landscape' (Sedlacek and Tödtling, 1997). It encompasses *land* ministries and the Styrian Economic Development Agency (SFG), chambers of commerce and labour, three universities, Christian Doppler laboratories and Joanneum Research (a non-university research institute owned by the *land*), training organizations and seven technology and innovation centres. SFG is the most central organization, semi-public but owned by the *land* government. It supports innovative activities, provides direct financial incentives and soft infrastructure measures. Suggestions have been made to decentralize SFG to local offices. There is good interaction with industry associations and chambers. The universities have strong industrial liaison functions and interact closely on spin-off and start-up business support, sharing staff and working closely with Joanneum Research. Along with the *land* government, SFG and Joanneum are key players formulating innovation policy, initiating the Styrian Technology Policy Concept aimed at building up innovative clusters and based on strong organizational and firm co-operation and communication. Still, it is argued by Sedlacek and Tödtling (1997) 'this research base is not integrated into the Regional Innovation System as much as it could be', and there is a need for more thematic co-ordination.

Wales is double the size, demographically, of Styria but has lower GDP per capita indicators. There are nine universities with over twenty designated centres of expertise but few free-standing public research laboratories. Training and Enterprise Councils mediate the skills development and management training functions. Industry has numerous (over twenty) localized or functional supply chain 'clubs' and there is a Wales Trade Union Congress and Wales Confederation of British Industry. The main centres for innovation promotion and support are the Welsh Office (WO) (from 1999 this will be supervised by the new Welsh Assembly) and its economic development executive the Welsh Development Agency (WDA). There is reasonably close and increasing interaction between these upper-level bodies, as signified by recent Welsh Office papers seeking consultation on a Welsh know-how centre advocating strong university-industry-development agency co-operation to further innovation. Innovation support exists in the technology transfer divisions of the WO and WDA, joint producers of the EU-funded Regional Technology Plan for

Wales, an ERDF-Article 10 pilot project, now extended to over twenty other European regions. There is, however, weakness in venture capital with only one main private organization, 3i, and the remainder being public through the WO and WDA. There are skill shortages for technical grades and firms have some difficulty in identifying precisely where to go, initially, for enterprise support (Schall and Cooke, 1997a). The system in Wales is rather hierarchical and loosely-coupled at the sub-system level and perhaps less co-ordinated than Styria.

Finally, the Basque Country has high regional autonomy, including tax-raising powers of some significance. Key actors in the innovation system are the Basque Department of Industry which guides innovation through the Regional Development Agency (SPRI), the sectoral technology centres, also owned by SPRI and the Ministry, and the overall planning function which has resulted in a third Science and Technology Plan 1997–2000 which adopts a systemic approach based on sectoral cluster-building and stronger university-industry interaction. There are strengths in the Basque system, but deficiencies lie in the industrial fabric where there are weak clusters and few Basque global player firms. Institutionally or culturally speaking there is not a high prioritization for innovation outside the public sphere. Moreover, in general, there is a rather low accustomization to interfirm co-operation by SMEs, although many interact closely with their technology centres. An exception to this is the Mondragon system where finance, production, training and innovation are tightly coupled in what is a model of a highly interactive innovation sub-system of high competitiveness (Basque Team, 1997a).

In summary, for these four regions with high infrastructure and policy organization capacity we can see clearly that their model of systemic innovation constitutes a co-ordinated network approach with elements of loose-coupling at the sub-system level. Each has a lead ministry with economic development executive powers either internal (Baden-Württemberg) or external (SFG, WDA, SPRI) to the government.

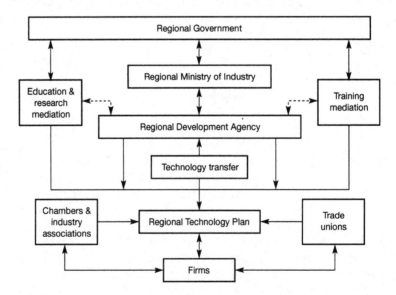

Figure 5.5 Co-ordinated network model of systemic innovation organization

Each has technology and workforce mediating functions operating through the regional governance structure and universities or research institutes, laboratories or technology centres conducting research and advanced skills provision. There are overlapping relationships with firms in vertical or horizontal networks and inter-action between knowledge centres and firms, both large and small. Crucially, each region has in place the guidance of a consensus-based Regional Technology Plan, Policy Concept, Science and Technology Plan or Future Commission vision. The co-ordinated network model of systemic regional innovation organization is represented in Figure 5.5.

4.1.2. Multi-level governance of innovation

Because Baden-Württemberg is not in receipt of Structural Funds its relations to the EU are focused, for innovation matters, on the Framework Funds. Other global interactions are independent matters, mainly for universities and research institutes, although the *land* has pursued an active policy of building transnational regional networks within the EU, most notably as leader of the 'Four Motors for Europe' initiative, and beyond. Moreover, the Steinbeis Foundation has established technol-ogy centres in other regions and countries. However, in terms of MLG the main relationship is with the federal government. As Kaufmann *et al.* (1997) note there is a strong impact and influence of the national level regarding the financial sector, research and innovation programmes and industry associations. Co-operative feder-alism entails joint *land* and federal funding of research, universities and scientific equipment though a funding gap has appeared with partial withdrawal of project funding at federal level. To increase SME development, the *land* seeks to increase EU innovation funding and established, in 1990, a Commissioner for European Affairs, EU branches at key research centres and sought EU funding for business research. The Baden-Württemberg mission to Brussels has a key priority in lobbying for science and technology funding and support for *land* firms and research bod-ies.

The Styrian MLG approach is comparable, though as an Objective 2 and 5b region it receives Structural Funding. Funding for innovation depends substantially on the federal level which has initiated several new funds for innovation research. The Austrian Association of Technology Centres and the Innovation Agency promotes interaction and knowledge exchange. Global firms have a presence in Styria and these are beginning to have a role, through cluster-building policies, in the regional innovation system, not least through transferring know-how. University depart-ments and firms are increasingly involved, the European Programme for Technologies and Training (APS) being the Styrian co-ordination office for the EU Framework Programme. As yet, Styria has not secured RITTS or RIS projects though it is involved with partner regions in a EU Information Society project focused on university-industry-regional development agency interactions. Thus the Styrian innovation system depends increasingly on national and, recently, EU funding support for regional innovation initiatives.

Wales is not as dependent on the UK level for innovation funding and organiza-tional development as the two *länder* discussed, except that university research funding is organized at UK level and academics must bid competitively for these projects as they do for EU Framework Programme funds. The main UK level guidance mechanism is the Technology Foresight Programme which sets research priorities and demands closer university-industry interaction on research funded by the Research Councils. Numerous SME innovation-support programmes were managed by the Welsh Office.

European Structural Funds with some SME and innovation support elements mean that interaction with the EU is important and, with local matched funding, worth some £100 million per year. Increasingly, efforts are being made to link Regional Technology Plan priorities to Structural Funds for implementation purposes. This is a live issue for future spending priorities within the Structural Funds more generally, since, as experimental programmes, Article 10 initiatives are not yet in the mainstream of Structural Fund spending priorities. A major step forward in developing systemic regional innovation would be the mainstreaming of Regional Technology Plans, or Regional Innovation Strategies, as they are now called, into Structural Funds Single Programming Documents.

The Basque Country has exclusive power over scientific and technological research in co-ordination with the Spanish state (Basque Team, 1997a). Still, approximately £30 million will be allocated by the state in the Basque Science and Technology Plan 1997–2000 and about £10 million is anticipated from EU programmes. Basque innovation policy is highly influenced by EU policy as shown by the fact that EU technology priorities are the subject of special promotion by the Basque government. The Technology Centres (EITE) participate significantly in EU innovation programmes and the funds allocated have risen to third place in terms of funding sources. Apart from funding, the organizations, and action lines pursued, are endogenously developed but the interrelationships of the Basque government and the EU in terms of policy priorities and development are closer than those with Madrid.

Thus, we may conclude that our four regional cases of stronger innovation systems' potential split fairly simply into two groups. The German and Austrian cases are far more integrated in organizational and policy terms, especially with respect to co-operative funding, with their federal government than with the EU. That is not say that the EU is not important, but it is much less so than the federal multi-level governance system, with significant involvement from the local level. By contrast, Wales and the Basque Country, with high levels of regional autonomy, resting on their regionalist traditions within fundamentally unitary states, depend on their state for funding but much less for organizational and policy development. Here, the stronger influence on priorities and motivating ideas for innovation is the EU and, though finance from Brussels is less than that from the state or region, the value of that involvement in promoting interaction and innovation networking is rather significant. In terms of the future, mainstreaming RTP-RIS outputs as Structural Funds inputs would strengthen the prospects for systemic innovation in these kinds of reconversion region.

4.1.3. *Knowledge application and exploitation: organizational – industrial links*

As has been shown elsewhere in this volume, firms, particularly SMEs do not make use of the organizational infrastructure for innovation support as much as they could or as much as they use contacts with other firms, exhibitions, trade fairs and journals for accessing innovation information. The reasons seem conclusively to be that they rely on the initiative being taken by organizations who must convince them of their value, there is an information gap regarding what is on offer, the costs of consultancy raise fears among SMEs, and there is a sense that it is not clear which of many organizations can help most. Probably the Baden-Württemberg system is least open to these criticisms. Large firms definitely make good use of Fraunhofer and industrial research institutes for technology applications work, the Max Planck basic research institutes and universities are given commissions. For SMEs, the technology-transfer activities of the Steinbeis Foundation, chambers of industry and commerce, and consultants are widely accessed to solve innovation problems throughout the *land*.

In Styria, Wales and the Basque Country, lead agencies such as SFG, WDA and SPRI are major sources and routeways to innovation finance, technology, information and advice as well as supplier development know-how. In Styria and Wales, the universities and research institutes have become more intensively used, partly through promotion activities such as the network-building by the Technical University of Graz and the Cardiff University Innovation Network. In the Basque Country this is only true of the small Mondragon University, but the technology centres have strong sectoral client bases. Funding is a major and valued activity of the development agencies and ministries. Locally, technology centres in Wales and Styria build strong and long-lasting links with SMEs and assist with information, premises, advice and, to some extent, even technology auditing, sometimes with the support of the EU STRIDE programme. Training services focused on innovation are rather rare, though SPRI and the Styrian training service do some IT training for firms.

Perhaps the key problems concerning the information gap, the costs of consultancy and unsureness about which organization to approach could be assisted, as Sedlacek and Tödtling (1997) suggest, by taking the following steps:

1. Building up co-ordinated strategies which focus on the demand of the region.
2. Increasing the budget for co-ordinated information campaigns.
3. Building up common information pools on regional firms, e.g. databases, for contacting potential innovators.
4. Awareness training for SMEs to increase their readiness for co-operation and external contacts.

These points tend to underline the one that was made earlier, namely that there is a need for a process such as that experienced in Wales, of bringing together in various settings over 600 firms and innovation organizations as occurred with the Regional Technology Plan, deriving statements of future needs and visions from the actors but then – and this is the crucial point – ensuring that funding is likely to be available to implement these. Hence, there is a need to link together the inputs, which all these regions are capable of producing because of their strong regional infrastructure and policy organization, to achievable and reasonable outputs in the sense of concrete, funded projects. Here the role of the MLG relationships between supranational, national and regional levels are of fundamental importance. Within such an approach, special local initiatives based on a programme of assisting universities and research institutes to work more closely with SMEs, without such centres facing the danger of losing touch with their client-group as they become more involved in EU and national projects, as happens somewhat in the Basque Country, could be of vital importance. And helping to establish a division of labour between organizations, so that channels to problem-solving are clear and understood, would be a great bonus.

4.2. Regions with medium regional innovation systems potential

4.2.1. Knowledge generation and diffusion

The regions in this category have strengths and weaknesses of significance for the organization of innovation support. In straightforward terms, they fall into two sub-categories. Friuli and Wallonia have regional governments but these are not as effectively mobilized for regional innovation support as those in the preceding category, even though Wallonia, in particular, has, in principle, amongst the greatest regional autonomy of all within the reformed federal Belgian system as well as Objective 1, 2 and 5b status. Even Friuli, as part of a Special Statute region in Italy, has some autonomy with respect to industry and innovation support but appears not to use it or not to use it effectively in a context where *local* interactions, especially centred upon industrial districts, are a more normal mode of innovation interaction. Friuli has a small area of Objective 2 but mostly 5b status.

By contrast, Brabant and Tampere have, in effect, no regional level of government, in the sense of democratic assemblies, hence low infrastructural and policy organizational capacity at regional level. But both have good instances of local policy development in support of innovative actions and close links with their member-state in the implementation of policies emanating from the appropriate national ministries. Both areas are recent beneficiaries of EU structural support due to substantial job losses in their local economies. Thus the Tampere region receives European Social Fund and ERDF support as well as Community Initiative programmes and Fourth Framework programme funding. This variously filters down through the Ministries of Labour and the Interior, through national innovation agencies or directly to regional universities, research institutes, and firms. In Brabant, Objective 2 status in 1993 stimulated regional actors to develop their own initiatives, launch activities and increase networking. The crises in Philips and Daf stimulated consensus, delegation of SPD programming by the Province and the establishment of a co-ordination agency to prepare it.

Wallonia has numerous potential organizations for promoting regional innovation including a powerful regional administration, universities and research centres, employers' organizations, chambers of commerce and a co-operative agency in the Council of Scientific Policy, but as RIDER (1997b) says: 'The main weakness of the system lies in the *absence* of political players capable of giving impulse to new orientations in the regional policy' (emphasis added). Regional policy is reconversion-oriented more than innovation-oriented. It lacks long-term vision, a culture of risk, clear targets in terms of sector and does not take into account the needs of SMEs. Consultative bodies involve many organizations, but their efficiency is reduced by conflicts between strong political lobbies. Co-operations exist within distinct spheres such as research organizations who have established joint research centres, an association of business innovation centres, regional organizations and agencies linked to EU actions. European programmes have had a strong impact on the development of European activities. In terms of innovation support, the main weaknesses are overlaps, fragmentation, bureaucracy and lack of flexibility. Programmes, though, are not suited to innovation and training. Systemness seems more visible at provincial rather than regional levels.

In Friuli, too, the role of the public organizational support infrastructure for innovation in firms is by no means clearly visible despite the presence of actors such as the regional government, universities and research institutes, technology transfer centres and social partner organizations. Although Friuli can make laws, the latest on regional industrial policy (1992) is largely ineffective. The key actors are the regional government, universities and the Friulia Bank but in the industrial districts it is the firms and their associations. The region and the university address firms, providing services but not many in innovation. Trieste Science Park provides consultancy and finance aimed at attracting biotechnology firms. Friulia Bank runs a competition for innovative firms, but technology centres are not perceived by firms to be market-oriented or effective. The role of the region has diminished with the decline of traditional Italian 'clientilism'. Co-operative projects are 'bottom-up', as in the furniture producing triangle through CATAS. The innovation system is seen as local, autonomous and market-oriented.

The key policy actors for regional innovation in Brabant are, first of all, national bodies, particularly the Ministry of Economic Affairs, mainly responsible for national innovation and regional policies and education for universities and research. Previously the EU funding regions had few resources for innovation activities for physical infrastructure. The province of North Brabant does not have innovation policy responsibilities but the local level (e.g. South East North Brabant centred on Eindhoven) can take innovation support actions. SRE is a consortium of city councils which led to the establishment in 1997 of the province status for South East Brabant and it has developed innovation action plans, partly funds a Development Agency and works in close collaboration with, for example, the Innovation Centre. *NV Rede* is the development agency which implements Structural Funds Projects such as company consultancy and finance for SMEs and start-up firms. *Stimulus* is the body responsible for organizing the quest for EU-funded projects such as improving industrial networking and support for technology training. There are two universities, a branch of TNO, the contract research organization and an industrial design college, and these interact with firms on innovation. The systemic nature of innovation linkage is based on a small village culture.

Tampere region has some similarities to Brabant, having weak regional bodies but strong links to national-level innovation organizations. It acts as a sub-system in the Finnish national system of innovation (Kautonen and Schienstock, 1997a). The core is the Technology Development Centre (TEKES), the Technical Research Centre of Finland and Tampere University of Technology. Interaction with firms through science parks, incubators and technology centres is locally very high. Promotion of new business ventures, co-ordination of resources for innovation needs, awareness raising and human resources development are conducted. A new regional risk finance system is in place. The municipal level, namely the city of Tampere, is an important shareholder in most public technology organizations. The system is based upon 'islands of intensified cooperation which lack mutual coordination due to the rapid expansion of measures to support innovation activities of industry' (Kautonen and Schienstock, 1997a). There is a lack of co-ordination, in particular, between education and employment policies and technically-oriented innovation policy.

Hence, each of these regions for different reasons shows greater systemic potential at the local than the regional level, a fact which is less surprising given the absence of regional government in Brabant and Tampere than it is in Wallonia and Friuli which have quite strong and established regional assemblies with significant powers. It would be wrong to try to encompass these cases in a single model, although localised systemic interaction is a not inappropriate term to use to designate them. Locally speaking, Brabant and Tampere have interactive innovation relationships to challenge or compare with those of Styria and Baden-Württemberg whereas regional innovation is worse in Wallonia and Friuli than it is in Wales and the Basque Country. The conclusion, therefore, is that regional autonomy may be necessary but is certainly not a sufficient condition for the development of systemic regional innovation, while strongly systemic tendencies can be found operating in local situations where regional government and governance are largely absent.

4.2.2. Multi-level governance of innovation

For innovation purposes, the governance relationships of greatest importance for at least three of the regions in this category are local-national with EU funding and interactions of varying degrees of importance. Wallonia is perhaps exceptional in that, as RIDER (1997a) put it: 'Because of the regionalization of Belgium, the dependence on the national system is very low ... European policy has played an important part in the development of transnational and interregional activities'. PACTE, INTERREG, CRAFT and STRIDE programmes have been accessed by Wallonia but the Objective 1 programme for Hainaut has created conflicts because other sub-regions are demotivated due to concentration of funds in Hainaut, the regional administration lacks absorption capacity for paperwork and funds, and recipient localities are conservative and non-innovative in mentality.

Friuli looks to Italy for Italian research funds administered by the Ministry for Universities and Research and innovation funds managed by the Ministry of Industry. The provinces of Pordenone and Udine were main recipients but because of EU sanctions the Special Rotating Fund for Technological Innovation has had to be substantially revised and was not subsequently refinanced. Recent legislation on incentives for innovation and SME support, giving tax reliefs and capital subventions for consortia of at least five SMEs in one version and at least 50 SMEs in another can be accessed. As Schenkel (1997) says: 'It would be too obvious to observe that the main European influence in shaping regional policy has been negative ... the role of the Structural Funds cannot easily be denied even if it is not possible to determine the extent the regional innovation system is shaped or influenced by it'. The main international links are conducted by the *universities* in Friuli.

In Brabant and Tampere, as we have seen, MLG is, again mainly local-national with a weak regional presence but increasing recent accessing of EU Structural and Framework Funds. In Brabant, as Boekholt (1997) says: 'The impulse from the European Funds has certainly increased the number of initiatives, and projects, some of which will have an impact on networking and commercial activities'. The decentralization of policy-formulating influence to the local level clearly works successfully in the Brabant case. There are large numbers of innovation projects in Tampere region and these operate transnationally, nationally and regionally. Many of the EU programmes are relatively unfamiliar to regional actors although the Technical University, VTT and TEKES participated in some before 1995. Nevertheless EU Funds have encouraged increased and intensified co-operation involving 30 partnerships centred on Fourth Framework projects, 50 ESF projects, 200 ERDF projects plus community initiatives. Yet, for innovation, national programmes predominate again with TEKES, Academy of Finland and various national innovation programmes being the backbone providers. There are also some regional programmes, again, usually carried out in partnership with TEKES and such like.

4.2.3. Knowledge application and exploitation sub-system: organizational-industrial links

In Wallonia, the main target of innovation support organizations is SMEs but only 20 per cent of regional SMEs have innovation projects; barriers being stated as lack of time, skills, financial and human resources. Thus innovation support services only play a small part in the activities of the organizations compared to management training, technical problem-solving, product testing and so on. While most try to improve co-operation with enterprises, these animation, informal co-ordination, training convention and spin-off support activities tend to reflect the organization of the support infrastructure which is fragmented, unconnected, over-lapping and, basically, non-systemic. Future policy should develop holistic support packages to identified business sectors, involving firms in the definition and implementation of strategy. The Friuli case is dualistic, with universities and large firms linking to national innovation programmes, and SMEs in districts innovating informally amongst themselves. Banks, business services and training organizations tend to have the closer links with regional SMEs. Regional organizations tend to be reactive towards local firms while local organizations are more proactive. In answer to the question why Friuli's system is as yet immature this could be a matter of institutional learning and the way forward is to build on a bottom-up approach as in Wallonia.

This seems to be occurring relatively successfully in Brabant and Tampere, where the absence of regional government has not hindered the development of local organizations promoting innovation amongst networks of SMEs, with the assistance of national and, to a lesser extent, EU enterprise support measures. In both countries technical universities play an important role in developing links with both large and SME firm populations. Technology-transfer, support for start-up firms, technology parks and incubators are successfully managed and make some contribution to assisting these economies recover from their difficulties in the past. This points the way, perhaps, and underlines the potential importance of EU, national and regional intervention with a support programme of university-led innovation support for enterprises.

4.3. Regions with low regional innovation systems capacity

4.3.1. Knowledge generation and diffusion

In these three regions, there is, as E. de Castro and Nogueira (1997) report of Centro 'the absence of a regional innovation system'. Therefore, it is more important to discuss the barriers to innovation development than dwell on the details of organizational interactions or practices which may be of limited scope. Having said this, Centro has some organizational infrastructure despite the very weak form of regionalization it displays within the highly centralist Portuguese unitary state. For example, the University of Aveiro is linked to the Telecommunication Institute and Institute of Systems Engineering and Computers in partnership with other Portuguese universities and other actors. There are specialist training organizations for the cork industry and technological centres for cork, footwear and ceramics, and there are offices of six industrial associations, a trade union, an SME Support and Investment Institute and the National Agency for Innovation (AdI) office plus a European Information Office.

While some of these organizations are effective, 'The role of the Institute for Development and Technological Innovation (IDIT) as a centre of support to technological innovation is totally null' (de Castro and Nogueira, 1997). The infrastructures are under-used and the initial investment is far from being paid off. Why? Because insufficient information about IDIT is disseminated and there is a lack of skilled personnel to set up R&D using existing equipment. The technological centres are better, conducting ISO 9000 certification and supporting innovation, not least through participation in EU funding from ERDF, CRAFT and the Framework Programme. SMEs co-operate because they have solutions to problems. These may be bridges to more advanced work with universities, and all the interface organizations relate to the University of Aveiro. AdI was created by the EU-STRIDE programme in 1993 and supports adoption of product and process technologies. The innovation barriers include SMEs being unaware of what little support infrastructure exists due to lack of time, resources and proactivity by organizations. There are many unnecessary bureaucratic requirements, insufficient co-operation and networking between firms and organizations, except the University of Averio, and an absence of dynamism.

In the Féjer region in Hungary, the position is predictably weaker from the point of organizational innovation support. The main actors are the Retraining Centre, the Regional Foundation for Entrepreneurial Development, the R&D Centre, the Regional Development Council, chambers of commerce and the Hungarian Employers Federation, only one of which could be said to have an innovation brief. Both colleges in the region 'felt they played a negligible formal role in innovation policy' (Makó *et al.*, 1997). The barriers to greater use and development of innovation support include, the dominance of foreign capital, the kind of production undertaken (mostly low-tech), university or college research not suited to industry needs, outdated equipment, and introversion by universities. Hence, once again, a programme to support a modern outlook towards university-industry linkage, funded by the EU and state after accession would begin to help Féjer evolve towards the role the University of Aveiro is also seeking in Portugal.

Lower Silesia may be better-placed to take advantage of such an approach since it possesses Wroclaw University of Technology and the University of the Economy, research institutes and Wroclaw Technology Transfer Centre. It also has business associations and some local economic development agencies. Wroclaw is the hub and the University of Technology is the core of whatever innovation activity occurs there. Finance for this is entirely public and extremely limited. Attempts are being made to start a technological park in Wroclaw, find ways of giving credit for innovation by firms and assisting technology transfer to firms. There is no innovation policy but a rising consciousness of its relevance to business competitiveness. To the extent innovation impulses occur, they are top-down in origin, from the centre of the unitary state. This may change dramatically with the establishment of strong, democratic regional governance and funding for coherent and co-ordinated projects centred upon the university-industry nexus and the development of an implement-able Regional Innovation Strategy funded with EU and accession of state resources. Until then, there will be little effective innovation in the modern sense in Lower Silesia.

4.3.2. Multi-level governance of innovation

This can be stated quite briefly; until Poland and Hungary join the EU and develop regions there is no real MLG, everything ultimately depends on a weakly-funded central state. There is little finance available for innovation; increased know-how transfer comes from whatever innovative interaction occurs between foreign multi-nationals and local supply firms. We noted in Chapter 2 how, in Poland and, probably, in Hungary too, once local firms interact with FDI businesses, rapid learning gains occur and indigenous firms can meet exacting technical quality and delivery standards in relatively few years. However, in both these countries there is an obvious need for large-scale investment from outside the countries in both basic, hard infrastructure and softer innovation-supporting social and technically-expert infrastructure. The EU Structural and Cohesion Funds are likely to be the main future source of such capital injections.

Centro offers some glimmerings of a vision for the way such investment might go, but lessons must be learned form the remaining relative weakness of innovation support in the region. While Portugal has received Structural and Cohesion Funding since accession, too much of the resulting investment has been concentrated in Lisbon and, to a lesser extent, Porto. This is because Portugal does not in any serious way have regions which can act as a counterbalance to this process of sucking in investment capital to metropolitan areas and then failing adequately to absorb it. Poland looks likely to avoid this temptation by establishing strong regions, Hungary needs to follow suit. Moreover, while both countries need investments in basic infrastructure, they need to learn the lesson from Portugal that competitiveness is a crucial prerequisite. which depends partly on innovativeness and a regional innova-tion strategy backed with resources and support for university-industry networking, training, technological and other interactions.

4.3.3. Knowledge application and exploitation: organization-industry links

All three regions are weak in promoting innovation organization – industry linkages, though under EU tutelage, Centro has made some limited progress. The University of Aveiro and the Technological Centres are clearly pointing the way for others. But it is striking how frequently the same criticisms of organizational innovation support occur in all but the most accomplished of regional innovation systems. These include, primarily, a lack of information or even knowledge that such organizations exist and what they do, a reactive 'sitting waiting for the telephone to ring' mentality on the part of innovation support staff, a lack of time or unwillingness to find it on the part of SME managers to think, let alone act, on innovation, an absence of sufficient or appropriate finance to promote innovation, a deficiency in co-ordination of the agencies that may exist, even weakly, to support innovation and a lack of focus and tendency for different agencies to do similar things, are amongst the barriers to successful innovation support.

These weaker regions are mainly different in their innovation support infra-structure needs from stronger regions because they are massively underdeveloped. But the route that they can take is comparable at its core whether they are weak or strong. Organizational support for innovation works best in a setting with strong regional, democratic governance or, failing that and in smaller countries, strong local bases for democratic governance and good MLG linkages to the national level and beyond. The MLG linkages beyond the region are also important where regional assemblies exist. Within that framework of resource access, two kinds of facility are associated with good support for innovation. Either universities with close industry links or research or technological centres with such links. The combination of good governance and interactive knowledge centres is a probable key to regional innovation success.

5. Concluding remarks

This has been a wide-ranging chapter trying to pin down key elements for successful organization of innovation support in an increasingly complex environment characterized by multi-level governance of regional innovation, notably in the EU. What have we found about this new landscape of multivariate regional, innovation, and systems competence and capability? The following six points seem most immediate:

1. In an MLG system, the competence and capability to interact at all appropriate levels upwards and downwards is a distinct advantage. Regions are highly appropriate levels at which to target modern, interactive innovation strategies.
2. The effects of EU policies towards supporting innovation are likely to become greater as innovation moves up the Structural Funds budgetary agenda. Support for regional innovation systems is needed in preference to existing piecemeal policies.
3. Regional innovation requires a package of innovation measures covering finance, management and workforce training, marketing training and competitiveness advice as well as more conventional technology transfer.

4. Regions have different innovation and MLG systems models and this may take some time to change, if change is even deemed necessary towards some European norm.
5. The EU regional innovation norm should be that every LFR receives funding for a RIS which is implementable using Structural Funds. 'Mainstreaming' is vital.
6. Each implementable RIS must have at its core a strong university-industry innovation networking programme.

CHAPTER SIX

Emerging Regional Innovation Policies: Present Profiles[1]

1. Introduction

Relations between the local, regional, state and European innovation policy levels have been undergoing transformation for a good two decades. The recent emergence of local and regional innovation strategies and policies signifies more than increased self-governance devolved from national policy levels. The trend is a multi-directional influence between all levels: European, national, regional and local. Whereas national science and technology policies heavily shaped regional innovation systems for decades, now there is evidence that national policies are taking account of regional diversities.

In Chapter 5 we assessed the policy dimension of specific cases. These reported on the organizational structure of each region. We established in the case studies which were the decisive actors shaping innovation policy, and the extent to which these policies were relevant to the various organisations.

2. Public policy in regional innovation systems

The public policy domain shapes the regional innovation systems directly and indirectly. It is the national level that has the largest influence on the institutional set-up of regional innovation systems. As Lundvall phrased it: 'In the real world the state and the public sector are rooted in national states and their geographical sphere of influence is defined by national borders.' (1992, p. 13) However, the regional policy level has adjusted this national institutional structure to the diversity and specificity of its area and is increasingly empowered to do so with European support. The main policy actors that operate on the regional level are:

- Local, sub-regional and regional government agencies, in particular departments or ministries for economic development and planning (in some cases also agriculture and fisheries, and tourism).
- Territorial bodies of national government agencies dealing with regional matters (e.g. the Welsh Office).
- Regional Development Agencies (e.g. the Styrian Economic Development Agency or *NV Rede* in Brabant).
- Organizations in charge of implementing the European Structural Funds.

---

[1] The comparative analysis made in this chapter is based on the empirical work of each of the REGIS teams in this TSER project. The author of this chapter takes full responsibility for the interpretation of this material.

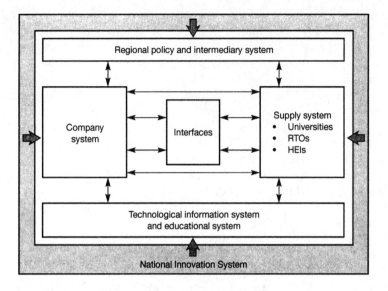

Figure 6.1 A simplified model of a regional innovation system

- In a number of cases regional elected bodies such as the Basque and Wallonian regional governments, the *länder* in Baden-Württemberg and Styria, and from 1999 the Welsh Assembly.

Innovation, science and technology policies are in general one element of any region's economic development policy. Few regions have a separate department or organization dealing with these matters: Baden-Württemberg has a Ministry of Industry. SMEs and Technology, a Ministry of Science and a Commissioner for Technology. Wallonia has a Ministry for Technology, Research and Energy. In all other regions, S&T is part of the Department of Industry or Development Agencies, if there is any public organization involved at all.

In addition to these decision-making and administrative bodies we distinguished a whole range of non-profit and representative organizations which use their influence to shape innovation policy, such as chambers of commerce, technology centres, universities, trade associations, etc. The relative weight of these types of organizations, and which public agency has a lead role, varied heavily between the different regional contexts. Figure 6.1 shows a simplified model of a regional innovation system.

Each of the elements of the regional innovation system, the Research and Technology Development (RTD) suppliers, intermediaries, educational system and industry, is affected by past and present policy interventions. The institutional elements of the Regional Innovation System (RIS) related to science, technology and education, are particularly shaped by national, regional, local and European policy-making, since their funding, their organizational structure and activities are largely dependent on public resources and policy decisions. The business sectors in the regional system are heavily influenced by the international, national and regional policies, by means of the regulatory, financial and fiscal frameworks and the Science and Technology (S&T) support systems.

The national systems of innovation literature emphasizes the importance of public policy as a significant shaping factor. 'The public sector plays an important role in the process of innovation. . . . it is involved in direct support of science and development, its regulations and standards influence the rate and direction of innovation, and it is the single most important user of innovations developed in the private sector.' (Lundvall, 1992, p.14). Nelson and Rosenberg (1993) focus on the role of science and technology and its institutions as principal vehicles which determine the national systems. Public policy is discussed mainly as the funder of both public and private R&D. The influence of policy is of a more indirect nature: 'certainly the policies and programmes of national governments, the laws of a nation, and the existence of a common language and a shared culture define an inside and outside that can broadly affect how technical advance proceeds. ... [however the Japanese model] 'has enhanced the belief that an explicit national technology policy can be effective' (Nelson and Rosenberg, 1993, pp. 16–17).

Lundvall and Borrás (1997) distinguish three levels of policy in the globalized learning economy:

1. Policies affecting the pressure for change (competition policy, trade policy and the stance of general economic policy).
2. Policies affecting the capability to impose and absorb change (innovation policy and human resource development).
3. Policies aiming at caring about losers in the game of change (social policies and transfer of income to weaker regions).

Whereas innovation policy addresses the capability to innovate and adapt to change, regional policy is seen by Lundvall and Borrás (1997) mainly as a policy for the redistribution of wealth. The REGIS research shows that regional policy is no longer solely focused on re-distribution, but increasingly on affecting the capabilities to impose and to absorb change. At the core of the 'clever' regional innovation systems are regional authorities who have widened their focus from investing regional support funds in infrastructures and attracting foreign companies, to investing in the capacities of indigenous industries and the competences of local people. This shift in attention illustrates that learning is taking place at the regional policy level.

The REGIS project looked at how decisive these policy interventions were in changing the capacities and directions of the regional systems. The general pattern that we found is that policy facilitates business innovation, the build up of competences in institutions and people and the frequency of their interactions. However, in none of the cases were policy interventions so powerful that they could change the direction or dynamics of the regional innovation system. In some of our cases policy does give additional stimulus to dynamism already present in the economic structure (Wales and the Basque Country particularly) and in other cases it intensified the lock-in effects (Baden-Württemberg, Wallonia, Centro, Friuli) through institutional inertia. Hence, the recent role of innovation policy in regional innovation systems is one of facilitating and awareness raising, rather than one of steering the direction of the innovation dynamics, except perhaps in the Basque Country where it is part of an international industrial policy to build clusters.

3. Strengths and weaknesses in innovation competences

Innovation policy is not a clearly defined set of interventions or activities that can be applied to all situations. Despite a growing 'best practice' culture in European policy due to the fact that countries and regions are increasingly learning from each other, there is no 'ideal model' for innovation policy. It is a set of actions consisting of various direct and indirect ways to support:

- the creation of new knowledge in R&D organizations and companies;
- the exploitation of new knowledge and technologies through commercialization;
- the absorptive capacity for new knowledge and technologies by firms, organizations and individual users;
- the diffusion of new knowledge and technologies to a wider set of users;
- the awareness building among less innovative companies.

The borderlines between policies for innovation, industrial policy, human resources development and education and training are not always clear cut. The latter two have much broader objectives than stimulating the innovation capabilities of industry. For example, conducting an innovation project in a small company by a graduate placement scheme serves both innovation, employment and human resources objectives. Co-ordination between these policy domains is the exception rather than the rule.

Chapter 5 on governance showed the difference in regional autonomy concerning the formulation and implementation of economic development and innovation policies. The degree to which the local or regional policy level is dependent on national decision-making differs from country to country. We have seen in Chapter 5 that the level of self-governance and control over regional budgets in the German *länder* is much higher compared to the Portugese regions which have a very low degree of self-governance. The innovation policies in the REGIS cases reflect these differences, not only in the level of empowerment but also in policy capabilities of dealing with the issues around science, technology, the learning economy and competitiveness. Regional economic development policy has traditionally concentrated on a strategy of providing the physical infrastructure for industrial development and/or attracting (foreign) investors to the region often with financial incentives (tax exemptions, grants, cheap land and facilities).

In the last decade policy-makers became increasingly aware of the notion that innovation policy should be pursued at regional as well as national level. A pattern is emerging where regional governments increasingly focus on innovation in indigenous companies, supporting inter-firm networking and local research-industry interfaces. At the same time national governments are mainly responsible for science and research policy, in which they shape the regional R&D landscape by supporting, or withdrawing support from, Research and Technology Organizations (RTOs) and universities. Gradually central governments are devolving authority to lower policy levels to deal with specific aspects of innovation policy. The REGIS study confirms this shift of innovation policy tasks being taken up by regional policy makers. Nevertheless we see that national policy has certain domains where few regions have any authority, such as the funding of universities and RTOs and the funding of industrial R&D.

The following key public tasks are performed at the regional and national levels to shape and support the innovation systems:

- providing R&D subsidies to (high-tech) firms
- funding of universities
- support for research and technology organizations
- support for sector-based technology centres
- encouraging research-industry interfaces
- innovation services for SMEs
- cluster policies
- public support for risk capital and innovation financing
- education and training

These tasks are performed by a mix of regional, and national-public and semi-public agencies, and we can distinguish both differences and commonalities in the policy division of labour (see Table 6.1). For instance, funding of universities is a national policy in many of our cases except in Baden-Württemberg, the Basque Country and Wallonia. Wales is an exceptional case where the Welsh Office was a territorial ministry of the national government, located in Wales. We will categorize the (pre-Assembly) Welsh Office tasks as national policy, whereas the initiatives of the Welsh Development Agency are regional. Also Wallonia is a special case being in a country where the federal policy level has lost importance and the majority of policy tasks are performed in the three regions of Wallonia, Flanders and Brussels. In addition, many regions have regional subsidiaries of national RTD support organizations that implement regional action lines mainly designed at the national level.

Of course, European Commission policy also enters the regional arena through three channels:

- The European Structural Funds (SFs), i.e. the European Regional Development Fund (ERDF) and European Social Fund (ESF) with financial support for both economic and social development;
- the EU's RTD support, particularly RTD funded by the Framework Programmes;
- the Article 10 and other regional initiatives for innovation strategy development such as Regional Technology Plans (RTPs), Regional Innovation and Technology Transfer Strategy projects (RITTS), and Regional Information Society Initiatives (RISI).

Whereas the REGIS regions all had support from the EU Structural Funds, with the exception of Baden-Württemberg and the two non-EU regions, the level of authority to determine the usage of these funds differs greatly between countries. For instance in South-East Brabant the policy decisions on SF projects and Action Lines were determined by the regional actors themselves, whereas in Centro the usage of Structural Funds is determined primarily by national policy organizations.

Universities and research organizations in the regions benefit particularly from participation in the Framework Programmes. Even in a small region such as Tampere, which only recently entered the EU, companies and research institutes participated in about 30 EU RTD projects. In Friuli there were almost 100 EU RTD

Table 6.1 Overview of innovation policy tasks and level

	R&D subsidy to (high-tech) firms	Funding of universities and fundamental science	Funding of RTOs	Sector-based technology centres	Encouraging research-industry interfaces	Innovation support for SMEs	Cluster networking policy	Public support for risk capital
Centro	Not at regional level, primarily at national level	Primarily national level	At national level	Nationally based, partly regionally implemented	In Centro mainly by University of Aveiro	Strong at regional level but through national agencies	Not a policy line	Not available
Baden-Württemberg	Primarily at national level but some support at regional level	Mix of regional and national support	Mix of regional and national support	Strong regional character and funding (Steinbeis)	Initiatives from universities themselves	Mix of regional and national support	Through regional technology transfer system	Mix of regional and national funds
Basque Country	From both regional and national funding	Strong regional component, funding from national and regional sources	Strong regional component, funding from national and regional sources	Strong regional component, funding from regional sources	Hardly any initiatives	Mix of regional and national support	Strong regional policy support for three main clusters	Funds at regional level
South-East Brabant	Some at regional level (EU funding) but primarily at national level	National level	National level with no spatial goals	National level, but not major initiative	Universities and HEIs with regional policy support	Mix of regional (EU) and national support	Through regional policy organizations	Some investment funds regional, VC mainly national

Table 6.1 *Continued*

	R&D subsidy to (high-tech) firms	Funding of universities and fundamental science	Funding of RTOs	Sector-based technology centres	Encouraging research-industry interfaces	Innovation support for SMEs	Cluster networking policy	Public support for risk capital
Friuli	National level	Primarily national level	Primarily national level	At regional level (not many)	Hardly any initiatives	Regional and EU funds	Hardly any initiatives	Regional investment funds
Lower Silesia	National level	National level	National level	No information	No information	National	Not a policy line	Not available
Styria	Primarily national level	Primarily national level	One regionally funded RTO, rest national	Some at regional universities and RTOs	At the two universities with regional support	Mainly national	Regional initiatives in one cluster: automotive	Regional investment funds
Székefehérvar	National level	National level	National and EU level	Not a policy line	Not a policy line	National	Not a policy line	Not available
Tampere	National level	National level	National level	At national, but also strong initiatives at regional level	Regional initiatives	Primarily national but also regional programmes	University and regional initiatives	Regional by Development Fund Finland
Wales	Some regional, but mainly national	Primarily national level but with Welsh Office	Not very strong policy domain	Regional around universities	Regional mainly by universities themselves	Mix of regional and national	Regional initiatives by WDA	Some regional, mainly private

Table 6.1 *Continued*

	R&D subsidy to (high-tech) firms	Funding of universities and fundamental science	Funding of RTOs	Sector-based technology centres	Encouraging research-industry interfaces	Innovation support for SMEs	Cluster networking policy	Public support for risk capital
Wallonia	At regional level	At regional level	Mix of national and regional level	Mainly in universities	Not many policy initiatives	Regional level	No initiatives present	Mainly private
Main trend	Primarily at national level	Primarily at national level	Mainly national level but regional input in empowered regions	Mix of regional and national support	Often at initiative of universities, sometimes with regional policy support	Mix of regional (EU) and national programmes	Either regional initiatives or no policy at all	Large variety in availability

projects with participants from the region, and a majority of the participants from industry. Although financially the EU RTD funding is only a fraction of the member-states' public expenditure, the opportunities to collaborate internationally were well appreciated.

Wales participated in one of the third type of EU initiatives, i.e. the RTP pilot Action of DG XVI. The impact on the regional innovation policy was considerable: 'The Regional Technology Plan is seen as essential in that it has brought regional actors together and stimulated discussions that would otherwise never have occurred on that scale. This resulted in the development of a regional consensus on key issues and actions for Wales' (Schall and Cooke, 1997a).

Table 6.1 shows at what policy level the above-mentioned tasks are performed. The table shows that there are certain trends, but there is no general model for subsidiarity, i.e. no clear cut rule can be established regarding what is done at what policy level. The differences in national contexts, the size and administrative positions of regions, as discussed in Chapter 5, determine which policy tasks are performed where.

We can see from Table 6.1 that there are some innovation support activities that are pursued mainly at specific levels:

- at the national level: support for industrial R&D, funding for basic science and universities and other semi-public RTOs,
- at both national and regional level: sector-based technology centres and support for SMEs. The regional support for the latter is mostly backed by EU funding.
- at regional level: support for clusters and the establishment of research-industry interfaces. Although the latter happens most often on the initiative of the universities and RTOs rather than as public policy action. A considerable number of the REGIS regions have set up a venture capital or investment fund with public resources.

In Chapter 7 we discuss whether a 'natural' subsidiarity model could be developed from this present situation.

Regional public agencies might play a larger role in innovation policy, nevertheless the competences to perform these policies, the available resources to develop initiatives, the path-dependency on former routes to innovation support and the socio-political context in which policy-makers have to operate, all determine the degree to which regional innovation support answers the firm's needs. Since policy strategies and instruments cannot be simply copied from the national level, regional public organizations require a degree of 'learning' regarding 'best policy practices' in the context of their region.

Policy competences at regional level include questions such as:

- Do policy-makers have a broad or narrow (technology or high-tech industry-oriented) view of innovation issues?
- Do regional policy-makers interact with the business community, the science and technology community and educational organizations?
- Is innovation dealt with as an integrated policy area or is it departmentalized?
- Do the key decision-makers share a common view on the regional innovation strategy, or are initiatives developed in a haphazard fashion?

- Do policy-makers help to set up interfaces between the publicly funded S&T organizations and industry?
- Do the regional institutions have a sophisticated, mixed policy portfolio addressing the needs of local industry?

The REGIS project showed a large variety in regional innovation policy capabilities, ranging from areas with hardly any innovation initiatives (Centro, Féjer, Silesia) to regions with a well-developed system of support (Basque Country, Wales, Baden-Württemberg). The other regions are somewhere between these extremes with policy competences being built up gradually. Regions that developed a specific regional technology policy strategy are Baden-Württemberg (Zukunftkommission 2000), South-East Brabant (Regional Technology Plan) Styria (Styrian Technology Policy Concept), Wales (Regional Technology Plan) and the Basque Country (Plan of Industrial Technology 1993–96 and Science and Technology Plan 1997–2000). Tampere has recently started an initiative to develop their Regional Strategy with the aim to achieve more synergy from their many individual initiatives and programmes. Other regions conduct policy initiatives on a project-by-project basis.

The following graphic (Figure 6.2) gives the position of each of the regions on two variables: empowerment (the authority and resources to pursue regional policies) and innovation policy competence. The arrows relate to shifts in empowerment and competence building that are taking place at the moment.

The graph shows that a high level of empowerment, i.e. where regional policy-makers have the authority and resources to develop innovation policies, does not necessarily mean that the appropriate competences are built up to support the innovation system. It also shows that regions with a medium level of empowerment (Styria, Tampere and South-East Brabant) can develop a high level of policy competence: if some needs are catered for by the national government and the

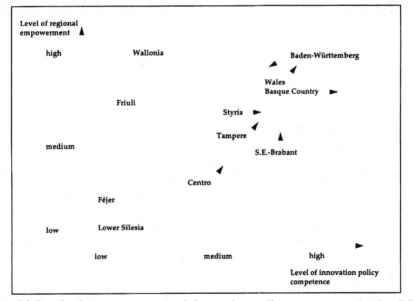

Figure 6.2 Level of empowerment and innovation policy competence in the REGIS regions

region also has European support, then the regional policy strategy and actions can be of high standard. Nevertheless, it is clear that the regions performing very well in terms of policy competences have a history of reasonably independent governance and are geographically large (Basque Country, Baden-Württemberg and Wales).

Centro in Portugal is an example of a region highly dependent on the national system of innovation, with relatively few opportunities and resources to shape its own regional innovation system. The weakness of the administrative region in combination with a severe concentration of RTD-related financial and human resources around Lisbon, make it difficult for the region to re-design its own future with support from existing policy. Therefore no overall innovation strategy has been developed by its main policy actors (E. de Castro and Noguiera, 1997)

In Friuli support for innovation comes for a large part through national financial schemes, focused on the purchase of technologies and the improvement of productivity. Due to stricter EU regulations on financial support to firms, many subsidy and loan schemes have been abolished, leading to the end of the 'golden age' of regional industrial policy in Italy. Firms are fiercely independent and competitive and are not very keen to develop linkages with the institutional and policy agencies. At the same time the regional institutions are quite passive in their approach to industry. Given these conditions, there is not a powerful policy-driven approach to the regional innovation strategy in Friuli (Schenkel, 1997).

Although Wallonia has a high degree of authority over its innovation policy and a ministry dealing with Science and Technology issues, the REGIS surveys found an absence of a policy vision and an unfocused innovation support. 'It lacks long-term vision, culture of risk, clear targets in terms of sectors, and does not take into consideration SMEs' specificities and marketing issues' (RIDER, 1997a). The gap between the institutional support system and the needs of industry appears to be very wide. In addition, a lack of sophisticated interfaces between research and industry hinders the opening of new technology trajectories. The reconversion from an economy with heavy industry and large regionally-owned companies, to a more varied economy with firms in growth markets has not taken place as successfully as in Wales and the Basque Country. With the powerful regional administration, the lock-in effect in industry is reinforced by the lock-in in the institutional sphere (RIDER, 1997a).

The region with the longest history of decentralized innovation policy and a high level of policy empowerment is clearly Baden-Württemberg. We saw in Chapter 5 that the level of institutional support is very high and provided in a 'near-to-industry' and decentralized manner. The policy awareness of regional clusters is strong and support is adapted to these specializations. Much of this support infrastructure is provided by the *Land* in combination with a vast number of national support mechanisms. The long history is at the same time its weakness: the institutionalization of the regional innovation system is hampering adaptation to globalization and changes in production modes (Kaufman *et al.*, 1997).

Other regions with a reasonably high level of empowerment are the Basque Country and Wales. The support system and the recently emerging innovation policy are designed and implemented to fit the specific circumstances of the regional economy. In the case of Wales a transition is made from the traditional type of regional development policy focused on inward investment, towards a more innovation-oriented policy. A very dominant Welsh Development Agency has had a significant influence on the regional innovation system. Initiatives are set up to improve the innovativeness of indigenous firms as well as the launch of high-tech industries such as medical technology. However a relatively autonomous science and technology system dependent on the national policy level has hindered a significant reorientation towards the needs of industry (Schall and Cooke, 1997a).

The Basque Country has a high degree of autonomy in formulating and implementing their own regional policies. Therefore a strong cluster-oriented policy involving the strongest industrial sectors is at the core of regional development policy. The political actors, particularly the Department of Industry, Agriculture and Fisheries, play a key role in shaping the institutional system. The region has its own science and technology strategy as an overall policy framework. However, this is considered to be top-down rather than consensus based. The key bottlenecks to innovation found in the Basque Country require changes in legislative and fiscal regulations, which is the task of the central government, and outside the scope of the Basque region (Basque Team, 1997a).

The region of South-East Brabant which does not have a high level of empowerment from its national political setting, has however achieved it through European Structural Funding, whereby they have autonomy to design and implement regional innovation policies. Despite the fact that formally South-East Brabant had only a weak and unclear administrative position, regional identity and institutional structures are so strong that higher policy levels have granted it a considerable level of autonomy in economic development issues. The institutional RTD system is however almost entirely dependent on the national policy level. The one-off character of European funding could endanger the newly developed initiatives and competences in the innovation policy arena (Boekholt, 1996).

Styria has government autonomy and policy through its status as *Land* in the Austrian Federal Republic. However, the study showed that despite this political status, innovation policy in Styria remains highly dependent on national funding and also increasingly on European funding. Although national state-owned companies are key business actors the institutional system has weak links with industry, so providing the regional policy system with fewer opportunities for moving towards the support of indigenous economic development (Sedlacek and Tödtling, 1996).

The Tampere region, despite its relatively low level of empowerment (no administrative region, few resources and small in size), has initiated many policy actions to support regional innovation. One of the main problems REGIS analysis found was that this support is too focused on technological issues, neglecting the organizational and commercial aspects of innovation. In addition the policies are pursued in a haphazard fashion, without co-ordination between policy domains such as SME innovation, ICT initiatives and human resource development. One of the challenges here is to intensify public–private partnerships (Kautonen and Schienstock, 1997a).

The Féjer region and Lower Silesia are still in the transition process from planned economy to market economy. 'Institutional thickness' has to be established after its severe restructuring. Public policy also has to be stabilized to find an equilibrium between focusing on new foreign investors and indigenous start-up companies. In the Féjer region local business linkages and support services seem more dominant than those of central government. However, public policy in general gives a low priority to science and technology issues and a very narrow approach to innovation issues. Creating an innovative culture and increasing awareness is not high on the policy agenda. (Makó *et al.*, 1997a). In Lower Silesia government efforts are barely recognized as having any impact on the issue of innovation. Interventions are mainly regulatory and fiscally oriented. Initiatives sponsored by the EU are more visible than any national or regional initiatives (Galar *et al.*, 1997).

The fact that the needs of many firms identified in the firm survey were not met by the support systems reveals that the supply of expertise and services does not match the innovation bottlenecks experienced by the firms in our survey. We can sum up the weaknesses in the regional innovation systems, and the policy strategies that underlie them, as follows:

- In regions with a rich institutional infrastructure the accessibility and transparency of the innovation support system (where can you find the support, which organization has the most suitable expertise, and so on) were considered to be poor.
- Small companies felt excluded from the regional technology transfer initiatives and RTD support programmes; the technology and innovation centres seemed to have a tendency to focus on the technologically competent companies.
- The surveys and face-to-face interviews revealed a disappointment from the view of the entrepreneurs concerning the quality of the services of (public) innovation and technology services. In many REGIS cases the competences on offer did not match the expertise needed.
- A huge gap in culture and working practices of regional knowledge suppliers (mainly universities) on the one hand and regional firms on the other hand was reported frequently. Traditional technology transfer activities did not seem to have great impact on the improvement of these relationships; in many regions the two sub-systems operated separately.
- Few innovation support services were available to provide vital information on existing and available knowledge and technologies which is needed by companies pursuing an incremental innovation strategy.
- The awareness that training is lacking but is an essential element of improving competences in the firms was not met by subsequent policy actions to stimulate improvement.
- Regional and local government tackle innovation in a haphazard way through the implementation of individual projects. Despite the fact that five regions had an overall technology policy plan, few regions had a vision or an overall strategy combining elements of economic development, science and technology, SME policy and human resource development.
- Regional policy-makers have the tendency to focus on the technological aspects of innovation without taking into account that innovation is linked to a broader set of issues such as management and organizational innovation, availability of finance, access to existing information and expertise, human resource development, commercial opportunities and so on.
- Regional governments do not have much influence on the specializations in universities and in RTOs performing applied research. Subsequently the research

strengths of universities and RTOs do not necessarily match the industrial strengths of the region. There is little scope for giving incentives to redirect this.

- Lock-in effects in the local RTD competences at universities and RTOs do not stimulate a shift to other technology markets.
- Firms perceived the lack of innovation finance as a major bottleneck for innovation. But we note that a large number of the regions had put in place venture capital and investment funds. Thus, it is the match between firms with innovative projects and the financiers assessing potential projects that seems to be a major problem.
- We found few cases where central and regional government co-ordinate and complement their innovation policies systematically. In the best cases, regions complement activities which are not on offer from the central government, in many cases similar activities took place at national and regional level.

These weaknesses were present in a substantial part of our REGIS cases, however, not everywhere. The same is true for the strengths that we found in a fair number of our regions:

- Regional organizations have developed and implemented many tools to support co-operation between firms (supplier-buyer initiatives, sectoral initiatives, informal meeting platforms, cluster projects) and between firms and the local research and technology organizations, which are fine-tuned to local circumstances.
- Because of proximity in the regions, networking can take place on a person-to-person basis, which facilitates both tacit knowledge exchange and trust building, which are crucial elements of strategic co-operation. This eases the facilitating role of public policy.
- Public governance agencies are increasingly aware of the importance of supporting their indigenous firms as the motor for growth and employment, instead of relying solely on inward investment and science park developments. Often with the support of EU funds an increasing number of initiatives and programmes are set up to help SMEs with a broad range of services.
- At the regional level, top-down policy strategies are under pressure since regional stakeholders usually have a more direct access to governance agencies. Policy strategies based on consensus building and taking account of the needs of the actors involved are more easily pursued on the local and regional level since communication can take place regularly. European Commission policy strategy actions such as RTP, RIS and RITTS projects, which are now widespread over Europe, encourage this approach.
- Local initiatives to improve university-industry links are becoming more sophisticated. In the most advanced regions, traditional technology transfer offices that aim to 'sell' a university's technological knowledge are being transformed into units which try to solve problems and interact with people from industry.

Each region performs differently on all these strengths and weaknesses and a general recipe for innovation policy cannot be derived from these points. The general trend that the REGIS regions show is one of increasing competences in innovation policy and institutional learning at regional, national and European policy levels.

4. The challenges for regional innovation policy: towards a systemic approach

The description of regional innovation systems showed that in general innovation policy has a tendency to be fragmented and haphazard and, even more problematic, it does not fit the needs of its users – the firms. To increase the systemic nature and efficiency of innovation policy, regional governments face a number of challenges to improve their support and policy strategies in the future:

1. The key actors in the regional system do not have a long history in formulating, designing and implementing innovation policies. In this sense they are at the start of the learning curve; generally displaying a strong tendency to tackle innovation from the linear innovation process approach. Thus, the first challenge is to facilitate the policy learning processes which looks internally (matching policies with regional needs) and externally (what can be learnt from best practices elsewhere?).

2. Large parts of the innovation policy arena lie outside the domain of regional authorities, notably the functioning of the RTD support system. Therefore regional governments have done little to anchor the S&T organizations into the regional economy. In fact regional authorities have few incentives to do so, if financial resources come from national sources and the evaluation of the efficiency of support services lies outside the regional authority's scope. Universities are assessed on the basis of their academic achievements, not on their contribution to regional industry. Only in those regions where technology organizations are controlled by regional authorities can incentives for better co-operation with industry have an impact. A second policy challenge is to encourage local actors (research and technology suppliers and users) to improve their communication and understand each other's practices as a first step to further co-operation. Regional policy-makers can facilitate these processes even if their are no 'sticks' to enforce this.

3. For regions lacking institutional richness and an economy with innovative firms, bridging the gap between restructuring traditional sectors and investing in the new growth area is a huge step. This is at the same time a challenge in the sense of the opportunity for leapfrogging into high-technology sectors, and a threat when policy decisions to launch a new area are not based on sound business arguments. Too often, regional policy-makers have engaged in 'high-tech fantasies' (Massey *et al.*, 1991) where economic growth was sought in activities with no market potential or from people without entrepreneurial skills. The third policy challenge is to find the appropriate balance between building the future strategy on present strengths and encouraging new technology markets to emerge in order to avoid lock-in effects;

4. The discrepancy between the expertise and innovation support offered and their utilization by SMEs, indicates on the one hand that innovation policies are not fine-tuned to the real problems of firms and on the other hand the lack of awareness in SMEs of the importance of exploiting external knowledge. Thus top-down innovation policies, developed without consulting its users and stakeholders, leads to inefficient innovation support strategies. This leads us to the fourth policy challenge, i.e. that regional governments should develop policies

that have the consensus of regional stakeholders and address the needs of regional firms. At the same time they should not avoid difficult choices on behalf of the most efficient services and actions, in order to avoid institutional lock-ins.

The next chapter discusses how these challenges can be tackled to design the policy for the future.

CHAPTER SEVEN

Future Policy Options

1. Introduction

The previous chapter discussed the present positions and performances in innovation policy in the REGIS regions. This chapter will draw upon these lessons to elaborate on the challenges that European regions face. First we will discuss why regional innovation policy has become more prominent in the past decade. Then we will address the weaknesses identified in the regions' innovation policies. To make the regions better equipped to face the challenges of globalization and the social problems attached, the REGIS project has come up with a number of recommendations for policy-makers. As we have stressed several times, the co-ordination and collaboration between regional, national and European policy hierarchies is vital for best practice at all levels. The time when solely national governments decide on issues of innovation, science and technology has passed as the REGIS project clearly illustrates. It is finding the appropriate balance between these levels which remains an unsettled matter.

2. Emerging regional innovation policy

As we have seen throughout the REGIS research, the local, regional, national and supranational policy levels today are strongly interdependent. The firm survey showed the degree to which firms have links inside and outside their region and countries. The organizational interviews and analysis demonstrated the intertwining of governance, RTD infrastructures and policy support at all spatial levels. In the globalized economy regional boundaries have opened up and none of the actors can allow themselves to look solely on what is happening in the limited space of the region.

The research confirmed that the relations between regional national and European governance levels and the direction of influence are in transition. The national state level is becoming less dominant in many of the countries under review. National science and technology policy has had a strong impact on the regional innovation system. The number and character of universities and research laboratories in a regional innovation system is a combined result of historical developments, intentional and unintentional science policies.[1] The current research specialization in a region is not necessarily related to the industrial specialization or needs in that area.

---

[1] Saxenian (1994) showed how the concentration of defence research contracts to a small number of research organizations had a large, but unintentional, impact on the emergence of both Silicon Valley and Boston 128.

Encouraging innovation, in particular technological innovation, has traditionally been the domain of national state policies. In the 1950s and 1960s when innovation was considered to be triggered primarily through R&D, science policy was the main mechanism to shape national innovation systems. National policies determined the type of research system put into place or reinforced (university based, semi-public research facilities, sectoral R&D facilities). Industrial development was facilitated through industrial policy, aimed at particular sectors of the economy or at a number of national champions. The two domains remained separate for quite a long time.

In the late 1970s, early 1980s, when the defeat of defensive industrial policies became apparent, policy attention moved towards the industries of the future. In most European countries support for traditional industries such as textiles and mining was reoriented towards support for the information technology and engineering sectors. At the same time discussions on the relevance of science for society asked for more industry-oriented research. Here technology policy blended the elements of both policy areas. Following eagerly what was happening in Japan, where large policy efforts were put into developing the IT industry, European state policy efforts were directed towards the key technologies for the future: new materials, information technology and biotechnology were the areas in which all nations focused their R&D efforts. It was still the national state level where the main decisions were taken. This was also the period in which the European Commission started to enter the arena in a more serious manner, following a similar technology policy approach: R&D investment in a few key technologies (nuclear energy, IT, new materials and biotechnology). Encouraging innovation was mainly about funding R&D efforts in a specified number of emerging technologies.

In the late 1980s when the limited success of the linear approach in terms of boosting competitiveness reached the policy echelons, encouraging innovation became a much wider concept. R&D was not assumed to be the sole source of innovation, and issues such as absorptive capacity, interactive learning and innovation management, were included in new policy concepts at the national level of most of the European states. In addition the notion that SMEs have an important role to play in economic development became widely accepted. Technology policies turned into innovation policies addressing the 'soft issues' as well as the 'hard technology'

The emergence of the regional and local levels in encouraging innovation can be seen as a direct result of this change in policy attitude at the national state level. Interactive learning assumes many information channels and feedback links which partly rely on personal contacts (see Kline and Rosenberg, 1986; Lundvall, 1988). Therefore proximity becomes an advantage since it can increase and intensify the possibilities for exchange of information. Innovation support services which contain personal counselling and knowledge of the specific situation of the firm works better on the local and regional levels than on the national level. The policy response in countries such as France, the UK and The Netherlands was a national network of localized support services. It is now much more accepted that particularly for innovation actions that involve networking and adaptation to sectoral circumstances, fine tuning policy support should be done close to the firm.

The European Commission has been slow to adapt its technology oriented approach, with the RTD Framework Programmes defined around technologies rather than innovation issues. Gradually their pre-competitive research orientation has been complemented by a commitment to address both societal issues and industrial competitiveness. The exception to the Commission's technology orientation were some of its 'exploratory pockets' where more integrated approaches were developed and tried at the regional level. A number of initiatives such as Regional Technology Plans (RTP), Regional Innovation and Technology Transfer Strategies (RITTS) and Regional Innovation Strategies (RIS) were launched in the mid-1990s in an increasing number of European regions. These programmes are demonstrating a great impact on the regional policy making culture and the role of innovation in shaping regional economic development. In this sense the EU initiatives have empowered regions to develop their own policies, irrespective of their national government's stance on this. Regional and local institutions are recognized to play an important role, mainly in the diffusion of (technological) knowledge.

In financial terms the European Structural Funds have had a much larger impact on the regions. A trend is clearly visible that EU Regional Policy is shifting from the 're-distribution' philosophy, where funds were used mainly for investments in the physical infrastructure, to policies dealing with the capability to 'impose and absorb change' through innovation policy and human resources development. Chapter 5 describes how European Structural Funds helped to empower regions to develop innovation oriented policy instruments.

There are more factors involved in the emergence of the local, and particularly regional, levels. The socio-political climate is pointing towards subsidiarity and devolution. Communities are claiming more self-empowerment and responsibility in various policy areas. This asks for some rules of thumb on which aspects of innovation policy should be addressed and at what policy level. We have seen in Chapter 6 that there is no clear cut division of labour. However we can say in broad term that national policy deals with the funding and policy formulation related to universities and research and technology organizations (RTOs), i.e. shaping the core elements of the science and technology institutions. In many cases the national government provided the structure and funding for SME support programmes, and intermediary services, which were implemented at regional level with adaptations to the local specifities. Networking and cluster-type initiatives were typically undertaken by regional actors, including specific university-industry linkages. The REGIS cases did make clear that good co-ordination is necessary to avoid overlaps in public initiatives, and confusion among users of the services.

Globalization is another factor behind the 'emerging regions', in so far as it encourages international firms to relocate certain business functions to those areas where value added is expected to be highest. It is exactly this globalization that has made regional diversity an important science and technology issue again, since those areas which can offer good competitive conditions (whether this is low cost labour, skilled labour, research facilities or access to markets) have a better chance of attracting and sustaining business investments. Knowledge has become a key commodity in international markets. This internationalisation of regional capacities has again raised the interest of national science and technology policy makers in regional specialisation patterns. As Tödtling (1994) rightly concluded, only a few regions of a country can develop high-technology networks. The consequence is that a consider-able number of national governments are tending towards a new type of 'picking winners' strategy: i.e. picking the winning regions. Sternberg (1996) showed how in some of the highly industrialised nations, focus of support on a few centres of excellence in science and research has had an intentional or unintentional effect on regional specialisation patterns. The trend towards nationally supported 'high-tech clusters' could reinforce the polarisation between regions in terms of industrial development and employment. None of the REGIS regions are intentionally labelled as a 'winning region' by their national government,[2] but the turn around in policy perception from regions as 'problem areas', to regions as 'promise areas' will no doubt influence the thinking on regional innovation systems.

Globalization and European integration have restricted the nation states' possi-bilities for intervention in the economy. At the macro-economic level parameters are set by either the European Union or the international markets. Therefore the interest in meso-level policies, i.e. for industrial sectors or, more fashionable clusters, has returned to national policy agendas. The internationalization of R&D makes even the science and technology policy domain less national than ever before. The literature suggests there is evidence that international sourcing of R&D and the creation of international R&D partnerships, particularly by large companies, are a growing phenomenon.[3] How far this trend will manifest itself in 'local presence' of these firms at those places where the knowledge is located is only starting to be studied. The trends have reinforced the interest in stimulating and facilitating regionally embedded pools of expertise and ways to anchor foreign investors to national and regional innovation systems. This policy strategy is particularly pursued in the most industrialized countries with high labour costs such as Germany, Austria, The Netherlands and Sweden (Boekholt *et al.*, 1998).

Although there are good arguments for the enthusiasm towards empowerment of regions, there are several potential pitfalls involved in this development:

- Many regional and local governments have limited experience in developing S&T policies, they are at the start of the policy learning curve. Without access to a pool of policy experience at other levels, re-inventing the wheel will occur fre-quently.
- There is a tendency for increased inter-regional competition for attracting busi-ness investments from elsewhere and sub-optimal duplication of support efforts. The small scale and size of regions can have disadvantages in setting up specific facilities or developing expertise which could also be available in a neighbouring region. Co-ordination of support efforts seems necessary.
- An inward look at regional innovation bottlenecks and developments carries the risk of developing strategies that reinforce lock-in effects. International market

---

[2] Although Baden-Württemberg, considered as Germany's success story, is endowed with a relatively large number of semi-public S&T institutions.

[3] See for instance Jungmittag, Meyer-Krahmer and Reger, Globalisierung von FuE und Technologiemärkten-Trends, Motive, Konsequenzen, conference paper 'Globalisierung von FuE und Technologiemärkten, Konsequenzen für die nationale Innovationspolitik', Bonn 1–2 December 1997; Ruigrok W., van Tulder R., 1995, *The Logic of International Restructuring*, Routledge, London.

and technology developments should be taken into account seriously. Incremental steps based on present competences might not be sufficient for longer term growth. Benchmarking of the competitive position of sectors and the matching technological expertise of the RTD infrastructure, with international state-of-the-art, should be part of a region's future perspective.

It is the task of European and national policy-makers to help overcome these negative side-effects of regional empowerment. As will be discussed below, inter-regional exchange of best practices and co-ordination at the national level should complement regional activities.

3. Towards systemic regions

The first chapters in this book illustrate the large variety between the regions in terms of economic performance, RTD capabilities and policy competences. Therefore it does not make sense to derive one set of policy conclusions for all regions. The conclusions for strategies have to be adapted to the situations in the regions. On the basis of our study we can distinguish four basic models each needing a different emphasis in policy approach.

- *Regions in transition*, i.e. Lower Silesia and the Féjer region are both dealing with the transition from a planned economy to a market economy, which has severe consequences for the RTD efforts and the governance structures.
- *Institutionally thin regional innovation systems* As Amin and Thrift (1994) have pointed out institutional thinness does not only occur in the obvious cases where few institutions are present, but also when they have neither high levels of interaction nor any common patterns for collective representation or common directions. This means that the support infrastructure for industry is fragmented, opaque or in some cases even of low quality. The examples in our study seem to point to Wallonia, Friuli, and Centro.
- *Dualized regional innovation systems* Here regions have a considerably well organized and interacting institutional structure with RTD centres and universities. They also have a relatively dynamic and interactive industrial network where most of the knowledge exchange takes place between co-operating firms and between the competent high-technology firms and the R&D organisations. However, the two parts of the innovation system are not well connected to each other. Examples here are South-East Brabant, Styria, Tampere and the Basque Country.
- *Interactive regional innovation systems* These are RISs where a critical mass of elements in the system collaborate and interact intensively and mutually reinforce the dynamics in the innovation strategies of its actors. The system has sufficient openness to be able to access external information and feedback and adapt to changes required by the 'outside world'. None of the REGIS regions fit this description perfectly although Baden-Württemberg and, to a lesser degree, Wales come close.

The key challenges for each of these types of region are different, depending on both the institutional set-up and the competitiveness of firms and sectors. Table 7.1

Table 7.1 Priority challenges for four 'types' of regions

	Regions in transition	Institutionally thin regions	Dualized regional innovation systems	Interactive regional innovation systems
RTD Infrastructure	• Emphasis on building up infrastructure • International S&T networks	• Access to external S&T expertise • Refocus existing organizations • Renegotiate with central government	• Develop two-way technology transfer mechanisms • Incentives for academia-industry relations	• Improve efficiency and client orientation RTD organizations • Incentives for academia-industry relations • Technology foresight
Innovation support for firms	• Access to available technologies • Management capacities • Awareness raising	• Access to external knowledge sources • Access to new markets and customers • Interfirm networking	• Improve access for less competent firms • Improve information on knowledge supply • Interfirm networking	• Improve access for less competent firms • Incentives for R&D co-operation • Inter-firm networking
Innovation policy vision	• Learning from international best-practice and ideas	• Develop indigenous strengths • Attract public (national, EU) and private knowledge intensive investments and expertise	• Towards a networked innovation system	• Refocus towards new technology markets

illustrates the broad lines of the challenges for each of these regions, without attempting to exclude other routes.

We should stress that the boundaries between the four models are not clear cut, and regional innovation models may have characteristics of two types. Neither does this model assume that each region develops along a logical development path from thin, to dualized to interactive stages.

However the 'ideal model' would be for regions to develop a more systemic approach, i.e. an interactive system, since the assumption is that innovation is an interactive learning process in which knowledge diffusion accelerates the speed of the process.

In Nelson and Rosenberg's (1993) view on national innovation systems, the elements in the system are not necessarily all working towards the same goal, let alone designed to do so by policy:

> There is no presumption that the system was, in some sense, consciously designed, or even that the set of institutions involved works together smoothly and coherently. Rather the 'systems' concept is that of a set of institutional actors that, together, plays the major role in influencing innovative performance. (Nelson and Rosenberg. 1993 pp. 4–5)

And since there are so many actors involved in innovation, there is 'no sharp guide to just what should be included in the innovation system and what can be left out' (Nelson and Rosenberg, 1993, pp. 4–5). The same holds true for innovation policy which can be defined very narrowly, i.e. relating to science and technology, or in a much broader sense, i.e. involving the support to firms to 'master and get into practice product designs and manufacturing processes that are new to them' (ibid.). Whereas the core of innovation policy still deals with the creation and use of science and technology for commercial exploitation, a much broader set of policies has come to the foreground which has an impact on the innovation capabilities of firms. Organizational innovations, management capacities, finance for innovation, and continuous training are a few of the key elements. An interactive innovation policy is one where the boundaries between science and technology development, SME support, education and training, and industrial policy have faded away. Public policy, and not only at the regional level, is not used to tackling problems in such an integrated manner. On the contrary these policy domains are usually compartmentalized in different departments and agencies, competing for power rather than co-operating to tackle the policy issues. In the vast majority of REGIS cases innovation policy is a newcomer to the public agencies and therefore not strongly embedded in the governmental hierarchical structure. So there is a strong argument concerning the need for 'institutional learning' to take place within the policy arenas.

In the 'interactive regional innovation system' a vital characteristic is that there is some level of consensus about the region's future direction in terms of economic development, competitive opportunities and routes to innovation. As said, this consensus or systemness cannot be planned or built and is likely to fail if it is pursued as a top-down policy by a dominant policy actor. The previous chapter showed that, in general, lines of innovation policy action in the regions are haphazard and piecemeal. One of the key issues here is the lack of communication for involving the broad range of stakeholders in a region. This leads to policies designed by the public sector that either do not match the needs of regional industry or follow the wishes of those groups of firms that are best in articulating their needs. Our surveys and interviews with firms confirmed this conclusion: a common criticism was that the support programmes and services were either not appropriate or were considered suitable for a particular target group only, most often large companies.

4. Designing for the future: policy support in regional innovation systems

Despite the differences in the development models described in the last section, REGIS did uncover several innovation policy deficits that apply to all regions. In the previous chapter we discussed the bottlenecks and weaknesses in the innovation policies of the REGIS regions. These were, in broad terms:

- a lack of policy vision and long-term strategy among the government agencies, and instead a haphazard and piecemeal approach to supporting innovation;
- a gap between the needs of industry, especially SMEs, and the expertise and services provided by the S&T and innovation support infrastructures;
- sub-optimal networking and collaboration between the relevant organizations;
- few policy efforts to address the low awareness, particularly with SMEs, of the importance of innovation and training;
- sub-optimal co-ordination of policies between regional, national and European policy levels.

What follows on from these considerations are recommendations for future action on three spatial levels: Regional governments, Member-states and European Commission.

At the Regional policy level we propose the following key actions:

1. Innovation should not be treated remotely but should be at the core of regional economic development policy:
   - Designate funds and resources to define an overall medium term innovation strategy in the region in close *consultation* with the relevant stakeholders in the community.
   - An effective innovation policy should be based on solid knowledge of the region's economy. Develop *information tools* and monitoring systems to be kept informed of the strengths and weaknesses of the regional economy.
   - Find access to other regions to *learn from ideas* and good practices, instead of reinventing the wheel.
2. Improve the linkages between research and industry.
   - Technology transfer initiatives have too often been set up in a one way direction: universities market their knowledge to industry expecting that interest will follow automatically; requests from industry to work on problems are not always considered in a serious and professional manner. Regional actors can learn from interesting initiatives set up in Europe where technology transfer is tackled by a multi-disciplinary problem solving unit working in close consultation with their industrial partners. Since person-to-person contacts are vital here, these initiatives can be best developed locally. We will elaborate on this matter in the section on national actions.

- Management seminars, 'open laboratory' days and Alumni activities are all low threshold activities which can help to develop personal networks between universities and industrialists.
- Small firms in general do not have the resources nor the expertise to conduct a particular innovation project from start to finish. A direct solution could be a subsidized graduate placement for a limited time. We have seen such policy instruments in several of our REGIS regions (Germany, UK, The Netherlands and in planning in Austria) which appear to have had a good impact on the firm and created employment following the assignment for the graduate.

3. Increase the use of the innovation support system by:
   - Creating transparency: the general picture that came out of the firm surveys was that there are too many support organizations; their competences overlap and the quality of their services are not always up to standard. This problem arises throughout Europe and can be addressed in several ways. One is to create 'first stop shops', i.e. one single entry point for requests for information and help which subsequently refers the firm to the relevant institution or expert. Wales created Business Connects who have this responsibility, however it is functioning under severe criticism because of a reactive disposition. A second solution developed in some countries is the 'one stop shop', i.e. an organization that can deal with all problems put before them by firms. In The Netherlands the merger between the Chamber of Commerce, the Innovation Centres and the Centres for SMEs is an attempt in this direction, but whether it will work is too early to decide. The least effort that regions can make is to clearly publicize what expertise and support is available in the region and to provide clear 'signposts' for firms to find them.
   - Pro-active approach to industry by intermediaries addressing more clearly defined target groups and catering for different kinds of support needs. The REGIS study revealed that large parts of the industrial community do not (wish to) use the support infrastructure or knowledge available in the region. Intermediaries which are set up on the basis of some form of self-financing have a tendency to focus on the most promising group of firms. Even completely publicly funded intermediaries tend to limit their activities to firms that have the capabilities to conduct technology projects. Innovation support services should map their clientele more clearly and make a policy decision about which target groups are addressed for which problems. General awareness raising is necessary to enlarge the target group. Increasing the intermediaries' visibility through proactive marketing is a necessary step for a majority of the organizations we interviewed in REGIS.

4. Stimulate interfirm networking: REGIS showed that both firm collaborations are an important source of innovative ideas and that awareness of the advantages and willingness to co-operate is still very low in many regions. The regional level is most appropriate since networking relies on trust building between people, and proximity can help to increase the meeting frequency.
   - The roles that public agencies and other intermediaries can play are as varied as awareness raising, brokerage activities, encouraging RTD co-

operation through subsidies, supply chain development, providing discussion platforms and fora, and so on. The most active regions in this respect were Wales, South-East Brabant, and the Basque Country.

5. Link regional initiatives for human resource development with innovation issues:
   • Inadequate management capabilities appear to be a key problem for many firms. Training courses dealing with the broad aspects of innovation management for entrepreneurs and those who want to start up firms, could be developed in collaboration with higher education institution (HEIs) and universities. Management seminars do not only facilitate learning, they also encourage networks between industry and HEIs for future collaboration.
   • Another approach to tackle management deficits is to create SME networks which deal with management issues under the supervision of mentors from large companies. These types of initiatives have been set up in several European countries following its first successful experimentation 10 years ago in Flanders. Universities also play this role, for example, in Sweden.

At the National policy level:

The core body of innovation policy instruments is usually held by the national government agencies. The challenge is to complement the national instruments which cover generic issues, with regional instruments which cater for the specific needs of the region. These specificities can relate to the (sectoral) composition of the economy, particular deficits in S&T investments or human resources, specific social and community needs or simply the geographical location of the region in question.

1. Allow regions a considerable level of empowerment to develop actions and policies which are fine tuned to the local situation. Empowerment involves both having the legal authority and the financial resources to develop and implement strategies. REGIS showed that regions with a history of independence and their own financial resources managed best to develop an overall regional innovation strategy.

2. Encourage inter-regional communication and networking between policy makers to:
   • avoid inefficient overlaps in setting up support facilities which could be shared between regions or developed as a national scheme;
   • avoid too blatant regional competition for foreign investors and public resources;
   • share good ideas for 'best practice' on policy instruments;
   • stimulate 'institutional learning' in the domain of innovation policy.

3. National Science and Technology policy departments can work together with regional authorities and universities to encourage research-industry linkages; Possible elements are:[4]
   • adapt their regulations;
   • policies for universities and public research organizations, to provide more flexibility to set up regional technology transfer initiatives. Examples are

---

[4] Several of these initiatives mechanisms have been described in the REGIS case studies

allowing commercial contracts to be made outside university financial departments, exempting researchers working on industrial projects from academically oriented peer review systems, encouraging separate legal units in academia to work on research contracts;

- funding of joint academic-industrial 'competence centres' or specific R&D projects;
- supporting the access to research facilities (laboratories, machinery, test equipment) for SMEs as a first step to further collaboration;
- setting up university-industry exchange programmes. Examples of policy instruments exist in Germany, UK and the Netherlands where graduates spend a certain time in a company to conduct an innovation project. In some cases the laboratory facilities can be used for the research project and supervision is given by experienced researchers;
- develop support packages for young entrepreneurs for start-up companies. Many initiatives have been set up to help campus based start-up companies, as we can see from the REGIS case studies. The support on offer is usually restricted to cheap office space facilities and access to laboratories.

The European Community already plays an important role in the shaping of regional innovation systems. We have seen that European Structural Funds were used to set up support instruments for SMEs, Information Technology initiatives and human resource development. There were two weaknesses in the use of Structural Funds:

1. In some countries regional authorities have a limited influence on the use of Structural Funds. Action lines are developed at central government level or by representatives of the central government in the regions. The possibility to develop actions which are closely matched to the specific issues of the region in question become smaller if the layers in governance increase.
2. The transition from using Structural Funds for physical investments in infrastructure and one-off industrial support actions towards investment in sustainable innovation strategies for firms requires significant institutional learning by policy-makers. The competence to develop good practice innovation policies is not always present, and the risk of falling into the same traps that national policy-makers have done in the last decades (i.e. a too narrow approach to innovation, concentration on high tech sectors only, little understanding of innovation bottlenecks) is likely.

Therefore, we recommend three types of action to be intensified at the European Commission level:

1. Designate a larger amount of the Structural Funds for innovation and technology-based competitiveness strategies aimed at improving the long-term position of indigenous companies. The development of such action lines requires regions to engage in an intensive strategy debate within their region. Technological innovation is often considered as a strategy that leads to unemployment and therefore faces severe opposition by those affected in the short term. In the global market short-term strategies that reinforce the lock-in of traditional industries and products made at lower costs in other parts of the

world, are not a solid basis for future wealth creation. A combined innovation and human resource development effort seems imminent.

2. Provide regional authorities with the (financial) opportunities to develop so called 'consensus based' Regional Innovation Strategies. The present RTP, RIS and RITTs initiatives have contributed to the design of regional policies which have the commitment of a larger number of firms and stakeholders in the region. In the REGIS research the case of Wales was illustrative of the effect that a relatively small initiative (in financial terms) can have on the innovation awareness within in firms and institutions. One of the main achievements is that initiatives have been developed on the basis of consultations of the policies' users, from entrepreneurs, trade unions to educational institutions. Other REGIS regions have engaged in strategy exercises, often in a more top-down policy fashion. The main challenge is to link these strategy exercises with public–private investments to implement the Action Lines that have come out of them. An obligatory linkage between the allocation of Structural Funds and the pursuit of a Regional Innovation Strategy exercise could be considered. However, it must be noted that when strategy exercises are linked to the allocation of large amounts of funding the consensus element, which is now clearly present in the RITTS/RIS projects, will suffer.

3. Provide regions with an international learning ground for the exchange of ideas on best practice policy. Again the European Commission is already providing these opportunities to those regions participating in the RIS and RITTS action lines. Our research showed that there is a need for this type of cross-fertilization amongst European regions. Catching up with regions with more experience in innovation policy as well as learning from experiments in other types of regions could speed up the institutional learning process.

For all these strategies and initiatives at all levels, continuous learning and adapting to change is vital to avoid lock-ins and inefficient public initiatives. In order to do so, ex-post and on-going evaluation of actions, institutions and programmes against policy objectives, and against their impact on the problems they aim to address, cannot be disregarded. Only through the information gained from monitoring progress and evaluating effects can actions be redirected and improved.

The differences in structure and character between national and regional systems of innovation mean that the REGIS project cannot provide a blue-print, but it can point to processes intended to deal with the issue of subsidiarity for each region and country. However, the broad lines developed above show first of all that divisions of tasks can be made and secondly that regions should be given an important role to play in the future.

CHAPTER EIGHT

The Governance of Innovation in Europe: Conclusions and Policy Implications

1. Introduction

In the first chapter of this book we argued that the new international political economy was characterized by asymmetrical globalization, pervasive innovation as a key driver of business competitiveness, and an imperative for firms in Europe to increase their capabilities of exploiting knowledge capital in learning economies and information societies. Further, since nowadays so much of production is externalized in the supply chain these demands cannot be fulfilled within the internal hierarchies of large firms alone. Large firms are, in some crucial European cases, notably Philips and Siemens in electronics, hiving-off branches of their traditional business activity for privatization or acquisition. Competitiveness and market liberalization have created volatile conditions where yesterday's assumptions are today's uncertainties. Change-management skills are prized assets and innovativeness is at a premium. We need a new idea of partnership to interconnect business elements of a changing economic landscape that, at the turn of the millennium, gives the appearance of hyper-competitiveness more than the much-heralded closer integration.

Innovation is the most integrative of economic activities because it demands social interaction among diverse actors due to the complexity and heterogeneity of competences it now involves. Innovation is stimulated but not encompassed by R&D, particularly as innovation activities can easily involve smaller firms that may be specialist or users of R&D from elsewhere, or simply relayers of their own tacit knowledge. However, innovation is spatially highly uneven (CEC, 1997). Within the EU the disparities in levels of business expenditure on innovation are more than double between the most and the least prosperous EU regions. EU-funded research on 'islands of innovation' in the Archipelago Europe programme (FAST, 1992) showed most science-based innovation co-operation between firms and laboratories to be concentrated in only ten places such as London, Paris, Munich and Milan.

Although that report has been criticized for a too-narrow (R&D) based definition of innovation and a too-narrow range of industries studied, nevertheless most informed observers would not disagree that leading science and technology investment takes place in a few regional or member-state capital cities. This is undoubtedly connected with the importance of government R&D budgets for both public and private-sector research.

However, it has been stated over and over again that this is not necessarily a good way of spending scarce government resources: first, because it does not appear to have significantly improved the comparative innovative performance of large EU firms, who are major recipients; second, because it exacerbates the cohesion and integration objectives of the EU more generally by giving a subsidy to the richest locations at the expense of the poorest. We suggested that EU and also member-state research budgets should be directed away from large EU firms that have low innovative performance or are only innovative in declining technologies, and towards innovator firms and laboratories of any size working systemically and interactively to develop, in particular, radical innovations. This was because European industry is too attuned to conservative, incremental innovation which can occur within the confines of close buyer-supplier relationships quite satisfactorily, but it is poor at generating breakthrough innovations of the kind regularly produced in Japan and the USA.

If we are to follow the implications of our conceptual analysis we must be in a position to assess the viability of a different kind of innovation policy, better designed to meet the exigencies of changed times and a new international political economy. If over-concentration of scarce innovation inputs has produced disappointing results in terms of commercialization of new knowledge, what is the scope for spatial diffusion of appropriate incentive and innovation support for a wider array of firm sizes? This should not be seen simply as a decentralization of expenditure through the decentralization of government research laboratories in the hope that they can become locomotives of regional innovation in underdeveloped areas. That 'cathedrals in the desert' approach based on unfounded assumptions about the propulsive effect of growth poles has only produced further disappointment in France and also Japan, where it was pioneered. We seek a different, more evolutionary approach that, for regions of diverse kinds and stages of development, enables them to maximize innovation opportunity in connection with assets supportive, actually or potentially, of innovation within the region and beyond it. In other words, as we have noted, our interest has been in the prospects of developing or enhancing regional innovation systems. Remember that these are geographically proximate private and public governance arrangements facilitating the flow of appropriate innovation knowledge and information around a region to the advantage of its innovators.

2. The European context

We have seen that for regional innovation to be promoted, funding in sufficient quantities must be raised regionally through member-state science, technology and regional policy, and EU applied science or technology policy and regional funds, to enable the furtherance of systemic innovation. Moreover, delivery mechanisms or institutional and organizational means for implementing regional innovation policy must exist. Recognition of the viability of regional innovation policy, addressed with special emphasis to SMEs, must be the subject of a consensus at the highest levels of the EU and member-state decision-making machinery. The EU, in particular, has been a crucial influence in reinforcing regional administrative identity and eliciting it where previously weak or absent. It is important that the EU and the regions, with their shared interest in the application and commercialization of appropriate scientific findings, remain in strong funding and policy-delivery partnership for the further and continuing promotion of systemic innovation at regional level.

These are the essentials of the new regional policy with innovation promotion and the diffusion of a learning culture at its heart. It is advantageous that the EU macro-economy is stable and seems likely to remain so, but the condition whereby this is associated with low enterprise, inadequate innovation and high unemployment in many areas, must be changed. From our results there is enough programmatic work to be done to keep policy-makers busy for the foreseeable future if systemic innovation capability is to be spread wider thus enhancing European business competitiveness on a broader canvas. This does mean changing the past spatial focus of European Research and Technology Development policy, or at least, bringing the spatial focus into clearer alignment. The past concentration of expenditure in the EU's 'innovation islands' was an unintended consequence of action since those were the locations of technological and scientific expertise. But, as we have seen, basic research is very strong in the EU; innovation, which is conducted everywhere in relatively modest, incremental terms, is nevertheless comparatively weak. Action is needed that focuses on generic weaknesses and demonstrations of market failure that justify public intervention. The EU as a major source of regional and innovation-support funding is the key policy-player, well-attuned to the nuances and needs of regional innovation policies. The member-states will thus continue to fund most science policy according to their priorities, albeit adjusted to reflect Framework Programme guidance, and perhaps with increasing attention also on the need for greater exploitation of scientific findings.

There may be many objections to this approach but those which seek to resist change to the existing state of affairs do not have a very strong case given what has been said and written about Europe's innovation deficit. Beyond that, three objections that may be posed appear to have some merit. First, it could be argued that taking R&D funding away from large enterprises is hardly likely to contribute to their effectiveness as innovators, so Framework Programme funding should continue to be given to large firms. Yet evaluations of these expenditures find consistently that they are valued as much, if not more, for their help in bringing firms from different countries together as they are for enhancing the technological capabilities of the larger companies. This is not least because these funds get lost in the total research budgets of large firms. Using scarce innovation resources for travel and meetings to discuss research activities that may already be being funded from internal resources, admittedly an exaggeration of reality, would clearly be unjustifiable.

There is a second, slightly more appealing objection, which is that although Framework Programme funding is a small proportion of total research funding for firms like Siemens, it is a far more substantial part of total public funding, and public funding is a way of getting large firms to engage in research deemed socially useful that they might not otherwise become involved in. Grande and Peschke (1997) argue this way, but the outcomes thus far are, once again, disappointing in that socially or environmentally useful innovation has been, if anything, harder to detect than innovation of world-beating quality in general. Nevertheless, this point, whereby a small 'tail' of EU funding can maybe 'wag the dog' of business research and innovation priorities is potentially of importance in encouraging innovation of the kind we have been discussing, interactive with SMEs and universities or other laboratories in networks which promote learning, change and innovation-based competitiveness enhancement.

A third, quite strong objection is that placing public innovation support funds with SMEs would massively weaken EU competitiveness because these are the least innovative of an already relatively weak population of firms in which large enterprises are the more innovative. But our results are valuable in showing why European SMEs are poor innovators. They are too closely tied to large firms who may be innovative by comparison with SMEs but are not especially radically innovative and clearly do not demand radical, and presumably not much incremental, innovation from their suppliers. Even though SMEs, like all firms, claim quite high rates of product and process innovation, detailed inspection by factory visits and face-to-face interviews reveal what is claimed is often development or adaptation, or even reconfiguration rather than innovation in the sense of commercialized output new to the market. SMEs are otherwise isolated, not networked, under-funded – especially for innovation – and poorly placed either to access technological information on a widespread and consistent basis or to find partners with whom to co-operate on innovation projects. In short, SMEs need help to fulfil their innovation potential, not least by some form of organizational innovation that enables them to become more engaged with the rest of the business world.

When Denmark entered the EU Single Market in 1993 it was feared that the economy (which is inordinately dependent on SMEs) would be unable to withstand competition from other EU countries. Because of this the Danish Ministry of Industry implemented a crash programme of network-building amongst SMEs in 1989. That programme was both the first to be implemented and to be evaluated and, as we noted in Chapter 1, found to have been less successful than first thought. Initially, it looked as though nearly half the firms joining networks with the backing of financial incentives and a trained mediator or broker to manage the network, typically of about seven firms each, had improved turnover ascribable to networking by just under 5 per cent over a three-year period. But a subsequent, more sober assessment suggested that in terms of network maintenance the programme failed in that most initial networks no longer existed, although some 100 or more had come into existence and persisted voluntarily.

Since the beginning of the 1990s we have learned considerably more about how to encourage fruitful networking. First, and perhaps most importantly, it is clear that firms entering networks, or other kinds of temporary partnership arrangements with other firms, ascribe greatest benefit to them in terms of business performance when the objectives for being in the network have been clearly articulated and agreed (Kingsley and Klein 1998; Shapira. 1998). Second, firms in networks either survive longer or perform less poorly in recessionary conditions, using measures such as employment and wage levels as well as turnover indicators, than matched firms not in networks (Brusco *et al.*, 1996; Uzzi, 1996). Finally, regarding innovation, weak ties or loosely-coupled networks are superior either to strong ties networks or individualistic firm strategies in the diffusion of technologies (Robertson *et al.*, 1996). These findings are important, especially for European SMEs, since, with a clear innovation goal firms may anticipate higher survival rates and more rapid learning through networks than by continuing as isolated actors. This may seem obvious but most European SMEs and their enterprise support agencies do not see it.

Importantly, the less tightly circumscribed the network form the better where learning is concerned. This point may be crucial in helping us understand a key reason why the pioneering Danish Technological Institute Network Programme received a relatively critical independent evaluation. There the programme required the rapid formation of networks and the swift formulation of legal contracts binding network members into co-operation for the duration of their funding period. This was one of the main criticisms made by firms of the programme and the reason why most left these formal networks. Nowadays it is better understood that network formation must entail an informal stage and that contractual obligations should be less binding. This is, of course, because of the all-important trust, reputational and customary nuances that represent the 'social capital' dimension of inter-firm SME collaboration (Putnam, 1993).

Our survey results clearly show that European SMEs are by and large not engaging in networking activity. While this may not be a demonstrable cause of low real innovation activity, it is clearly operating in association with it. Clear lessons are also now emerging of the kinds of advantages than can accrue for SMEs in appropriate kinds of networks which help meet key learning and diffusion deficits identified as weaknesses under present conditions. Many European SMEs have experience of inter-firm interaction through supply-chains, but these, principally vertical, networking relationships seem to place them in a position of 'capture' and even dependence upon larger, customer firms. This, too, is associated with, if not causal in relation to, the European paradox of comparatively low innovation. Even though larger firms are the more innovative they may not yet be placing sufficient innovation demands upon suppliers. Evidence for this is strong in one of Europe's richest supply-chain economies, Baden-Württemberg, where SME suppliers expressed grave concerns about their capabilities as serious innovators when Daimler-Benz proposed that they should take on more of this responsibility in response to heightened global competition from firms such as Toyota with its cheaper luxury vehicle, the Lexus (Cooke and Morgan, 1998).

There are some rays of light despite the relatively gloomy picture of European SME interactiveness with respect to innovation. This concerns the emergent evidence of more complex inter-activity in some regional economies, especially those that have a reasonable degree of devolution of innovation policy competence and, perhaps, a cultural predisposition to consensus and associational activity. These latter characteristics appear to be decisive, differentiating as they do regions with substantial devolution but lower interactivity of a systemic nature, from others in which both characteristics are high. We say more about this in the later sections of this concluding chapter, but we think the roles of trust and social capital warrant discussion here since we would concur with a number of authors such as Putman (1993) and Sabel (1996) that social capital may be the most important missing ingredient in economies that fail to develop adequately. If this is so, policy may need to be refocused further to address this new kind of 'market failure' in the learning economy.

3. Social capital, the missing ingredient?

Networking of the more formal kind under discussion here is a policy of whether to induce, or draw out, social capital amongst SMEs perhaps in association with knowledge centres and larger customer enterprises. Social capital involves norms of reciprocity, trust and networking for collectivities of individuals or organizations. It is to be contrasted with human capital which is primarily an individual attribute measured in terms of personal skills and qualifications. The aim is to enhance their competitiveness through engaging in joint innovation. However, our results show that, even in accomplished regional economies SMEs are not natural networkers (although there are isolated exceptions in, for example, north-central Italy) and in Europe's many less favoured regions they are even less so. Encouragement and incentives to become more open-minded towards inter-firm and firm-agency collaboration are vital prerequisites to developing a learning culture among European firms, universities and innovation agencies. Learning from good practice elsewhere must be facilitated but always with the cautionary note that social capital is many-faceted and not replicable in its entirety from one culture to another. Yet learning theory tells us that imitation through adaptation is one of the most powerful forces for transferring knowledge, and the concept of role models is a primary incentive for innovative learning to occur. What is needed in Europe, therefore, are regional role models, the economic conditions of which are relevant to the learning region. Thus the developmental pathway may be monitored, absorbed and the learning region shown the nuances of learning-by-adaptation and refined into the two types discussed next.

In his book on the subject, de Geus (1997) differentiates between learning by assimilation and learning by accommodation as a different means of adapting to the effects of a learning experience such as that discussed above. Learning by assimilation means that the learner already has existing structures in place into which new knowledge fits. Most businesses learn in this way, just as a bank is geared to assimilating information about, and responding to, an interest rate change throughout its diverse divisions. This is also the way in which learning occurs in educational institutions where learners are conditioned to receive information in certain ways – fundamentally through teaching – and such information is, in the absence of information overload, absorbed. Learning by accommodation is different in that the learner must change structures governing assumptions, understandings, conventions, habits and rules, and adapt to change by full involvement in the learning process and its implications. It means letting go of comfortable perceptions and world-views of the past, such as the assumption that economic life is fundamentally an individualistic competition, or that industrial relations are essentially a form of class conflict, and learning that co-operation and consensus are equally if not more important in economic life than individualism and conflict. Accordingly, whole sets of new skills and expertise have to be learned, either through pedagogy or experience, to articulate the revised world-view. Diplomacy rather than command, partnership in place of outright rivalry, and co-operation to complement competition are the kinds of social skills that are more closely associated with nurturing social capital.

Now, in the context of such complex socio-economic constructs as regions, this is even harder to achieve than in a firm where changing corporate culture is known to be difficult. The task was discussed in Chapter 2, where fairly comprehensive lists of postulated attributes of regions with strong and weak innovation systems potential were contrasted. The key problem is that there are many and diverse institutions and organizations whose conventional wisdom may need to be transformed through processes of learning by accommodation. Our research and previous work strongly suggests that if regional institutions are to change in relatively benign rather than crisis conditions, where options may be quickly closed off and where choices made become narrower and narrower, then double-feedback learning is the most likely way forward (Argyris and Schon, 1978). Some EU regional innovation programmes like RITTS and RIS, discussed in the previous chapter, have this intent but implementation of desired actions is often limited.

Double-feedback learning is based on self-monitoring and monitoring exemplars. Clearly, in a complex regional setting there should be a lead organization or means of bringing together key organizations. The former could be the business community, if it is institutionalized, but should be either the democratically elected public administrative authority or one or other of its legitimate functional agencies. The latter could simply be the expressed will of appropriate associations with relevance to the problem or who have the opportunities at hand to project their concerns publicly and establish a forum, convention or standing conference to elicit expertise and draw up implementable plans of action. Either way, associational practices involving numerous collective actors have to be mobilized. Now, the self-monitoring trigger for learning by accommodation is the question: to what extent are we achieving our goals for this region or regional economy? Even if goals are implicit and have to be made explicit, they are likely to be underpinned by some notion of improving regional prosperity. Research of some kind may be necessary to determine whether prosperity is being enhanced absolutely or relatively, but if the answer is in the negative, the case for action is strengthened.

The trigger related to monitoring exemplars may precede the first kind of monitoring, but more frequently it follows. That is, having identified a failure of goals-achievement, the questions arise of whether the ends or the means should be changed and how have comparably placed or even 'world best-practice' regions pursued a successful growth path? This is the point at which any number of conduits for policy-learning may be activated. It is also such a relatively common and repeated point in the development curve of regions and countries world-wide that, ideally, a supra-state organization such as the EU should be the first port of call, with a specialist task-force capability to advise the would-be learner region of better practice. By and large though, this is a point at which the learner region may invite the consultant in. How does this happen? Intellectually, as we noted in Chapter 1, this is an interesting and generally not well-understood process. However, certain possible routes can be identified by means of which sufficient knowledge is held to enable a tender document to be more or less sensibly drawn up.

Given the complexity of establishing and explaining regional economic excellence, particularly where concepts such as 'social capital' are involved, one route by which useful knowledge appears is through academic books and articles. The research department of an agency or firm might access such knowledge for future reference, or a staff change may have resulted in knowledge-transfer entering the arena. Alternatively, journalists might have either picked up through academic work or discovered and interpreted a new case clearly and articulately, with similar archiving results. A study-visit, organized by the regional administration or consultant, might also be an important means of providing a learning role model and stimulating the first steps away from learning by assimilation towards learning by accommodation. The next step in the process is the invitation to tender which will elicit expert consultancy advice, but advice which is likely to be of the learning by assimilation variety. Thus, Michael Porter's Monitor consultancy is a good example of an organization with a generic methodology through which it feeds appropriate local data, and arrives at recommendations regarding the primacy of clusters as economic development objects worth achieving. Where the consultancy cannot help the regional agency, authority or association move closer to a learning by accommodation position is in iterating the generic and the specific cases, something which can take months if not years to achieve and which is, accordingly, expensive and perhaps, as a consequence, something which could justifiably be subsidized by the public sector under market-failure rules.

Clearly, advocacy of clustering, networking and associational activities which promote inclusivity, co-operative interaction and consensus are all germane to the stimulation of systemic flows of information, knowledge, legitimacy and resources. To the extent that innovation is the focus of systemic regional innovation it may be enhanced by aligning with relevant linkages beyond the region. If it is under the circumstances of a globalizing, competitive, innovative world economy in which linkage and interactivity are key practices, that region, its institutions and organizations will have begun the process of learning by accommodation to the new realities. Such realities may mean a switching, or bridging from one industrial path-dependence to others, as we discussed in Chapters 6 and 7, by developing enterprise support policies for promising indigenous sectors or seeking to attract foreign investment in promising industrial fields. In either case, stimulating linkage with key support organizations in training, technology transfer, banking and knowledge generation is no longer an add-on but an essential part of the package. Through associationism of this kind, as well as others like sophisticated networking and clustering programmes, the social capital of the regional economy can, where necessary, be built up and exploited for collective benefit.

These, we have argued, are the reasons why regional innovation systems are, in principle, such a crucial element in the economy of the future. We think that Europe, where regions in many countries are historically relatively strong and becoming stronger administratively as more industries become decentralized and innovation policy takes root, has an advantage over competitor countries and even continents in this respect. Some of the most studied monitoring exemplars in the world are located in the EU, notably northern Italy, south-west Germany, Denmark, Wales and in the Basque Country. They all have in common an associational capability which translates into their 'economy culture' (Albert, 1993). In different ways and with differing degrees of success in economic terms they have shown that rugged individualism and cut-throat competitiveness are not the only ways of becoming either a favoured regional economy or ways of learning to recover from economic threat or adversity by accommodating to new realities. Thus, in our concluding remarks we propose to show grounds for confidence that this new, systemic view of regional economic co-ordination centred upon ensuring enhancement of innovation capability not only exists but can, by means of policy intervention, be generalized beyond a few privileged places to the wider population in less-favoured regions. And, in our belief, by pursuing policy action lines such as those summarized below, the overall innovation capability of the EU economy can be raised substantially. Of course, our prescriptions are not limited to Europe, they can also apply in other settings where sub-national administrative and knowledge-capital competences are found.

4. Regional firm competitiveness and innovation

Here, we move on to summarize the main findings of the research informing this book. We have seen in earlier chapters that regional innovation systems exist in a few of our eleven cases, but by no means in all. That is not to say that innovation is not present in all regions, indeed one of the surprising features of the study has been how much innovative activity is claimed by firms in all kinds of settings, though some of these claims were moderated in the light of deeper investigation. Moreover, a substantial amount of innovative activity produces results which are not new to the market, and a majority of innovative activity by surveyed firms is incremental, though involving some degree of partnership relationship among firms. This suggests that systemic innovation, involving important and well-established links between regional, but also nationally-located, firms and, to a lesser extent, regional and national innovation support organizations, is relatively common. Where the region is not the most important medium or milieu for interactive innovation, the local or national level often plays that role; seldom is it the case that the European or global levels are prominent in the process, except for EU innovation funding support.

Strong regional governance for innovation support and promotion seems to be a necessary, though by no means sufficient, condition for the existence of regional innovation systems. The cases of Baden-Württemberg, the Basque Country, Styria and, to some extent, Wales point to that. But strong regions like Friuli and, particularly, Wallonia, do not generate notable regional innovation systems, while South-East Brabant and the Tampere region are quite innovative although innovation is both more nationally-driven and locally-focused. The weakest systems are found in highly centralized governance settings with little local, let alone regional, purchase upon or influence over the evolution of regional innovation trajectories of firms or sectors. The Hungarian, Polish, and to a lesser extent, Portuguese cases exemplify this.

The key policy dilemma is how to produce a generic policy approach for enhancing regional innovation systems potential which may usefully be accessed by regions at different stages of economic development and with varying regional powers? Ten of the eleven regions examined, including those in Hungary and Poland, are recipients of.EU structural intervention funding, and these two accession countries will undoubtedly be recipients when they join the EU. Only Baden-Württemberg lies outside the regions in receipt of Structural Funds. Structural Funds, therefore, may be the key to promoting regional innovation systems in less favoured regions. This is one of our fundamental conclusions, as was elaborated in Chapters 6 and 7. There are two ways in which this could operate. Either the Single Programming Documents could become the vehicle requiring regional funding bids to be organized to include Regional Innovation Strategies plus, subsequently, funding bids for projects to realise the outputs of such strategies in physical terms. Or, if such 'mainstreaming' of innovation policy into Structural Funds budgets is deemed ineligible, regions should be encouraged to operate as if it were, in principle, acceptable, and propose projects which, in a more disaggregated way, enabled them to achieve the same outcome. In what follows, we elaborate upon the rationale for this general approach.

It was noted in Chapter 3 that a substantial portion of main corporate functions of firms in the surveys are located at regional level. Baden-Württemberg revealed high percentages of R&D activity, purchase of inputs, and the existence of comprehensive regional co-operation with only the sale of outputs being substantially less regional than towards higher market scales. Of the reconversion regions, the Basque Country and Styria were fairly regional in their outlook for R&D, competitors and co-operation, while the industrial district regions displayed less regional focus for key corporate activities, except competitors and co-operation in Friuli; and R&D and co-operation in Centro. Hence, there is a significant degree of autonomy to be found at regional levels though perhaps higher in the more economically developed regions examined. This suggests that initiatives to promote innovation at regional level should not meet insuperable barriers because of firms having to refer decisions to a head-office outside the region before engaging in interactive relationships.

Firms in all regions, including those in Hungary and Poland reported that quality and cost were the most important, or second most important, impulses driving their competitive behaviour. We conclude that these twin imperatives are the source of their demand to innovate. A generic position in which firms seek to ensure they have the human capital necessary to sustain competitive advantage is also present. Thus, innovation for surveyed firms is focused upon three pillars of corporate activity: enhancing quality, enhancing skills and minimizing cost; so affecting market prices. We conclude that these are the essential drivers of the innovative impulse and that firms are open to receiving external assistance in seeking to respond. Innovation policy must recognize the integrated nature of the quality/cost and skills development elements of the challenges faced by European firms, especially SMEs.

What have firms been doing themselves to meet these challenges? Organizational innovation is within their power to a considerable extent. The most widely practised organizational innovation on average has been the introduction of teamwork, and recognition of the importance of collaborative intra-firm practices in sustaining competitive advantage. Close behind it has been the achievement of the ISO 9000 organizational standard, frequently required nowadays to remain a supplier to increasingly demanding customers, particularly in the supply chain. Next, Total Quality Management (TQM) also reflects the recognition of quality as a key competitive instrument, and introduction of Information Technology (IT) and Just-In-Time (JIT) management further underline the organizational changes that have been relatively widely introduced. Most of these organizational innovations imply considerable workforce retraining as a consequence of reorganization. There is some evidence that these innovations are more intensively pursued in the high performance engineering and reconversion regions, though the differences between regional categories are not great, the transition regions being, understandably perhaps, less innovative in organizational terms. Where differences are significant they refer to innovation inputs such as R&D expenditure and employment. However, overall, less than half our sample had introduced organizational innovations, so the need for increasing awareness and assisting implementation remains sizeable in all regions. Here is a place for policy to offer support to an aspect of innovation – that related to firm organization – that may, in the past, have been under-emphasized.

We also noted how firms seem rather introverted or at least limited in their horizons regarding their sources of information regarding innovation. Fairs and exhibitions, customers, journals and suppliers, in that order, are the main sources and there is little detectable pattern according to regional categorization. Firms are learning most from the more familiar surroundings of other firms and the absorption of technical literature, rather than from consultants, industry associations, technology transfer centres or universities. When it comes to actual partnerships in the innovation process, customers and suppliers again score highly, though, interestingly universities and consultants rise up the rank-order considerably. Both seem to be used more when an innovation problem or opportunity is clearly specified than for more general accessing of information concerning innovation. Moreover both tend to be quite strongly regionally located, suggesting that greater dissemination and proactivity by regional universities towards their business community could result in benefits for both, as is also the case with consultants.

The results of innovation efforts by firms, alone or in partnership, may be thought to be rather disappointing. Our data echo very closely the findings of the Community Innovation Survey (CIS), albeit for a slightly different period. The CIS results refer to 1990–92, ours to 1993–96. The percentage of product innovations new to the market in the CIS survey was 48 per cent and in our research 44 per cent. However, actual innovations averaged 67 per cent in our survey indicating a substantial proportion of product innovations being imitations or re-innovations new only to the firm not the market. The ratio is worse for process innovations, where an average of 50 per cent of firms in our 1993–96 survey reported producing them, but only 23 per cent were new to the market. There is some degree of necessary process innovation to generate product innovation but there must remain concern that there is a disparity between innovations and sales of innovations. Maybe the much-observed inadequacy of finance to enable firms to transform prototypes into commercial propositions has a part to play, and invites reflection on policies.

Constraints on innovation are stated by firms in our study to be, first, funding (or lack of it) and second, the costs of research personnel. Clearly, innovator firms experience serious barriers to conducting or realizing the potential of innovations because of funding limitations. After funding, management time is cited as the next most important constraint, followed by workforce skills and know-how. Hence the need to enhance workforce skills to sustain competitive advantage runs into a barrier because research personnel are expensive and appropriate skills are not always or easily available to assist in the pursuit of product or process innovation. Clearly, the funding and training environments are operating less than optimally, suggesting the need for policy attention. These problems are generally more pronounced in the less-favoured regions than in the high performance engineering and upstream reconversion regions.

When firms interact with the public innovation infrastructure, something that is done on a modest basis compared to inter-firm interaction, regional and national universities are the most important interlocutors with 24 per cent of firms linking with universities in their region and 22 per cent linking nationally. However, small firms (employing less than 50 people) do this between 30–50 per cent less than firms in general; medium-sized (50–200 employees) do so at the average level (i.e. 24 per cent regional, 22 per cent national) while large firms (over 200 employees) do so between 75–90 per cent more than the average. Larger firms also co-operate noticeably more than average with research institutes, technology transfer and training organizations. Thus larger firms make much the most use of the innovation support infrastructure at both regional and national levels while small firms significantly under-use it. This may be because small firms are adaptors rather than innovators, or there may be more barriers to making such links. If the latter is true then the support infrastructure may well be failing small firms, bearing in mind some of its elements are designed to assist them, especially at regional level. So there may be a role for policy in stimulating small-firm networks that might form the critical mass necessary for better information supply, learning opportunities and joint financing to help overcome the barriers to a fuller use of appropriate services. If insufficient innovation support services are available regionally, there may also be a role for policy to supply them.

Overall, the results for policy consideration from the research into innovation processes of firms and the innovation support infrastructure show some generic features. There is the question of complementarity between the multiple levels of the EU innovation support infrastructure. Regional universities, technology transfer agencies and training organizations are conveniently used, on a modest basis, where they exist and offer a valued service. Funding for innovation support is often organized at national level and firms access this intelligently as appropriate, except for small firms. Also specialist research institutes and services as well as specialist training services may be organized and accessed nationally for reasons of efficiency. At the EU level, more generic funding programmes and services, including international networking focused on innovation, is an appropriate task. However, small and less innovative firms are not well-reached by the innovation system at any level, perhaps because of a lack of intermediaries or other barriers. Therefore, a policy to improve this could be a valuable initiative led by the EU but implemented regionally. Consciousness of the value of networking by firms is rather low and there may be a case for EU support to promote more pre-competitive collaboration among SMEs. Finally, improving the capability of SMEs to engage in bridging technologies to newer sectors, would be valuable.

Existing innovation policies have begun to recognize the importance of the regional level for organizing innovation support to firms. However, so far policies have been piecemeal and have tended not to recognize the fact that for firms, innovation includes quality, organization, management, marketing and training aspects as well as those dealing mainly with technology. But regional competences are not evenly distributed within the EU and hardly exist in the rest of Europe. Nevertheless, much funding in support of economic development from the EU is absorbed with a regional focus. There is a clear case for strengthening regional absorption capability, reemphasizing the centrality of innovation support as a key focus for expenditure and encouraging transfer of learning opportunities concerning the management of regional innovation policy from strong to less-favoured regional innovation systems. This is especially important regarding innovation support for SMEs. Moreover, there is a widespread lack of respect for many elements of the regional innovation support infrastructure that exists, except in the most highly developed regional cases like Baden-Württemberg or Styria, or local cases with good links to the national level, such as in Brabant and Tampere.

A number of policy challenges must be faced in preparing for future improvements to regional innovation policy. First, there is the question of *policy learning* which is two-dimensional: ensuring that regional bodies understand their own strengths and weaknesses as sites for promoting innovation; and comparing that situation with other regions, learning from their experiences, and adjusting lessons learned back to the context of the learning region. Second, the question of policy communication and co-ordination within the region, or the formation of regional *policy networks* is important for improving intra-regional policy co-ordination to support innovation. Bringing universities and other normally external bodies into such policy network arrangements is desirable. A third challenge may be called building *policy bridges*, meaning encouraging through use of incentives the graduation of firms from stagnating or declining sectors into those with growth prospects, without making these bridges impossible by trying to leapfrog into wholly new, perhaps high-tech industries. Finally, regions need to develop *policy consensus* about action lines agreed by all the major regional stakeholders regarding the appropriate future innovation strategy to be pursued. This should then be monitored, evaluated and adjusted in line with changing policy conditions and evolving policy goals.

5. Future policy

We now come to the presentation of our thoughts for the future of regional innovation policy within a regional innovation systems perspective. It is probably true to say that at all levels, but especially that of the EU, innovation policy has been equated with technology policy. One of the strong findings of our research is that, for firms, innovation is intimately tied to issues of competitiveness and is to be understood, in consequence in relation to finance, quality and skills issues as well as being inextricable from social, political and cultural relationships. All firms recognize this and have communicated it to us, but small firms are mainly left out of the innovation support picture, while only one-fifth of medium-sized firms make regular use of the support infrastructure, larger firms being the main beneficiaries. Some EU initiatives such as RITTs and RIS recognize this and bring together all the actors of consequence in a region to build a regional culture of receptivity to innovation. We would urge this approach on all regions, especially the less favoured, but add that there must be funding mechanisms, via regional policy, to enable projects to be implemented.

A key aim is that less-favoured regions of the many kinds we have identified should evolve towards a more systemic approach based on the concept of interactive innovation, emulating but not copying the condition enjoyed by more developed regional economies. Receiving, learning, absorbing and adapting appropriate experiences from elsewhere should be facilitated in pursuing this aim. Equally, broader aspects of innovation, concerning firm organization, management competence, skills development, quality management and finance for innovation must be addressed, particularly for SMEs. In other words a regionally integrated innovation policy is now required, linking SMEs, not necessarily excluding large firms, but also including regional and relevant national and even international support organizations. A

Regional Innovation Strategy at EU level is needed to express consensus and guide action towards achievable innovation goals.

This places innovation at the heart of regional economic development policy, complementing and gradually displacing an older tradition of regional development policy as concerning investment in 'hard' infrastructures with one more attuned to the promotion of 'soft' infrastructures at regional level. Part of this process involves learning from elsewhere as well as understanding internal needs alone. By listening to the difficulties firms have, such as – insufficient management time to think about innovation – it may be deemed more valuable to subsidize the appointment of a graduate 'innovation assistant' to deal with the problem than to try to teach an old dog new tricks. If universities are not committed to encouraging spin-off firms, as in the Basque Country, then technological centres could take on such a function. There is a great need to improve transparency concerning services that are on offer for regional firms who constantly find it hard to identify a route towards help regarding finance, information, technology and partners with respect to innovation. Again, an innovation assistant will probably be more familiar with, for example, accessing useful Internet information than the hard-pressed SME manager.

Innovation organizations, understandably, concentrate their efforts on receptive firms but they should be required to make efforts in assisting slow learners as well as fast trackers. Moreover, our evidence shows that SMEs may benefit from being encouraged to form self-managing networks through which they can engage in informal know-how trading, benchmarking and, collectively, identification of possible innovation projects of generic value. Such networks, supported by regional innovation agencies, should be in a position to bid for Structural Funds to co-fund joint strategies and implement their findings as appropriate. Such projects may well be broader than mere technology transfer and involve organization, marketing and skills-development as adjuncts to innovation. Universities and other knowledge generation and diffusion agencies should be encouraged to play a key role in these networks along with firms.

Hence, we conclude that some already existing and important EU regional economic development resources like the Structural Funds can be a main vehicle for promoting nationally and regionally co-funded promotion of systemic regional innovation in less favoured regions. Other experimental approaches like RITTs and RIS could be 'mainstreamed' usefully into Single Programming Documents which are the means for realizing development through approved projects. SMEs working in networks, supported by innovation organizations, should be main recipients of such funding in so far as innovation is the focus. Innovation itself should be more broadly defined to capture firm-relevant dimensions of the process. This, we believe, is a viable approach to designing regional innovation systems for the future.

References

Albert, M. (1993) *Capitalism Against Capitalism*. London: Whurr Books.

Amin, A. and Thomas, D. (1996) The negotiated economy: state and civic institutions in Denmark, *Economy and Society*, 25, 255–81.

Amin, A. and Thrift, N. (1994) Living in the global, in A. Amin and N. Thrift (eds), *Globalization, Institutions and Regional Development in Europe*. New York: Oxford University Press. pp. 1–22.

Archibugi, D. and Pianta, M. (1992) *The Technological Specialization of Advanced Countries*. London: Kluwer.

Archibugi, D. and Michie, J. (eds) (1997) *Technology, Globalisation and Economic Performance*. Cambridge: Cambridge University Press.

Argyris, C. & Schon, D. (1978) *Organizational Learning: A Theory of Action Perspective*. Reading, MA: Addison-Wesley.

Arrow, K. (1997) Economic growth policy for a small country, in A. Gray (ed.), *International Perspectives on the Irish Economy*. Dublin: Indecon.

Asheim, B.T. (1996) 'Learning regions' in a globalised world economy: towards new competitive advantages of industrial districts? Paper presented at the European Urban and Regional Studies Conference, Exeter.

Autio, E. (1998) Evaluation of RTD in regional systems of innovation, *European Planning Studies*, 6, 131–40

Aydalot, P. and Keeble, D. (eds) (1988) *High Technology Industry and Innovative Environments: The European Experience*. London: Routledge.

Basque Team (1997a) Report: Structure of innovation organizations, report to EU-TSER project, 'Regional Innovation Systems: Designing for the Future'. University of the Basque Country, Department of Applied Economics.

Basque Team (1997b) Report on face-to-face interviews with firms, report to EU-TSER project, 'Regional Innovation Systems: Designing for the Future'. University of the Basque Country, Department of Applied Economics.

Bechtle, G., Kaufmann, C. and Becker, D. (1997) The case Baden-Württemberg: a tightrope walk between risk and safety, innovativeness and sterility, report to EU-TSER project, 'Regional Innovation Systems: Designing for the Future'. University of Bamberg, Department of Sociology.

Benko, G. and Dunford, M. (eds) (1991) *Industrial Change and Regional Development: The Transformation of New Industrial Spaces*. London: Belhaven Press.

Boekholt, P. (1996) South-east Brabant: profile of a regional system of innovation, report to EU-TSER project, 'Regional Innovation Systems: Designing for the Future'. Brighton: Technopolis.

Boekholt, P. (1997) The organisations in the regional innovation system, report to EU-TSER project, 'Regional Innovation Systems: Designing for the Future'. Brighton: Technopolis.

Boekholt, P. and van der Weele, E. (1998) South-east Brabant: a regional innovation system in transition, in H. Braczyk, P. Cooke and M. Heidenreich (eds), *Regional Innovation Systems*. London: UCL Press. pp. 48–71.

Boekholt, P., Clark, S., Sowden, J. and Nichoff, M. (1998) *An International Study on Initiatives to Build, Develop and Support 'Competence Centres'*, Amsterdam: Technopolis.

Boffo, S. and Pugliese, E. (1997), Results of the face-to-face interviews to firms: the case of Friuli, report to EU-TSER project, 'Regional Innovation Systems: Designing for the Future'. University of Udine, Department of Sociology.

Borrás, S. (1998) EU multi-level governance patterns and the Cohesion Fund, *European Planning Studies*, 6, 211–26.

Braczyk, H.-J., Cooke, P. and Heidenreich, M. (eds) (1998) *Regional Innovation Systems: The Role of Governances in a Globalized World*. UCL Press: London.

Brusco, S., Cainelli, G., Forni, F., Franchi, M., Malusardi, A. and Righetti, R. (1996) The evolution of industrial districts in Emilia-Romagna, in F. Cossentino, F. Pyke and W. Sengenberger (eds), *Local and Regional Response to Global Pressure: The Case of Italy and its Industrial Districts*. Geneva: International Institute for Labour Studies 17–36.

Business Week (1998) 'The 21st Century Economy', *31 August, 56–146*

Camagni, R. (ed.) (1991) *Innovation Networks*. London: Belhaven.

Caprio, G. & Klingebiel, D. (1996) Bank insolvencies: cross-country experience, Policy Research Working Paper 1620, Washington DC: World Bank.

Castells, M. and Hall, P. (1994) *Technopoles of the World: The Making of Twenty-first Century Industrial Complexes*. London: Routledge.

CEC (1996) The Green Paper on Innovation. Luxembourg: Commission of the European Communities.

CEC (1997) Second European report on science and technology indicators. Luxembourg: Commission of the European Communities.

CEC (1998) The globalising learning economy: implications for innovation policy. Luxembourg: Commission of the European Communities.

Chesnais, F. (1993) The French national system of innovation, in R. Nelson (ed.), *National Innovation Systems*. Oxford: Oxford University Press. pp. 192–229.

Cohen, W. and Levinthal, D. (1990) Absorptive capacity: a new perspective on learning and innovation, *Administrative Sciences Quarterly*, 35, 128–52.

Cooke, P. (1992) Regional innovation systems: competitive regulation in the new Europe, *Geoforum*, 23, 365–82.

Cooke, P. (ed.) (1995) *The Rise of the Rustbelt*. London: UCL Press.

Cooke, P. (1997) Regions in a global market, *Review of International Political Economy*, 4, 348–79.

Cooke, P. (1998) Introduction: origins of the concept, in H. Braczyk, P. Cooke and M. Heidenreich (eds), *Regional Innovation Systems: The Role of Governances in a Globalized World*. London: UCL Press.

Cooke, P. Moulaert, F., Swyngedouw, E., Weinstein, O. and Wells, P. (1992) *Towards Global Localisation*. London: UCL Press.

Cooke, P. and Morgan K. (1993) The network paradigm: new departures in corporate and regional development, *Environment & Planning D: Society and Space*, 11, 543–64.

Cooke, P. and Morgan, K. (1994a) The regional innovation system in Baden-Württemberg, *International Journal of Technology Management*, 9, 394–429.

Cooke, P. and Morgan K. (1994b) Growth regions under duress: renewal strategies in Baden-Württemberg and Emilia–Romagna, in A. Amin and N. Thrift (eds), *Globalization, Institutions, and Regional Development in Europe*. New York: Oxford University Press. pp. 91–117.

Cooke, P. and Morgan, K. (1998) *The Associational Economy: Firms, Regions and Innovation*. Oxford: Oxford University Press.

Cooke, P. and Schall, N. (1996) Regional profile and Welsh innovation system, report to EU-TSER Project 'Regional Innovation Systems: Designing for the Future'. Cardiff University, Centre for Advanced Studies.

Cooke, P., Uranga, M. and Etxebarria, G. (1997) Regional innovation systems: institutional and organizational dimensions, *Research Policy*, 26, 475–91.

Cooke, P., Uranga, M. and Etxebarria, G. (1998) Regional systems of innovation: an evolutionary perspective, *Environment & Planning*, A, 30, 1563–1584.

Cooke, P., Manning, C. and Huggins, R. (1999) Industrial liaison and academic entrepreneurship in Wales, *Entrepreneurship and Regional Development*, (forthcoming).

Crevoisier, O. (1997) Financing regional endogenous development: the role of proximity capital in the age of globalization, *European Planning Studies*, 5, 407–16.

Dalum, B. (1995) Local and global linkages: the radiocommunications cluster in Northern Denmark. Department of Business Studies University of Aalborg (mimeo).

DeBresson, C. and Walker, R. (eds) (1991) Networks of Innovators, special edition of *Research Policy*, 20(5), 1–17.

de Castro, E. and Nogueira, F. (1997) Report on regional innovation organizations, report to EU-TSER project, 'Regional Innovation Systems: Designing for the Future'. University of Aveiro, Department of Environment and Planning.

de Castro, Nogueira, F. and Gonzales, C. (1996) Regional innovation systems profile of the Portuguese Centro region, report to EU-TSER project, 'Regional Innovation Systems: Designing for the Future'. University of Aveiro, Department of Environment and Planning.

de Geus, A. (1988) Planning as learning, *Harvard Business Review*, March–April, 70–74.

de Geus, A. (1997) *The Living Company: Growth, Learning and Longevity in Business*. London: Nicholas Brealey Publishing.

de Vet, J. (1993) Globalisation and local and regional competitiveness, *STI Review*, 13, 89–121.

Dierickx, I. and Cool, K. (1989) Asset stock accumulation and sustainability of competitive advantage, *Management Science*, 35, 1504–13.

Dosi, G. (1988) Sources, procedures and microeconomic effects of innovation, *Journal of Economic Literature*, 26, 1120–71.

Dosi, G., Freeman, C., Nelson, R., Silverberg, G. and Soete, L. (eds) (1988) *Technical Change and Economic Theory*. London: Pinter.

Edquist, C. (1997a) Introduction: systems of innovation approaches – their emergence and characteristics, in C. Edquist (ed.), *Systems of Innovation: Technologies, Institutions and Organizations*. London: Pinter. pp. 11–35.

Edquist, C. (ed.) (1997b) *Systems of Innovation: Technologies, Institutions and Organizations*. London: Pinter.

Enright, M. (1996) Regional clusters and economic development: a research agenda, in V. Staber, N. Schaefer and B. Sharma (eds), *Business Networks: Prospects for Regional Development*. Berlin: de Gruyter. pp. 190–214.

Esteves, C., de Castro E.A., Rodrigues, C. and Nogueira, F. (1997) Report on face-to-face interviews with regional firms: Aveiro region, report to EU-TSER project, 'Regional Innovation Systems: Designing for the Future'. University of Aveiro, Department of Planning and Environment.

Etkowitz, H. and Leydesdorff, L. (1997) *Universities and the Global Knowledge Economy*. London: Pinter.

Etxebarria, G., Gomez Uranga, M., Intxaurburu, G. and Ozerin, L. (1996) Regional profile of the Basque Country, report to the EU-TSER Project 'Regional Innovation Systems: Designing for the Future' University of the Basque Country. Department of Applied Economics.

FAST (1992) Archipelago Europe: islands of innovation synthesis report. Brussels: MONITOR/FAST Programme.

Florida, R. (1995) The industrial transformation of the Great Lakes Region, in P. Cooke (ed.), *The Rise of the Rustbelt*. London: UCL Press. pp. 162–76.

Freeman, C. (1987) *Technology Policy and Economic Performance: Lesson from Japan*. London: Pinter.

Freeman, C. (1994a) Innovation and growth, in M. Dodgson and R. Rothwell, (eds), *The Handbook of Industrial Innovation*. Cheltenham: Edward Elgar.

Freeman, C. (1994b) The economics of technical change, *Cambridge Journal of Economics*, 463–514.

Galar, R. and Kuklinski, A. (1997) Regional profile of Lower Silesia, report to EU-TSER Project 'Regional Innovation Systems: Designing for the Future'. University of Warsaw, Euroreg.

Galar, R., and Waskiewicz, J. (1997) Report on the REGIS survey in Lower Silesia, report to EU-TSER project, 'Regional Innovation Systems: Designing for the Future', University of Warsaw, Euroreg.

Gibbons, M., Limoges, C., Nowotny, H., Schwartzman, S., Scott, P. and Trow, M. (1994) *The New Production of Knowledge*, London: Sage.

Grabher, G. (1993a) The weakness of strong ties: the lock-in of regional development in the Ruhr area, in G. Grabher (ed.), *The Embedded Firm: On the Socio-economics of Industrial Networks*. London: Routledge. pp. 255–77.

Grabher, G. (ed.) (1993b) *The Embedded Firm: On the Socio-Economics of Industrial Networks*. London: Routledge.

Grande, E. and Peschke, A. (1997) Missing links: transnational cooperation and policy networks in European science policy-making, Working Paper No. 6. Technical University of Munich, Department of Political Science.

Grandinetti, R. and Schenkel, M. (1996) The economic development of Friuli-Venezia-Giulia, report to EU-TSER project, 'Regional Innovation Systems: Designing for the Future'. University of Udine, Department of Sociology.

Gray, A. (ed.) (1997) *International Perspectives on the Irish Economy*. Dublin: Indecon.

Hakansson, H. (ed.) (1987) *Industrial Technological Development: A Network Approach*. London: Croom Helm.

Hassink, R. (1996) Technology transfer agencies and regional economic development, *European Planning Studies*, 4, 167–84.

Heinelt, H. and Smith, R. (eds) (1996) *Policy Networks and European Structural Funds*. Aldershot: Avebury.

Henry, N. and Pinch, S. (1997) *A Regional Formula for Success? The innovative region of Motor Sport Valley*, Birmingham University, Department of Geography.

Henton, D., Melville, J. and Walesh, K. (1997) *Grassroots Leaders for a New Economy*. San Francisco: Jossey-Bass.

Herrigel, G. (1989) Industrial order and the politics of industrial change: mechanical engineering, in P. Katzenstein (ed.), *Industry and Politics in West Germany*. Ithaca, NY: Cornell University Press. pp. 185–220.

Herrigel, G. (1996) Crisis in German decentralized production, *European Urban and Regional Studies*, 3, 33–52.

Hirst, P. and Thompson, P. (1996) *The Globalization Question*. Cambridge: Polity.

Hodgson, G. (1993) *Economics and Evolution: Bringing Life Back into Economics*. Cambridge: Polity.

Hooghe, L. (ed.) (1996) *Cohesion Policy and European Integration*. Oxford: Clarendon Press.

HUD (1996) *America's New Economy and the Challenge of Cities*. Washington DC, Department of Housing and Urban Development.

Joanneum Research Institute (1995) *A Technology Policy Concept for Styria*. Graz: Joanneum Research Institute.

Johnson, B. (1992) Institutional learning, in B. Lundvall (ed.), *National Systems of Innovation: Towards a Theory of Innovation and Interactive Learning*. London: Pinter. pp. 23–44.

Kaufmann, C., Becker, D. and Bechtle, G. (1997) Organisations in the regional innovation system of Baden-Württemberg, report to EU-TSER project, 'Regional Innovation Systems: Designing for the Future'. University of Bamberg, Department of Sociology.

Kaufmann, A. and Tödtling, F. (1997) Innovation in Styrian companies: university-based cooperations along traditional trajectories, report to EU-TSER project, 'Regional Innovation Systems: Designing for the Future'. University of Economics Vienna, Institute of Urban and Regional Studies.

Kautonen, M. and Schienstock, G. (1996) Profile of the Tampere Region, report to the EU-TSER Project 'Regional Innovation Systems: Designing for the Future'. University of Tampere, Work Research Centre.

Kautonen, M. and Schienstock, G. (1997a) Innovation organisations and technology policy in Tampere region, report to EU-TSER project, 'Regional Innovation Systems: Designing for the Future'. University of Tampere, Work Research Centre.

Kautonen, M. and Schienstock, G. (1997b) Report on firm interviews: the case of Tampere region, report to EU-TSER project, 'Regional Innovation Systems: Designing for the Future'. University of Tampere, Work Research Centre.

Kelly, K. (1998) *New Rules for the New Economy*. London: Fourth Estate.

Kingsley, G. and Klein, H. (1998) Interfirm collaboration as a modernisation strategy, *Journal of Technology Transfer*, 23, 65–74.

Kline, L. and Rosenberg, N. (1986) An overview of innovation, in R. Landau and N. Rosenberg (eds), *The Positive Sum Strategy*, Washington DC: National Academy Press.

Krugman, P. (1991) *Geography and Trade*. Cambridge, MA and London: MIT Press.

Krugman, P. (1994) The myth of Asia's miracle, *Foreign Affairs*, November-December, 63–75.

Krugman, P. (1995) *Development, Geography and Economic Theory*. Cambridge, MA, and London: MIT Press.

Krugman, P. (1997) Good news from Ireland: a geographical perspective, in A. Gray (ed.), *International Perspectives on the Irish Economy*. Dublin: Indecon, pp. 38–53.

Landabaso, M. (1997) The promotion of innovation in regional policy, *Entrepreneurship and Regional Development*, 9, 1–24.

Lazaric, N. and Lorenz, E. (eds) (1998) *Trust and Economic Learning*. Cheltenham: Edward Elgar.

Levitt, T. (1983) The globalisation of markets, *Harvard Business Review*, May/June, 92–102.

Lundvall, B. (1988) Innovation as an interactive process, in G. Dosi, C. Freeman, R. Nelson, G. Silverberg and L. Soete (eds), *Technical Change and Economic Theory*. London: Pinter.

Lundvall, B. (ed.) (1992) *National Systems of Innovation: Towards a Theory of Innovation and Interactive Learning*. London: Pinter.

Lundvall, B. and Borrás, S. (1997) The globalizing learning economy: implications for technology policy at the regional, national and European level, paper to EU-TSER Workshop on 'Globalization and the Learning Economy: Implications for Technology Policy'. Brussels, April.

Lundvall, B. and Johnson, B. (1994) The learning economy, *Journal of Industry Studies*, 1, 23–41.

Maillat, D. (1991) The innovation process and the role of the milieu, in E. Bergman, G. Maier and F. Tödtling (eds), *Regions Reconsidered: Economic Networks, Innovation and Local Development in Industrialized Countries*. London: Mansell, pp. 103–18

Maillat, D. (1995) Territorial dynamic, innovative milieus and regional policy, *Entrepreneurship and Regional Development*, 7, 157–65.

Makó, C., Ellingstad, M. and Kuczi, T. (1997), Székesfehér region: survey results and interpretation, report to EU-TSER project, 'Regional Innovation Systems: Designing for the Future'. Hungarian Academy of Sciences, Budapest.

Makó, C. and Kuczi T. (1997) Weak regional policy: key role of the regional human capital (firm interviews in the Székesfeher region), 'Regional Innovation Systems: Designing for the Future'. Hungarian Academy of Sciences, Budapest.

Makó, C., Novoszath, A. and Kuczi, T. (1997) Organisational innovation in Féjer region, Hungary, report to EU-TSER project, 'Regional Innovation Systems: Designing for the Future', Hungarian Academy of Sciences, Budapest.

Malecki, E. (1991) *Technology and Economic Development: The Dynamics of Local, Regional and National Change*. Harlow: Longman.

Malmberg, A. and Maskell, P. (1997) Towards an explanation of regional specialization and industry agglomeration, *European Planning Studies*, 5, 25–42.

Marin, B. and Mayntz, E. (eds) (1991) *Policy Networks: Empirical Evidence and Theoretical Considerations*. Frankfurt and Boulder, CO: Campus/Westview Press.

Marks, G, Scharpf, F., Streeck, W. and Schmitter, P. (1996) *Governance in the European Union*. London: Sage.

Marshall, A. (1919) *Industry and Trade*. London: Macmillan.

Massey, D., Quintas, P. and Wield, D. (1991) *High-tech Fantasies: Science Parks in Society, Science and Space*. London: Routledge.

Moravscik, A. (1993) Preferences and power in the European Community: a liberal intergovernmental approach, *Journal of Common Market Studies*, 31, 473–524.

Moulaert F. and Tödtling F. (eds) (1995) The European geography of advanced producer services firms, *Progress in Planning*, vol. 43, parts 2–3.

Nelson, R. (ed.) (1993) *National Innovation Systems: A Comparative Analysis* Oxford: Oxford University Press.

Nelson, R. and Rosenberg, N. (1993) Technical innovation and national systems, in R. Nelson (ed.) *National Innovation Systems: A Comparative Analysis*. Oxford: Oxford University Press.

North, D. (1993) Institutions and economic performance, in U. Mäki, B. Gustafsson and C. Knudsen (eds), *Rationality, Institutions and Economic Methodology*. London: Routledge. pp.242–64.

O'Donnell, R. (1998) Post-Porter: exploring policy for the Irish context 'Sustaining Competitive Advantage', in NESC (ed.) *Sustaining Competitive Advantage*. Dublin: National Economic and Social Council.

OECD (1996) *Networks of Enterprises and Local Development*. Paris: OECD.

Oman, C. (1996) *The Policy Changes of Globalisation and Regionalisation*. OECD Development Centre, Policy Brief, no. 11. OECD: Paris.

Pavitt, K. (1995) Academic research, technical change and government policy, in J. Krige and D. Pestre (eds), *Science in the Twentieth Century*. London: Harwood pp. 35–58.

Porter, M. (1990) *The Competitive Advantage of Nations*. New York: The Free Press.

Putnam, R. (1993) *Making Democracy Work*. Princeton: Princeton University Press.

Pyke, F. and Sengenberger, W. (eds) (1992) *Industrial Districts and Local Economic Generation*. Geneva: Industrial Institute for Labour Studies.

Rhodes, M., Heywood, P. and Wright, V. (eds) (1997) *Developments in West European Politics*. London: Macmillan.

RIDER (1997a) Regional innovation systems in Wallonia, report to EU-TSER project, 'Regional Innovation Systems: Designing for the Future'. University of Louvain, RIDER.

RIDER (1997b) Report on the firms survey: face-to-face interviews, report to EU-TSER project, 'Regional Innovation Systems: Designing for the Future'. University of Louvain, RIDER.

Robertson, M., Swan, J. and Newell, S. (1996) The role of networks in the diffusion of technological innovation, *Journal of Management Studies*, 33, 333–59.

Rosenberg, N. (1976) *Perspectives on Technology*, Cambridge: Cambridge University Press.

Ruigrok, W. and van Tulder, R. (1995) *The Logic of International Restructuring*. London: Routledge.

Sabel, C. Kern, H. and Herrigel, G. (1989) *Collaborative Manufacturing: New Supplier Relations in the Automobile Industry and the Redefinition of the Industrial Corporation*. Cambridge, MA: MIT.

Sabel, C. (1989) Flexible specialisation and the re-emergence of regional economies, in P. Hirst and J. Zeitlin (eds), *Reversing Industrial Decline*? Oxford: Berg, pp. 17–70.

Sabel, C. (1995) *Experimental Regionalism and the Dilemmas of Regional Economic Policy in Europe*. Paris: OECD.

Sabel, C. (1996) Learning-by-monitoring: the dilemmas of regional economic policy in Europe, in OECD (ed.), *Networks of Enterprises and Local Development*. Paris: OECD.

Saxenian, A. (1994) *Regional Advantage: Culture and Competition in Silicon Valley and Route 128*. Cambridge, MA: Harvard University Press

Schall, N. and Cooke, P. (1997a) Organizational innovation in Wales, report to EU-TSER project, 'Regional Innovation Systems: Designing for the Future'. Cardiff University, Centre for Advanced Studies.

Schall, N. and Cooke, P. (1997b) How do firms innovate? a Welsh case study, report to EU-TSER project, 'Regional Innovation Systems: Designing for the Future'. Cardiff University, Centre for Advanced Studies.

Scharpf, F. (1976) Theory of *Politikverflechtung*, in F. Scharpf, B. Reissert and F. Schnabel (eds), *Politikverflechtung*: Theory and Empirics of Cooperative Federalism in Germany. Kronberg: Scriptor. pp. 3–30.

Scharpf, F. (1988) The joint decision trap: lessons from German federalism and European integration, *Public Administration*, 66, 239–78.

Schenkel, M. (1997) Report on innovation organizations, report to EU-TSER project, 'Regional Innovation Systems: Designing for the Future'. University of Udine, Department of Sociology.

Schienstock, G. in collaboration with Roponen, P. (1998), Regional competitiveness, cooperation and innovation: a comparative study of eight European regions. Work Research Centre, University of Tampere.

Scott, A. (1996) Regional motors of the global economy, *Futures*, 28, 391–411.

Sedlacek, S. and Tödtling, F. (1996) Regional economy and innovation system of Styria, report to EU-TSER project, 'Regional Innovation Systems: Designing for the Future'. University of Economics, Vienna, Institute of Urban and Regional Studies.

Sedlacek, S. and Tödtling, F. (1997) Organisations in the Regional Innovation System of Styria, report to EU-TSER project, 'Regional Innovation Systems: Designing for the Future'. University of Economics, Vienna, Institute of Urban and Regional Studies.

Semlinger, K. (1993) Economic development and industrial policy in Baden-Württemberg: small firms in a benevolent environment, *European Planning Studies*, 1, 435–64.

Senge, P. (1994) *The Fifth Discipline*. New York: Doubleday.

Shapira, P. (1998) *The Evaluation of USNet: Overview of Methods, Results and Implications*. Atlanta, GA: School of Public Policy, Institute of Technology.

Simmie, J. (ed.) (1997) *Innovation, Networks and Learning Regions*? London: Jessica Kingsley.

Simon, H. (1992) Lessons from Germany's mid-sized giants, *Harvard Business Review*, March–April, 84–95.

Smilor, R., Dietrich, G. and Gibson, D. (1993) The entrepreneurial university: the role of higher education in the United States in technology commercialization and economic development, *International Social Science Journal*, 45, 1–11.

Smith, K. (1997) Economic infrastructures and innovation systems, in C. Edquist (ed.), *Systems of Innovation*. London: Pinter, pp. 86–106.

Storper, M (1995) The resurgence of regional economies, ten years after: the region as a nexus of untraded interdependencies, *European Urban and Regional Studies*, 2, 191–221.

Storper, M. and Scott, A. (1995) The wealth of regions: market forces and policy imperatives in local and global context, *Futures*, 27, 505–26.

Storper, M. and Scott A. (eds) (1992) *Pathways to Industrialization and Regional Development*. London: Routledge.

Sturm, R. (1996) *Economic Regionalism in a Federal State: Germany and the Challenge of the Single Market*. Occasional Paper No. 1, Tübingen, European Centre for Federalism Research.

Sturm, R. (1998) Multi-level politics of regional development in Germany, *European Planning Studies*, 6, 525–36.

Tödtling, F. (1992) Technological change at the regional level: the role of location, firm structure and strategy, *Environment & Planning A*, 24, 874–87.

Tödtling, F. (1994a) The uneven landscape of innovation poles: local embeddedness and global networks, in A. Amin and N. Thrift (eds), *Globalization, Institutions and Regional Development in Europe*. Oxford: Oxford University Press 68–90.

Tödtling, F. (1994b), Regional networks of high-technology firms: the case of the Greater Boston Region, *Technovation* 14 (5) 342–54.

Tödtling, F. (1995) Firm strategies and restructuring in a globalising economy. IIR Discussion Paper, 53. Vienna: University of Economics.

Tödtling, F. and Sedlacek, S. (1997) Regional economic transformation and the innovation system of Styria, *European Planning Studies*, 5, 43–64.

Uzzi, B. (1996) The sources and consequences of embeddedness for the economic performance of organisations: the network effect, *American Sociological Review*, 61, 674–98.

Van Doren, P. (1996) Wallonia regional profile, report to the EU-TSER Project 'Regional Innovation Systems: Designing for the Future'. University of Louvain, RIDER.

Von Hippel, E. (1988) *The Sources of Innovation*. Oxford: Oxford University Press.

White, C. (1997) Catalonia's pocket-sized multinationals, *Financial Times*, 7 January.

Womack, J., Jones, D. and Roos, D. (1990) *The Machine that Changed the World*, London: Macmillan.

Index